MW00895478

Collective Security within Reach

To Valerie,
With warm wishes for the success of your doctoral degree and future work!

Saraida
Sept. 2009

Collective Security within Reach

Sovaida Ma'ani Ewing

George Ronald
Oxford

George Ronald, *Publisher*
Oxford
www.grbooks.com

© Sovaida Ma'ani Ewing 2007
All Rights Reserved

*A catalogue record for this book is available
from the British Library*

ISBN 978-0-85398-519-8

Cover design: Steiner Graphics
Cover picture: Marion Prentice

Printed and bound in Great Britain
by Alden, Witney, Oxforshire

Contents

Dedicated to

Baharieh, my loving mother,
whose devotion and example inspire me
and whose constant encouragement sustains me

Ken, my beloved husband and friend,
without whom this work would not have been possible

and

Gigi, my daughter and dearest treasure,
for whom I hope this book will lead to a safer world

Foreword

We have stepped into the third millennium with eager anticipation and high expectation. The United Nations designated the final year of the last century as the 'International Year of the Culture of Peace' and the first year of the 21st century as the 'Year of Dialogue among Civilizations'. These noble intentions, unfortunately, continue to face new challenges as the world is engulfed by immense tragedies, grave concerns and endless violence. The last century has been the most violent in human history.

The first step on the road to peace should be an appreciation of the changing nature of conflicts. Gone are days of war between states for conquest, for the extension of spheres of influence in the name of ideology. Today's world and its problems are becoming increasingly more interdependent and interconnected owing to globalization and the advancement of science and technology. Most disturbing is that often today's atrocities are directed at people living in the same community or neighbourhood. Hatred and intolerance have blurred the vision of the perpetrators. The interdependency of the world, if not addressed with sanity, can result in a social, economic, nuclear or environmental catastrophe. Violence by non-state actors and internal conflicts have been on the rise, preoccupying state authorities which very often have resorted to preventive actions that violate civil liberties and fundamental human rights. Complicating the situation further has been the proliferation of weapons that can cause widespread death and destruction. This situation has become worse as access to these means of destruction has become easy with readily available technological and financial resources. Innocent, uninvolved civilians have been the main victims, a disproportionately high percentage being women and children.

The magnitude of these problems requires all human beings to work together to find new, workable, realistic solutions.

As we embark on our journey in the 21st century, we note the many promises that are within the grasp of humankind. We see immense possibilities. We have the power to change the world for the better. We have the technology and the wealth. With collective effort and will, we can eliminate hunger, eradicate disease, fight malnutrition and poverty and create a fulfilling future for all. We pay tribute to human creativity and genius for the progress achieved by humankind. For all the advances made – in science, literature, arts, management and medicine – the human mind has played the pivotal role. It has made the world a better place to live in.

But there is another side to the human mind as well. That other side is capable of breeding intolerance, harbouring hatred and inflicting pain on fellow human beings. It is this side of the human mind that poses the gravest challenge for humanity. Our challenge is to prevent the human mind from being consumed by ignorance, fear, violence, fratricide and intolerance. We have seen in the past century alone what these can do to undermine the progress of the human race. We have seen a culture of war and violence spread its venomous tentacles, threatening to destroy all that is good, moral and just.

The dawning of the new millennium gives us an opportunity to learn lessons from our past so that we can build a new and better tomorrow. One lesson learned is that to prevent history repeating itself, the values of non-violence, tolerance and democracy have to be inculcated in every woman, man and child. 'Since wars begin in the minds of men, it is in the minds of men that the defences of peace must be constructed,' says the UNESCO constitution. As former Secretary-General of the United Nations and Nobel Peace laureate Kofi Annan has said, 'Over the years we have come to realize that it is not enough to send peacekeeping forces to separate warring parties. It is not enough to engage in peacebuilding efforts after societies have been ravaged by conflict. It is not enough to conduct preventive diplomacy. All of this is essential work, but we want enduring results. We need, in short, a culture of peace.'

The efforts at peace and reconciliation have to be based on an understanding of this new reality. Global efforts towards peace and reconciliation can only succeed with a collective approach built on trust, dialogue and collaboration. For that, we have to build a grand alliance amongst all, particularly with the pro-active involvement and participation of civil society and young people. No social responsibility is greater nor task heavier than that of securing peace on our planet. Building a culture of peace is therefore the most practical way of addressing the root causes of conflict and violence.

Why do I put such emphasis on a culture of peace? Three reasons. First, it targets individuals. There cannot be true peace unless the mind is at peace. Second, it brings together all actors. In addition to states and international organizations, actions to promote a culture of peace can be undertaken by parents, family, teachers, artists, journalists, students and community and religious leaders . . . people from all walks of life. Third, it sets its goals not on the principle of an eye for an eye but on tolerance, solidarity and dialogue to settle differences and heal wounds.

There is obviously a need to approach the present global threats to peace and security in a fresh and creative way. The existing mechanisms that are available to the international community to address today's threats with all their complexities either have been subverted through unilateral action or are totally inadequate to tackle such challenges. The Security Council and other institutional means available have been abused to the point that they have become ineffective to a considerable extent. What is needed are fresh ideas and out-of-the-box thinking. Sovaida Ma'ani Ewing provides exactly this.

Ma'ani Ewing's comprehensive analysis of the current threats to peace and security identifies the inadequacies of existing mechanisms to deal with these threats. Her argument for the reform of the United Nations system in these areas is powerful and valuable. She lays out several 'principles' which underpin her concrete proposals for reforming the existing mechanisms as well as creating new ones. Her proposals for the extensive reform of the Security Council are particularly worthy of attention, providing substantive food for thought and, hopefully, action by the international community.

The political will we find so elusive in our quest for global peace is analysed by Ma'ani Ewing, who explains how political will can be developed through an institutional framework. She emphasizes the need for structures that have the potential to address the present and future requirements of international relationships and provides a checklist of such structures and mechanisms. In particular, she suggests that it is important to fill the vacuum that exists in the international system in its warning about possible flash points.

Ma'ani Ewing makes a strong case for the curtailment of national sovereignty as a vital stepping stone towards collective security and peace. In recent years there has been a growing opinion in support of this view. Although we seem far from creating the supranational authority, world government and world parliament proposed by Ma'ani Ewing, she succinctly describes the powerful effect that collective action has on international relations.

More than three decades of first-hand experience of the multilateral system tells me that the countries that should take action to put together workable structures for the future are likely to be the very ones that will stand in the way. Powerful nations in particular are the main obstacles to making the international system just and equitable. It is therefore necessary to engage people everywhere in discussion about how to make the international system much more effective, particularly its maintenance of global peace and security. A wide-ranging readership and discussions at various forums which look into the real potential and workability of the structures proposed by Ma'ani Ewing would do justice to the rich materials in her book.

The Bahá'í writings offer a vision of collective security and the references to them bring a much welcomed freshness to the main focus of Ma'ani Ewing's thought-provoking, well-researched and meticulously put together treatise.

Ambassador Anwarul K. Chowdhury
UN Under-Secretary-General
and High Representative
New York
28 June 2007

Introduction

Introduction

Our world is flailing in the face of successive threats to its peace and security. It is beleaguered by a set of recurring and intensifying crises. Every day seems to bring a fresh onslaught. On the one hand, we seem unable to rid ourselves of the scourge of genocide. From Rwanda, where an estimated 800,000 to 1,000,000 people were massacred in the space of a mere 100 days while the world stood by ineffectually, to Bosnia and Kosovo and now Darfur, genocide has become an ugly feature of our times. On the other hand, weapons of mass destruction continue to proliferate, increasing the likelihood that they will be used by accident or by a deranged state actor, or that they will fall into the hands of terrorists with no compunctions about using them. Meanwhile we stand by, paralysed observers of the grim destiny we are sowing, wringing our hands but unable to decide upon an effective course of action to halt this madness. Terrorist networks are becoming more sophisticated and may soon have access to technologies that will enable them to make biological and chemical weapons. Religious intolerance and hatred continue to plague our societies, providing us with yet another excuse to maim and kill each other. Roving militias and insurgents act with impunity, raping and pillaging communities, striking fear into the hearts of local populations and bringing about the collapse of nations, further destabilizing the international community as a whole. Organized crime decimates our social fabric by making drugs freely available, trafficking in women and children, and spreading corruption that weakens whole economies. Unfortunately our response as a community of individuals represented by our nations has been to lurch reactively from crisis to crisis, administering temporary and superficial relief at best. We are neither able nor willing to tackle these crises effectively and efficiently. We have been unable to devise a comprehensive system capable of effectively dealing with these fundamental problems that generate so much fear and sap so much of humanity's energy and resources. As citizens of this world community, we have lost confidence in our international institutions and governments to respond to our common problems adequately and collectively.[1] The questions we must ask ourselves are: Will we simply continue to repeat our past failures – bickering again and again about the most effective way to deal with the crisis of the day? Shall we continue to argue about whose turn it is to provide the resources to do what is needed, while countless more suffer? Will we engage in fruitless exercises of blaming each other in a futile attempt to assuage our guilt? Can we afford to continue as before?

These crises have taught us some valuable lessons, however, which we would do well to heed. First, like it or not, our world is very interconnected; so much so, in fact, that an apparently isolated crisis affecting one part of the world can have devastating effects on other parts. One striking example is the terrorist attacks of 11 September 2001 on the Twin Towers in New York City, which the World Bank estimates increased the number of people worldwide living in poverty by ten million. The World Bank also estimates that this one day of terror alone cost the world economy in excess of US $80 billion.[2] We share a common interest and therefore a strong incentive to apply ourselves seriously and find solutions for our common problems. Second, it is becoming equally clear that no one nation, no matter how powerful, has sufficient human and financial resources to allow it single-handedly to tackle all threats that abound, even if such threats were limited to halting the proliferation of weapons of mass destruction or combatting terrorism.[3] Even the most economically and militarily powerful nation in history, the United States, may not have the human resources to add a third military intervention, for instance, to handle a flare-up in northeast Asia, to its current engagements in Afghanistan and Iraq.[4] Moreover, the financial costs of such military engagements are already very high. It is estimated that the war in Iraq could end up costing between $461 billion and $646 billion by

2015.[5] The people of the United States are unlikely to be willing to bear this kind of cost for an unlimited period of time. Third, we have learned, largely thanks to the news media, which now beam pictures of atrocities right into our living rooms, that we all share in our humanity. All human beings fundamentally suffer in the same ways. Nothing moves us more than to see pictures of mothers mourning the senseless loss of their husbands and children.

It is time we drew on these lessons, earned at great cost of human life and suffering, and applied ourselves seriously to the task of pro-actively shaping a world in which crises are dealt with efficiently, justly and effectively – the kind of world we would want our children to inherit. The push for change must come from us, people at the grass roots who pay dearly with our lives for policies gone awry. First we must muster the humility and courage to acknowledge that certain of our laws and institutions no longer serve us as they should and must therefore be revamped or replaced as necessary. We must also recognize that what we lack is a well-thought-out, coherent and comprehensive system of collective security crafted not to address the crisis of the moment but to resolve all the crises that plague us, in a systematic, principled, unified, just and effective manner.[6] By 'security' I mean the right of all people to live free from the threat that they will be harmed by the wilful actions of their fellow humans, especially when those actions are taken by organized segments of society. Such threats include genocide, ethnic cleansing, proliferation of weapons of mass destruction, acts of terrorism, acts of rape, pillage and murder undertaken by militias or insurgents, and trafficking in drugs, women and children by members of organized crime syndicates.

Our world cries out for new thinking and creativity. Fortunately, the answers are already there. The Bahá'í writings, which have hitherto been little explored by the world, provide us with precisely what we need: a set of basic principles along with a blueprint for a just, efficacious and comprehensive system of collective security that will ensure the peace and security of our world. The task of this book is three-fold: to describe these Bahá'í principles and the elements of this blueprint, to see how far the world community has come in applying them and to propose practicable, high-impact next steps that can be taken in the short term to craft the kind of comprehensive system of collective security envisioned in the Bahá'í writings.

But new thinking and approaches are not enough. We must also forge consensus around a new approach.[7] We, the people at the grass roots of our communities, must hold our leaders' feet to the fire until they achieve consensus. Our role, as citizens of the world, is to familiarize ourselves with the problems that beset our global community and to examine and vigorously discuss any proposed solutions, including those in this book. We must continually demand that our leaders work untiringly and determinedly to agree with each other on the principles of a comprehensive system of collective security. Our leaders, in turn, must then exert every effort to implement their agreement in complete unity. The issues are too critical to leave to chance.

Once this is done, we must unite around the approach decided upon by pressing our leaders to convert collective thought into action. Sporadic, isolated bursts of collective action will no longer suffice. What is required is sustained, unified collective action by the nations of the world to deal with all crises threatening peace and security. History shows that without unity of both thought and action we will not succeed in ridding ourselves of the scourges that plague us. But recent history also has provided us glimpses of what can be achieved when we are unified. For instance, in February 2005 Faure Gnassingbé threatened civil war in Togo and unrest throughout West Africa when, in violation of Togo's constitution, he claimed the title of president after the death of his father. However, facing the stiff resolve and complete unity of the Economic Community of West African States as well as that of the 53-member African Union which suspended Togo's membership in the Union and imposed a travel ban and economic sanctions on Togo's leaders, Mr Gnassingbé agreed to step down peacefully only three weeks after he seized power and allowed elections to take place in accordance with the constitution.[8] Perhaps even more illuminating was Syria's withdrawal of its forces from the Lebanon in April 2005[9] after 29 years of its military domination of the country and eight months after United Nations Security Council Resolution 1559 was passed in 2004, which demanded the departure of all foreign forces, the disbanding of all Lebanese militias and respect for Lebanon's political independence. There were a number of factors that coalesced to set the stage for the international community and Syria's responses respectively. These included the former's outrage at Syria's apparent assassination of the veteran Lebanese politician and peacemaker Rafik Hariri. The willingness evinced by the United States to invade Iraq combined with its rhetoric about Syria's support for Iraq insurgents also played a part. However, it was ultimately the unified pressure applied by key countries including the United States, France, Jordan, Germany, Russia, Saudi Arabia and Egypt and the threat that the international community would both politically and economically isolate Syria that finally achieved this result.[10]

Part 1

Blueprint for a Viable System of Collective Security

Blueprint for a Viable System of Collective Security

In the middle of the 19th century a Persian nobleman's son by the name of Mírzá Ḥusayn-'Alí proclaimed to the world that He was the latest in a series of divine teachers sent by God from time to time in our collective history to guide and educate us in accordance both with our capacity to receive spiritual truth and with our needs. Bahá'u'lláh, as He came to be known, claimed that He had brought the answer to the ills currently plaguing humanity and urged both the religious and secular leaders of His day to examine His teachings and apply them for the good of their people. Bahá'u'lláh's revelation was prolific and amounts to over a hundred volumes of writing. These works, together with the interpretations of the two authorized interpreters, 'Abdu'l-Bahá and Shoghi Effendi, are collectively known as the 'Bahá'í writings'.[1] It is these writings that inspired the ideas on collective security in this book.

Understanding International Insecurity: Humanity in the Throes of Adolescence

Before attempting to solve any given problem, especially one involving human relations, it often helps to put the problem in context and to study the dynamics that drive it. Not only may we learn about possible solutions but the exercise can help motivate us to take the necessary steps to solve the problem. This is no less true of the global problems involving threats to our security and peace. The Bahá'í writings help us to put these problems into context and to understand what drives them.

The Bahá'í writings offer a powerful image to help place human society and its current problems in proper context. Imagine that humanity, as a collective whole, is an individual person. This person begins life as an infant and gradually develops into a toddler, a young child, an adolescent and finally a mature adult. Just as the individual passes through each of these stages, so does humanity as a whole. And just as each of these stages is marked by developmentally appropriate behaviour, so too are the stages of humanity's evolution and development marked by corollary behaviour. We need only to study the history of humanity to see how accurate this image is. One way in which this evolutionary behaviour presents itself is in the breadth of the community to which a society is willing to extend its loyalties. The wider the circle of loyalty, the more mature the community. So, for example, loyalty only to one's clan or tribe represents a less mature form of social organization than loyalty to a city-state or nation. As the members of a society become less self-centred and more willing to consider the interests of a broader social circle, the circle of unity expands and the society becomes more diverse and complex in its organization. So far, the highest form of social organization humanity has reached is a federation of nations in which the individual units are willing to cede larger degrees of sovereignty for the good of a wider collective whole.

The Bahá'í writings explain that the human race is now experiencing the final throes of its turbulent adolescence, marked by acts of rebelliousness and behaviour that push boundaries of propriety to their farthest limit. Wars, human rights atrocities, the proliferation of weapons of mass destruction, terrorism, brutal militias, insurgents and gangs, and our clinging to unfettered nationalism all reflect humanity's adolescent attempts to define itself and to establish what legal and moral boundaries it will not cross. The Bahá'í writings assure us, however, that this stage will pass and that humanity will make it to adulthood and maturity, shedding the upheavals of its adolescent years. Although our past and present appear bleak, we are promised that our future is unimaginably bright and glorious.

This perspective on our seemingly entrenched behaviour is not only critical to our understanding of why we have been behaving in this manner but, more importantly, provides us with the hope that these troubles, too, shall pass and that things will get better. Such hope, in turn, motivates and spurs us to do the work necessary to hasten the end of this adolescent stage and openly to embrace our maturity. The Bahá'í writings do not abandon us here. They go further and paint a picture of what our collective life will look like once we have attained maturity. This picture will not only help us recognize maturity once it arrives but also gives us a concrete vision and specific goals to accelerate the transition from adolescence to maturity. The writings tell us that the next inevitable stage in our collective growth will be marked by a grow-ing awareness of our oneness, which will result in increasing unity and in an understanding that we must owe our first allegiance to humanity as a whole. One of the critical components of this stage of maturity is the creation of a system of collective security as envisioned by Bahá'u'lláh – a system that will bring us the security and peace that we crave and deserve.

The Bahá'í writings also stiffen our resolve to do what is neces-sary by pointing out that our institutions, laws and the policies that drive them are there to serve our best interests and to bring us happiness. If they no longer fulfil these fundamental purposes or, worse still, if they are positively harming us and we are being sacrificed for their preservation, we should have no qualms about scrapping them and relegating them to the dust heap of items that have outlived their usefulness. Everything in this world, we are reminded, is subject to change and deterioration. We cannot expect institutions, laws and policies that we have built, however painstakingly, in the past to be exempt from this immutable law. Nor can we expect to be able to bring about the kind of positive transformation we all yearn for if we stubbornly cling to old ideals, social assumptions and outmoded ways of doing things. Having let go of the old, however, we must create policies, institutions and laws that meet the needs of our times. This requires that we be imaginative and apply the full force of our creativity. We must be willing to think outside of the box.

Tools to Craft a New System of Collective Security

The Baháʼí writings offer a set of tools to craft a new system of collective security to replace the outmoded institutions, laws and ways of thinking that humanity is outgrowing. These tools are a set of basic, operational principles that can never be compromised in our quest for ever-improved systems of international governance and international relations. We must be especially vigilant against expediency or short-term self-interest. The governing body of the Baháʼí Faith reinforces this point by saying we must raise the context in which we want to create a new, workable system of collective security 'to the level of principle, as distinct from pure pragmatism'.[2] They also say that 'Leaders of governments and all in authority would be well served in their efforts to solve problems if they would first seek to identify the principles involved and then be guided by them'.[3] We have a tendency, both in our individual lives and collectively as nations, to focus on our short-term interests without giving much thought or care to the consequences of our actions or omissions in the long term. Consequently, we often make decisions to act or not to act that haunt us in the future. Very often our solution to the crisis of the day sows the seeds of future crises. The only way to break this cycle is to step back, identify a set of core principles that will govern our international relations and upon which we want to build a system of collective security, and then forge international consensus around them. Having committed to this core set of principles, we guard against the perils of decision-making driven by expediency – i.e. our short-term interests – by unflinchingly adhering to them. The Baháʼí writings outline several core principles.

The Oneness of Humanity

First and foremost, we need to embrace in all its many ramifications the foundational principle of the oneness of humanity. All human beings are one in the sight of our Creator. No matter what the colour of our skin or our gender, no matter how rich or poor we are, educated or uneducated, no matter what our ethnic origins or nationalities, we are all animated by the same human spirit and live our lives for the same common two-fold purpose: to develop our virtues, thus assuring the continual development of our souls, and to carry forward an ever-advancing human civilization. We are all entitled to equal rights and opportunities to develop and advance ourselves. Indeed, the Bahá'í writings say that all of the problems of insecurity and lack of peace can be traced to the inability of our leaders to grasp this principle of oneness fully and to forge and reshape the machinery of our governments to meet the standards this principle implies.[4] Our goal, the writings say, should be to make the oneness of all the body of nations the 'ruling principle of international life'.[5] The process that leads to the achievement of this goal concerns itself with the nature of the essential relationships that bind states and nations together as members of an integral international community and will entail an organic change in the structure of society of a kind never experienced.[6] Indeed, the Bahá'í writings claim that operationalizing the principle of oneness 'represents the consummation of human evolution'.[7] It is the final, inevitable stage in the progression of human evolution that manifested itself in its early stages in the birth of family life and subsequently developed to achieve tribal solidarity, the creation of the city-state and later the creation of independent sovereign nations.

Justice, Equity and Fairness

This principle can, in some sense, be viewed as an outgrowth of the principle of oneness discussed above. It stands to reason that if we assume that we are all one and that others are as deserving as we are and entitled to as much benefit and good as we are, then we should treat all equally. This means that we should under no circumstance accord preferential treatment to one nation or group of nations over another. Applying this principle to the relationships between nation states will revolutionize our institutions, laws and policies and will contribute vastly to a more secure and peaceful world. For example, applying it to the United Nations Security Council would mean eliminating the power of any one of the five victors of World War II to veto whatever the rest of the world may want to do in the Council. Similarly, the international community would need to respond quickly and effectively in the face of genocide, regardless of whether it occurred on Europe's doorstep in Kosovo or farther from the centre of power in Rwanda or Darfur. Moreover, all nations would need to forgo their claims to possess weapons of mass destruction, rather than allowing a handful of nations to possess them while prohibiting others from acquiring them. The alternative, which entails allowing all nations to develop and possess weapons of mass destruction, is untenable as it would embroil us in a nuclear weapons race and create even more fear and insecurity than already exists.

Curtailing Unfettered National Sovereignty

For centuries the laws and institutions of international relations have jealously guarded the unfettered sovereignty of independent nations. Unfettered national sovereignty has outlived its usefulness. The anarchy inherent in it is 'moving towards a climax'.[8] Clinging to it is causing us more pain than gain. It is therefore time to re-examine its role in international life and curtail it.[9] In a world that is as interconnected as ours and in which the threats we face, including terrorism, organized crime, the proliferation of weapons of mass destruction and virulent disease, know no national boundaries, it is dishonest to continue to insist that national sovereignty is absolute. The international community has already demonstrated (although not entirely consistently), for example, that it will not allow nation states to treat their subjects with complete impunity and has reserved to itself the right to step in and protect peoples from atrocities such as genocide and ethnic cleansing. It is also counterproductive to insist that national sovereignty is absolute for such an attitude promotes narrow self-interest at the expense of the greater good and hampers our collective ability to arrive at global solutions to problems that are patently worldwide. The inability of our leaders to arrive at any decision to stop the dangerous proliferation of nuclear weapons despite their attempts at two separate world gatherings in 2005 amply demonstrates this point.

There is another interrelated principle at work here, which is also articulated in the Bahá'í writings. It is the principle that the advantage of the part is best reached by the advantage of the whole and that there can be no long-term benefit for a component part if the interests of the whole are neglected.[10] In the context of international relations, this means that the advantage of any one nation can best be assured by decisions that take into account and ensure the best interests of all nations.

Europe experimented with this principle in the aftermath of the Second World War when it found its economy in tatters and garnered tremendous benefits from doing so. A number of western European nations, in particular France, Germany, Luxembourg, the Netherlands, Belgium and Italy, recognized that they needed to have adequate access to coal and steel to successfully reconstruct their economies. More importantly, they recognized that their hitherto separate attempts to craft markets to maximize their individual advantage had been unsuccessful. They came to believe that pooling their coal and steel resources would work to their collective advantage and, by extension, to their individual advantage. They also recognized that one of the keys to avoiding another European war driven by the desire to control these critical resources would be the creation of a system in which they all had equal access to coal and steel. It was this felicitous combination of economic necessity and enlightened self-interest combined with a dose of idealism that led them to embrace a brilliant plan devised by Jean Monnet, Planning Commissioner for France, to pool European coal and steel under the management control of a supranational High Authority and to supply these resources on equal terms to nations willing to participate in this pool. Thus it was that in 1951 the six nations mentioned above entered into an agreement to create a European Coal and Steel Community (ECSC) and in 1952 the ECSC was born. Within two years the collective and individual advantage to the member countries was apparent: the total output of the ECSC was larger than the joint production of the six member countries had ever been before and prices were stabilized to the benefit of each of the six nations.[11] Moreover, the benefits to each of the six member countries of a peaceful existence with their neighbours, free of the human and economic costs of war, were incalculable. Indeed, so successful was the European experiment that it formed the foundation for a far deeper and broader integration between the nation states of Europe in the form of the European Union which, as of the summer of 2007, comprises 27 member states.

Although the laws and institutions governing international life should take into account the advantage of the international community as a whole, this does not imply that the concept of national autonomy ought to be eliminated altogether. In fact, such autonomy serves a useful and critical purpose in that it is essential for the avoidance of the evils of excessive centralization.[12] It also makes a distinct, identifiable entity responsible for the welfare and protection of a state's people, one that is accountable to them and to the international community for any failure to discharge this weighty responsibility.[13] What is needed is for us to broaden our loyalties to include the human race as a whole and to be willing to subordinate our national impulses and interests to the imperative claims of a unified world.[14]

Force as a Servant of Justice

Bahá'u'lláh's system of collective security does not assume that the use of military force will be abolished. Rather, force should act as the servant of justice. Not all force is evil and to be shunned. There will be instances in which force must be used for a larger good. 'Abdu'l-Bahá, the first authorized interpreter of the Bahá'í writings, states clearly that there are times when war becomes the 'powerful basis of peace' and 'ruin the very means of reconstruction'.[15] He also says that if war is waged for a 'righteous purpose', then 'this seeming wrath is mercy itself', 'this apparent tyranny the very substance of justice and this warfare the cornerstone of peace'.[16] At these times military force is like an aggressive medical treatment, such as chemotherapy to cure cancer. It is unavoidable that healthy, perfectly functioning cells will be destroyed along with the cancerous ones. However, the loss of some healthy cells is a price that must be paid if the patient is to be saved. To shy away from treatment for fear of killing a few innocent cells would be tantamount to suicide. While recognizing that force is a tool that must sometimes be resorted to in order to do justice to the body of humanity, the Bahá'í writings call for nations to reach a political agreement ending war as an instrument of international relations and suggest that force should be used collectively.[17] Doing this would significantly reduce human suffering as nations would bend the energies they currently waste on ruinous wars to crafting new tools for resolving conflicts. These tools would include creating a system of international relations based on clear rules rather than fuzzy policies, complemented by effective international courts with compulsory jurisdiction and the proper means to enforce their judgements. The tools would also need to include an international standing force capable of enforcing the will of the international community as expressed either by an international executive or an international court.

International Cooperation and Unity of Thought and Action

All nations must commit to international cooperation, without which nothing can be achieved and no system of collective security can, even if envisioned, be implemented and maintained. Nations all have an enormous incentive to commit to such cooperation, given that none of them, no matter how powerful, can fully protect themselves against all the threats to peace and security we face today. All nations are intensely vulnerable and their only prayer for security and peace is to act together in unity. The Bahá'í writings aptly express this reality in a metaphor in which the world of humanity is likened to the human body. No matter how small or seemingly insignificant a member of the body may appear, when it aches the entire body experiences that pain and shares in the suffering.[18] For example, even if we merely stub our little toe, the pain is felt by the rest of the body. The whole body is affected whether or not we like it. This is a reflection of the ultimate reality that the peace and security of our world and its well-being can only be attained when its unity its firmly established.[19]

Changing Institutions, Laws and Policies to Reflect the Needs of the Time

We humans must regularly remind ourselves that the purpose of our institutions, no matter how long they have been in existence and how noble and worthy a part they have played in our lives, is to serve our welfare and minister to our needs. This also applies to our laws, social assumptions, policies, political and economic theories and religious formulas. The minute they cease furthering our welfare, we must sweep them away. We must have no qualms about doing this, for a mere moment's reflection will assure us that one of the immutable laws of life is that change and decay will overtake us all. Why then should we expect our institutions and laws to be exempt from this universal law? It certainly makes no sense for us to crucify ourselves in order to uphold a particular political theory, law or institution.[20] Many of our social ills might have been avoided had our leaders correctly read the signs and requirements of our times and adjusted our system of economic and political institutions and reshaped the machinery of our governments to keep up with them.[21]

Elements of Bahá'u'lláh's Blueprint for a System of Collective Security

There are several parts to the Bahá'í vision of collective security. Each part could be considered separately and fully implementing any one of them would contribute immensely to world peace and security. But the power of Bahá'u'lláh's vision lies in combining all the parts. As we will see, these parts work together to create a seamless system to address the very divisions and weaknesses from which our current institutions and *ad hoc* policies suffer.

A Core Group of the World's Leaders Must Meet and Make a Pact

The Bahá'í vision of collective security begins with the idea that a 'certain number' of leaders should meet with the sole objective of finding ways to bring about international peace.[22] Their driving motivation should be to act for 'the good and happiness of all mankind'. These leaders must also be 'distinguished', 'high-minded' and 'shining exemplars of devotion and determination'.[23] This meeting should result in 'a binding treaty', which I will call the 'International Covenant'. This treaty should then be presented to the rest of the world for its 'sanction'. The Bahá'í vision is at once a call to action by the world's leaders and a promise to us, the people of the world, that the vision can and will come true if we work to achieve it.[24]

The Bahá'í vision incorporates several subtle points that can help steer us to make it a reality. First, it is sufficient for a core group of the world's leaders to meet initially; it is not necessary that all the world's leaders participate in that crucial first meeting and agreement. Upon reflection, this makes abundant sense. It is much easier for consultation to take place among a smaller group of people. Consultation in very large groups become unwieldy and loses its focus. Moreover, the rest of the world's leaders are likely to trust the outcome of any consultation among a core group if the members of that group have a proven track record of outstanding service (i.e. they are distinguished), have in mind only lofty goals that benefit everyone and are known for their single-mindedness, devotion and perseverance when approaching a task. The very fact that their only purpose in getting together will be to discuss the establishment of international peace will speak to their lack of self-interest, the loftiness of their ideals and their devotion. No one can object to a goal that will, by definition, benefit everyone and conduce to the happiness of the generality of humanity.

Second, once the core group has persevered and consulted diligently, it must present its conclusions in the form of a treaty to all the nations of the world for ratification. This is critical for the success of the endeavour. Each nation must bind and commit itself to uphold all the provisions of the International Covenant and to take appropriate action to punish any violation. The Bahá'í blueprint for a system of collective security outlines some of the critical topics to be covered in the International Covenant. These topics should form part of the agenda of the core group of high-minded and distinguished leaders.

CLEAR ESTABLISHMENT OF NATIONAL BORDERS

The International Covenant will include clear provisions fixing all national borders. Our experience over the last few decades attests to the critical importance of dealing with this issue once and for all. Numerous wars and conflicts have been sparked and many continue to fester and threaten to erupt because of competing claims to territory: Ethiopia and Eritrea, Palestine and Israel, Kosovo and Albania, India and Pakistan, Iran and Iraq, Iraq and Kuwait, North and South Korea, to name but a few. Much of the problem stems from the arbitrary manner in which borders were determined over the course of the last two centuries by external powers without taking into account either the wishes and needs of the local populations or any pre-existing borders. If we are to leave our adolescent stage with its tumultuous crises behind and move to the next stage of our collective development, then we must take the steps necessary to ensure that we remove border and territorial disputes as a trigger for violent conflict. The time is ripe for resolving these issues once and for all.

CLEAR DETERMINATION OF THE PRINCIPLES GOVERNING INTERNATIONAL RELATIONS

The International Covenant will also include 'the principles underlying the relations of governments towards one another'.[25] These principles encompass those basic tools and operational principles discussed above upon which a new system of international relations must be built. They will form the foundation from which responses to all international dilemmas, problems and conflicts will be derived. These principles are the fixed cornerstones of an international system of relationships. They must never be compromised or overridden in the name of expediency.

In addition to those discussed above, other principles may also be added. For example, it would make sense to agree upon the principle that nations will forgo the use of force as an instrument of international relations unless such use is collectively authorized.[26] Also, principles governing the circumstances in which force is to be made a servant of justice and used collectively to maintain peace and security must be agreed upon and established. Equally importantly, universal agreement about circumstances in which unilateral use of force is acceptable, such as in self-defence, must also be reached. Detailed recommendations on what the content of such principles might be are discussed further in the third part of this book.

CODIFICATION OF INTERNATIONAL LAWS, AGREEMENTS AND OBLIGATIONS

The world has become so interconnected and relationships amongst states so complex and multi-layered that it is clearly time to streamline and codify the international rules and obligations that affect us all. At the moment, the international rules and obligations that govern nations in any particular subject area can be difficult to ascertain. The sheer multiplicity of treaties involving any single topic can make it hard for nation states even to understand their obligations, much less to implement them. Complexity makes it equally difficult for the international community to monitor compliance. Examples abound, ranging from environmental protection and conservation on the one hand to control of terrorism on the other. Another obvious benefit of clearly determining international obligations is that transparency will be assured. This is critical to building trust among nations, which in turn is an essential element for building and maintaining a successful system of collective security.

ARMS REDUCTION

The International Covenant will also address each nation's right to maintain armaments. According to the Bahá'í vision 'the size of the armaments of every government . . . [will] be strictly limited'.[27] Each nation will be allowed to possess arms only in a number that allows it to keep the peace within its borders and to maintain civil order.[28] The motivating factor driving this principle is that any increase in military forces by one nation will only serve to arouse the suspicion of other states who will then take steps they deem necessary to retaliate and redress the balance. So begins the well-known problem of an arms race with all the attendant rises in tension and the possibility of unintended accidents. Our world is all too familiar with this scenario – the Cold War was largely a study in precisely this phenomenon leading us to the ludicrous comfort point of mutually assured destruction.

The Bahá'í vision implies that the International Covenant will contain details regarding the number of armaments that each nation is allowed to have. In order to be able to arrive at suitable figures, groundwork will need to be done and detailed studies and analyses will need to be conducted to inform the decision of the world's leaders.

COLLECTIVE ENFORCEMENT

The lynchpin of the entire Bahá'í blueprint for a viable system of collective security is the principle that if any government were to violate any provision of the treaty 'all the governments on earth should arise to reduce it to utter submission' and if necessary 'the human race as a whole should resolve, with every power at its disposal, to destroy that government'.[29] The Bahá'í writings envision that this principle will constitute the underlying foundation of the International Covenant.[30] Such a vision requires a level of commitment and unity of purpose and action hitherto unseen in human affairs. It requires that the nations of the world assume collective responsibility for the peace and security of our planet and that they will support their verbal pledges by actual preparation for collective action.[31] 'Be united, O concourse of the sovereigns of the world', rings the commanding call of Bahá'u'lláh. '. . . Should any one among you take up arms against another, rise ye all against him, for this is naught but manifest justice'.[32] However, unity in adhering to this principle will ensure the peace and security of our planet. 'So powerful is the light of unity', says Bahá'u'lláh, 'that it can illuminate the whole earth'.[33] No nation should be allowed to upset the equilibrium of the world's peace. If one country poses a threat to the peace, it must be effectively dealt with on a collective basis. The costs in human suffering alone are too high to countenance any failure to act on the part of the international community as a whole. The Bahá'í writings assure us that if this 'greatest of all remedies be applied to the sick body of the world, it will assuredly recover from its ills and will remain eternally safe and secure.'[34] This sort of mechanism for ensuring our collective security is a prime example of the organic change in the structures and machinery of governance called for in the Bahá'í writings, structures that will incarnate and reflect the truth that we are all one.[35] For effective collective action to be taken on a systematic, fair and effective basis, two things are necessary: detailed agreement upon the principles and rules that will trigger collective action and a viable mechanism for enforcing the rules. The latter leads us to the next component element of the Bahá'í blueprint for a viable system of collective security, namely, the creation of a standing army.

CREATION OF A STANDING ARMY

Application of Bahá'u'lláh's principle of collective security presupposes and necessitates the creation of a standing army and a world police force, envisioned in the Bahá'í writings as a combination of forces of different nations that will eventually comprise federated units in a world federation of states.[36] This force is to be used as an instrument for collective action by the international community in service of several goals. These include maintaining the peace and organic unity of the planet,[37] which can be threatened in a variety of ways, including the intentional violation by a state of any provision of the International Covenant, enforcing the decisions of a World Court to be established by the treaty, enforcing a single code of international law[38] and enforcing the laws of any future international legislature.

CREATION OF AN EFFECTIVE WORLD COURT

An essential element of Bahá'u'lláh's blueprint for a system of collective security is the creation of a 'Supreme Tribunal' whose purpose it will be to contribute to the establishment and maintenance of universal peace.[39] It will do this by acting as the first port of call for nations and other constituent elements of the international system (presumably at this stage in the development of world order this would include international and regional organizations and other international actors such as transnational corporations) when disputes arise between them which they are unable to resolve by other means such as bilateral or multilateral negotiations, good offices and mediation, conciliation, arbitration or other relevant mechanisms of conflict resolution. The intent is that by referring conflicts to the Supreme Tribunal for final resolution, nations will no longer resort to the use of force to resolve their disputes. The Bahá'í writings emphasize that the Supreme Tribunal should give expression to the principle of the oneness of nations and humanity by ensuring that justice is brought to bear in all its decisions. The writings describe several salient characteristics for the Supreme Tribunal to be effective.

Mode of Election

First, the manner in which the Supreme Tribunal's judges are elected must inspire trust. The judges must be perceived to be truly representative of the peoples of the world, fully competent, free of bias and independent of the wishes of any particular nation or group of nations. They must be seen to be fair-minded and interested in rendering just and equitable decisions untainted by political pressure. To this end the Bahá'í writings propose that all the parliaments of the world elect two or three representatives who are highly regarded and distinguished in their country. The precise number of those elected should be proportionate to the population of that country. They should be well versed in international law and international relations and aware of the essential needs and requirements of the world. Their election should be confirmed by all the component parts of the legislature, including the upper house of parliament or the congress. It should also be confirmed by the executive branch, including the cabinet, and either the president or monarch. In this manner those elected will truly represent both the people and the government. From among the entire body of representatives elected around the world the members of the Supreme Tribunal should then be elected.[40] Details of how this election will be conducted and who will be entitled to vote for the members of the Supreme Tribunal will presumably be decided by world leaders in the future.

Compulsory and Binding Jurisdiction

The Supreme Tribunal must have compulsory jurisdiction. It must be able to adjudicate all disputes between nations, even when the parties concerned do not voluntarily agree to submit their case to its jurisdiction.[41] All its judgements must be viewed as final and binding on the component parts of the international system. The Bahá'í writings seem to indicate that these will include at the very least member states, as well as a future international legislature and international executive.[42]

Enforceable Decisions

Without a mechanism with which to enforce its decisions the Supreme Tribunal would be toothless and greatly weakened. Its judgements would stand in danger of being rendered meaning-less in the face of wilful disregard and blatant impunity or even mere delay and dilatory action on the part of recalcitrant nations. It would then be unable to play its vital role of maintaining peace and security and of resolving disputes so that the parties do not resort to violent means for their solution. In the event that a nation neglects its duty to implement the Tribunal's binding decisions promptly and effectively, the Bahá'í model provides that all the nations will act collectively to enforce the Tribunal's judgement, relying upon the international army discussed above.[43]

Relationship with Other Organs of an Evolving Federated System

One of the issues that must be decided in the future, as our inter-national institutions continue to evolve in the direction of a world federation as envisioned by Bahá'u'lláh, is the exact nature of the relationship between the Supreme Tribunal and other organs of a world federation.[44]

PROGRESS TOWARDS A FEDERATED INTERNATIONAL GOVERNMENT AND EQUITABLE DISTRIBUTION OF THE WORLD'S RESOURCES

The Bahá'í system of collective security envisions the eventual creation of a world federated system in which unity in diversity is a prime principle. This means that although the machinery of international governance is unified and there is unity of thought in world undertakings, the peoples of the world are not required to think, behave or live uniformly. Rather, the diversity of peoples and cultures will be actively cultivated and celebrated. Moreover, all nations within this federated system will willingly cede all claims to make war, certain rights to impose taxes and all rights to maintain armaments except what is required for self-defence and the maintenance of order within their borders.[45] The creation of such a system will go a long way towards ensuring the peace and security of the planet. The world's experience with federated states and even close cooperation of states that falls short of federation demonstrates that the various component units are less likely to resort to violence when disputes arise among them. The Bahá'í writings point to the United States of America as a successful example of federation and urge us to consider emulating this example on a global scale. In this regard 'Abdu'l-Bahá, successor to the Prophet-Founder Bahá'u'lláh and authorized interpreter of His writings, when visiting America early in the 20th century, advised a US government official that the best way he could promote the interests of his government and people was to strive, in his capacity as a citizen of the world, to assist in the eventual application of the principle of federalism underlying the US government to the relationships between the nations of the world.[46]

The Bahá'í blueprint for such an international federation envisions that it will comprise a number of organs including a world legislature or parliament whose members are to be elected by the citizens of each country respectively and confirmed by their respective governments. This legislature will ultimately control the resources of all the component nations and will enact laws that are necessary to 'regulate the life, satisfy the needs and adjust the relationships' of all peoples.[47] To this end, the Bahá'í writings envision that the 'economic resources of the world will be organized', its sources of raw materials 'tapped and fully utilized', its markets 'coordinated and developed' and the 'distribution of its products' 'equitably regulated' by the federation.[48] In short, the goal is to establish a world federal system, which will rule the whole earth and exercise unchallengeable authority over its vast resources, bending its energies to the exploitation of all the available resources for the benefit of all.[49] The federation will also include an international executive with an international standing military force at its disposal that will have the unchallengeable authority to enforce the laws enacted by the legislature, including the single code of international law and the judgements handed down by the Supreme Tribunal. It will also safeguard the organic unity of the whole commonwealth.[50] The federated state will also include a Supreme Tribunal as discussed above.[51]

What is most compelling about this vision, however, is the assertion in the Bahá'í writings that the achievement of this kind of organic unity will signal the coming of age of the entire human race. It will mark the last and highest stage in our collective evolution on this planet. When coupled with an emerging world community, the consciousness that we are all citizens of one world and the founding of a world civilization and culture, this world federation will be regarded as the furthermost limit in the organization of human society.[52]

Part 2

What Have We Built So Far?

What Have We Built So Far?

The key to creating a more peaceful and secure world for ourselves and for our children is to start being pro-active, rather than merely reacting to crises as they flare up. We must not only have a vision of the kind of system of collective security that would bring us the peace we crave, we must also learn from our mistakes by gauging the progress we have made and correctly identifying the weaknesses of current institutions and policies. Only then can we decide what steps we need to take to move from where we are to the point at which our vision is implemented.

It is clear that the world has been moving, albeit unconsciously and often in fits and starts, in the direction of the Bahá'í vision. However, progress towards the Bahá'í vision has been uneven; sometimes we leap several steps forward only to slide a few steps back again. It is equally clear that most progress made in this direction has been made reluctantly. Unanticipated world events are forcing humanity to face up to its responsibilities and to react in progressively maturer ways. Much as a rebellious teenager would, we continue to resist the obvious choices that would alleviate our suffering because we prefer to cling to our old comfortable ways no matter how dysfunctional and self-destructive they might be. Despite this resistance, however, with each new crisis or series of crises we relent a little and inch closer to the Bahá'í vision.

For Bahá'ís, this entire process is evidence that the Greater Plan of God is at work.[1] God is working through social, economic and political forces to help humanity learn some fundamental lessons. Humanity is being provided with numerous opportunities to do the right thing, finally to learn its lessons, grow up and move on. Every time we fail to learn, the test is repeated. The test also intensifies with repetition. In the pattern of current affairs certain crises recur, such as genocide and nuclear proliferation; with each recurrence the stakes are higher. These crises are occurring in ever-quickening succession. It is almost as though the world were in labour, waiting to give birth to an effective system of collective security.[2]

Efforts at Collective Action by World Leaders

Particularly over the last 15 years, there have been several efforts to bring together the leaders of the world to consult and agree on solutions to some of the seemingly intractable problems facing the community of nations. These efforts have generally been driven by and held under the auspices of the United Nations.

Some of the most recent gatherings are of particular relevance to the topic of collective security. In early September 2000, heads of state and government of all 191 member nations of the United Nations came together at the Millennium Summit in New York City. The participants met to 'reaffirm [their] faith in the [UN] Organization and its Charter as indispensable foundations of a more peaceful, prosperous and just world'.[3] At the conclusion of the meeting the member states adopted a document entitled 'United Nations Millennium Declaration' in which their leaders recognized their duty to all the world's people, especially its most vulnerable, and stated that they were 'determined to establish a just and lasting peace all over the world in accordance with the purposes of the Charter'.[4] They articulated certain 'fundamental values' which they deemed 'essential to international relations in the twenty-first century'.[5] These include freedom, equality, solidarity, tolerance, respect for nature and shared responsibility. Under the heading of shared responsibility, the leaders noted that managing threats to international peace and security 'must be shared among the nations of the world and should be exercised multilaterally'[6] and that the United Nations must play the central role in managing such a responsibility. To translate these shared values into action, the leaders identified some key objectives. Among these was the objective of freeing their peoples from the scourge of war, whether within states or between them, and of eliminating the dangers posed by weapons of mass destruction.

The nations resolved to take several steps. They resolved to strengthen respect for the rule of law in international affairs by ensuring compliance by member states with the decisions of the International Court of Justice. To make the United Nations more effective in maintaining peace and security, they agreed to give it the resources and tools it needs for conflict prevention, peaceful resolution of disputes, peacekeeping and the like. They also agreed to ensure the implementation by states parties of treaties in areas of arms control and disarmament, international humanitarian law and human rights. The 191 assembled nations resolved to take concerted action against international terrorism and to accede as soon as possible to all the relevant international conventions. They furthermore resolved to strive for the elimination of weapons of mass destruction, particularly nuclear weapons, and to consider convening an international conference to identify ways of eliminating nuclear dangers and to take concerted action to end illicit traffic in small arms and light weapons.

Other areas in which the nations resolved to act are in the thematic areas of development and poverty eradication; protection of our common environment; human rights; democracy and good governance; protection of the vulnerable; meeting the special needs of Africa; and strengthening the United Nations. After this summit, the leaders agreed to adopt eight development goals which they aimed to achieve by the year 2015. The goals are to eradicate extreme poverty and hunger; achieve universal primary education; promote gender equality and empower women; reduce child mortality; improve maternal health; combat HIV/AIDS, malaria and other diseases; ensure environmental sustainability; and develop a global partnership for development.[7] However, all of these goals are development related and none of them involve establishing a mechanism for collective security.

Although the leaders of the world achieved much at the Millennium Summit, they did not achieve all that is envisioned in the Bahá'í writings and they manifestly failed to establish a lasting and effective system of collective security. First, although the Millennium Declaration recognizes and affirms that 'nations and peoples have become increasingly interconnected and interdependent'[8] it still overemphasizes the traditional notions of national sovereignty that, as recognized by the Baháʾí vision, now impede progress towards truly effective collective security. Second, the Millennium Declaration and its goals fail to address several components of collective security articulated in the Baháʾí vision and essential to ultimate success. For example, there is no mention of the need to revisit and clearly fix boundaries between nations. Similarly, although certain fundamental values are articulated as essential to international relations in the 21st century, they do not include such essential principles as the oneness of peoples and nations. The assembled nations resolved to strengthen cooperation between the United Nations and regional organizations, in accordance with the provisions of Chapter VIII of the UN Charter but did not address the need to create an international police force or standing army to enforce the decisions of the Security Council or the International Court of Justice. Regarding arms reduction and non-proliferation of nuclear weapons, they resolved to ensure the implementation by states parties of arms control and disarmament treaties and to strive for the elimination of weapons of mass destruction but took no concrete measures to reduce arms proliferation. Similarly, they resolved to ensure compliance with the decisions of the International Court of Justice but took no practical steps to establish an enforcement mechanism or to expand the Court's jurisdiction over member states who choose not to be bound by its decisions. No mention was made of the need to make the Court more credible and trustworthy by revamping how its judges are elected. Finally, the Declaration leaves unaddressed how to move the international community in the direction of a world federation or the placing of some of the world's critical energy and other resources in the hands of a supranational agency to be used for the good of the totality of humankind.

Despite its shortcomings, we can view the Summit as a prelude to one or more future meetings of world leaders in which they will act more boldly to devise a viable system for the maintenance of international peace and security. Indeed, since the Millennium Summit, leaders of the world have gradually come to recognize the severe weaknesses inherent in the current system of collective security and have evinced a certain willingness to find new solutions. This, in itself, is a big step in the right direction, as only after accepting that certain institutions, policies and laws have outlived their usefulness and should be discarded can any far-reaching reforms of the international machinery of governance be successfully attempted. Recognizing the flaws inherent in the current system, world leaders commissioned high-level panels of experienced and distinguished individuals who have served in leadership capacities at both the national and international levels to produce studies. Two such bodies and the reports they produced stand out for the far-reaching effect of their work.

High-Level Panel on United Nations Peace Operations

The High-Level Panel on United Nations Peace Operations, also known as the Brahimi Commission after its chair, former Algerian Foreign Minister Lakhdar Brahimi, was convened by the Secretary-General of the United Nations Kofi Annan on 7 March 2000.[9] It was tasked with thoroughly reviewing United Nations peace and security activities and making frank, specific and realistic recommendations for change that would help the United Nations conduct such activities better in the future.[10] In addition to Mr Brahimi, the Panel included distinguished personalities from around the world with a wide range of experience in conflict prevention, peacekeeping and peacebuilding. The Panel produced its report, known as the Brahimi Report, on 17 August 2000. The Secretary-General urged the General Assembly and the Security Council to expeditiously implement its recommendations, which he described as 'far-reaching yet sensible and practical' and 'essential to make the United Nations truly credible as a force for peace'.[11] His hope was that the report would be brought to the attention of the leaders attending the Millennium Summit and that they would begin the process of enhancing the capacity of the United Nations to meet the current future threats to world peace.

One of the important observations of the Brahimi Report was that the 'United Nations does not wage war'.[12] When the United

Nations has found that enforcement action is necessary, it has delegated such action to coalitions of willing states, authorizing them to act under Chapter VII of the UN Charter. The Brahimi Report made the critical point that the United Nations does not have a standing army or a standing police force designed for field operations.[13] It also highlighted the fact that many member states have argued against the establishment of such a standing army and police force and have resisted entering into reliable standby arrangements under which they would provide the United Nations with military personnel and equipment and civilian police and other civilian experts when called upon to do so.[14]

The United Nations Standby Arrangements System (UNSAS), launched in the mid-1990s to enhance the United Nations's rapid deployment capabilities, has yet to become a dependable source of military or police resources. UNSAS is essentially a database of military, civilian police and civilian assets and expertise that governments participating in it commit to make available for deployment to the United Nations peacekeeping operations upon request at various intervals of notice ranging from seven to 90 days. As of 2000 when the Brahimi Report was published, 87 member states participated in UNSAS, committing to deploy a total of 147,900 personnel. Of these, 85,000 were in military combat units; 56,700 in supporting positions to the military and 1,600 were military observers. This figure also included 2,150 civilian police and 2,450 civilian specialists.[15] Unfortunately, however, of the 87 states participating, only 31 have concluded memoranda of understanding with the United Nations setting out their responsibilities for the level of preparedness of the personnel they are offering to deploy. Further, the memoranda that have been agreed contain clauses that make their commitments conditional. In the name of protecting national sovereignty, these memoranda allow the participating nations to avoid their commitment to contribute those assets to a peacekeeping operation at the request of the Secretary-General. As a practical reality, many member states refuse to deploy formed military units to United Nations peacekeeping operations far more often than they agree to do so,[16] which leaves the United Nations ill-equipped to fulfil its most fundamental mandate – indeed, the very purpose for which it exists – namely, to preserve and restore peace and security to a war- and conflict-ravaged humanity.

The Brahimi Report made it very clear that the United Nations has been and will continue to be severely handicapped in its ability to ensure world peace and security if it is not provided the force it needs to translate its words into deeds. The reality is that many parties to conflicts neither have respect for nor fear of verbal condemnation by the Security Council. Only strong and forceful action at the direction of the Council will be convincing for some nations bent on disrupting the peace and security of others. As the Brahimi Report states, what is needed is *'Res, non verba'*.[17]

The Brahimi Report marked an important milestone in the recent evolution of collective action by the international community. A standing army and police force constitutes a pre-eminent element of the Bahá'í vision of collective security. The Brahimi Report authoritatively identifies the absence of such a force as one of the most critical problems that must be addressed before a viable system of collective security can be crafted. It is therefore clear that thoughtful men and women of influence in international affairs are beginning to revisit this gaping shortcoming in our international infrastructure.

High-Level Panel on Threats, Challenges and Change

On 3 November 2003 the Secretary-General of the United Nations informed the General Assembly that he had appointed a group of 16 eminent people from around the world to serve on a High-Level Panel on Threats, Challenges and Change, with the former Prime Minister of Thailand, Mr Anand Panyarachun, serving as its chair.[18] The High-Level Panel's terms of reference began with the following dramatic words, indicating the severity of the situation facing our world in the area of peace and security: 'The past year has shaken the foundations of collective security and undermined confidence in the possibility of collective responses to our common problems and challenges.'[19] The Panel was charged with examining both current and future major threats and challenges to international peace and security that faced the world and assessing how well existing policies and institutions had done in addressing them. Finally, it was to recommend how to change the existing international infrastructure, including the principal organs of the United Nations, to provide effective collective security for the 21st century.

The impetus for this Panel was provided by the painful events of the previous 12 months. In many countries terrorism had once again brought suffering and death to the innocent, violence had continued to escalate in the Middle East and Africa, and in the Korean peninsula and elsewhere the ominous threat of nuclear proliferation continued to loom ever larger. It was recognized that there were new threats to be faced as well as old ones in new and dangerous combinations (such as terrorism and weapons of mass destruction). There was also an evolving understanding that all of the threats, whether they endangered life and limb (such as weapons of mass destruction, terrorism and organized crime), or caused economic distress (such as corruption and organized crime) or health problems (such as pandemics), were linked. Finally, it was acknowledged that the nations of world disagree on how to respond to these multiple threats effectively. This, in turn, had led to a great danger, articulated by the Secretary-General in his address to the General Assembly in September 2003: the absence of an effective collective system for addressing these threats would lead certain nations to act unilaterally or in *ad hoc* coalitions to protect themselves. Such an approach would lead eventually to the lawless use of force, with or without justification, and undermine the fabric of the international system as we have known it for over 50 years. The answer to this dilemma did not lie in simply denouncing unilateralism. Rather, as the Secretary-General acknowledged, we need to 'face up squarely to the concerns that make some States feel uniquely vulnerable, since it is those concerns that drive them to take unilateral action'. He concluded by saying: 'We must show that those concerns can, and will, be addressed effectively through collective action.'[20]

The Secretary-General went on to state his conviction that humanity has come to a fork in the road and that this moment could be as decisive as 1945 when the United Nations was founded. The question to be decided was whether it was possible for us to continue on the basis of the rules drawn up in 1945 to govern international behaviour and the institutions crafted to make the world safe or 'whether radical changes are needed'. He added that 'we must not shy away from questions about the adequacy, and effectiveness, of the rules and instruments at our disposal'. Rather, the time was ripe for us to take a hard look at fundamental policy issues and at the structural changes that may be needed in order to address them.

The High-Level Panel's Report, entitled 'A More Secure World: Our Shared Responsibility',[21] known as the Anand Report, was released in December 2004. The Panel drew on a wide range of sources including governments, academic experts and civil society organizations, and the composition of the Panel itself was diverse. As the Secretary-General of the United Nations noted, that such a diverse group could reach consensus on some of the most divisive issues among peoples and nations and come up with farsighted but workable recommendations gave him hope that the nations of the world could do the same, giving new meaning to the name 'United Nations'.[22] The Report is extremely important and worthy of careful study and implementation, particularly in light of the Bahá'í vision of collective security.

First, the Report acknowledges and stresses the reality that our world is interconnected as never before and that the threats we face are also interconnected. Moreover, the threats are such that no nation can hope to conquer them by acting alone. We are all mutually vulnerable whether our nation is weak or strong, small or large. Every state requires the cooperation of other states to make itself secure.[23] Indeed, what we need are shared policies, collective strategies and institutions and a sense of collective responsibility if we are to confront these threats adequately.[24] The Report's central thesis is that we need a comprehensive system of collective security that addresses the security concerns of all states. However, the first step is to arrive at a mutual recognition of threats because what often happens is that a group of nations perceives certain threats as not being serious threats to international peace. So, for example, not all nations agree that HIV/AIDS is a threat to the peace of the planet. Similarly, there are nations that do not believe terrorism is a threat to the peace and security of the planet.[25] Unfortunately, our perceptions as to what amounts to a genuine or grave threat have hitherto been determined by where we live and the degree of our affluence and power.

The Report says that we need a new consensus that we all share responsibility for each other's security. What the Report does not say – but which is inherent in its conclusion – is the reality that we are all one people. The truth is that consensus about shared responsibility is hard to achieve if we do not first agree that we are all one and that no one nation or people should vaunt itself over another. Ultimately, it will only be when we truly embrace this principle of oneness as foundational to the relations between nations and peoples that we will come to regard a threat to one as a threat to all and will not denigrate the gravity of a threat simply because we believe it does not immediately impact on us. It is only when we come to regard ourselves as members of a single human body that we will rally to the defence of any member that is threatened. It is really only by accepting this fundamental principle of human relations that we can begin to build the feelings of true caring and mutual responsibility that the world craves and that result in action rather than empty words. The alternative, which we have long experienced, is that each nation will look out only for itself, mistrust will rule and we will not cooperate for long-term mutual gain.

Although the Report openly acknowledges that certain attitudes, policies and institutions must change, it warns against change for its own sake. Change must be of the kind that helps us to meet the threats that face us today. The most important change needed is that of our perceptions of what state sovereignty means. The Report argues that regardless of the perceptions regarding state sovereignty that prevailed when the modern system of nation states was established with the signing of the Treaty of Westphalia in 1648, today the notion of state sovereignty carries with it the obligation of a state to protect the welfare of its own peoples and meet its obligations to the international community at large.

Moreover, if a state is unwilling or unable to meet its responsibilities to protect its own people and not harm its neighbours, then an effective system of collective security requires that those responsibilities should be assumed by the international community.[26] Having said that, the Report emphasizes that the success of a viable system of collective security rests on the viability and strength of the states comprising the international system because states are still the front-line responders to today's threats. We must therefore try to enhance their capacity to exercise their sovereign responsibility.[27] The Report also recommends fixing certain institutional weaknesses so that we can respond effectively to current threats. These include the need for the Security Council to be more pro-active and to become more credible, legitimate and representative. There is also a great need for the General Assembly of the UN to focus on the most compelling issues of the day rather than get caught up in minutiae or topics that are irrelevant to our current problems and a waste of time.[28]

Another critical point made by the Report is that in discharging its responsibility to protect, the international community must act early, decisively and collectively against all threats, especially those that lead to large-scale death or those which undermine states as the basic unit of the international system.[29] All too often action has been taken too late, as in Rwanda, or half-heartedly, as in the Sudan. Moreover, a credible system of collective security must be effective, efficient and equitable.[30] Like the Bahá'í writings, the Report recognizes the fundamental principle that there will be circumstances in which effective collective security may require the use of military force.[31] For enforcement to be robust, however, the international community must have deployable military resources in the form of both personnel and equipment. The Report highlights the need for all members of the international community to do more to provide the United Nations with such resources. To date, most decisions to authorize military force have relied upon multinational forces to whom the United Nations delegates the right to use force to enforce the peace rather than on the United Nations's blue helmets, which are under the direct command of the United Nations itself. The latter have been more frequently deployed when the circumstances involve peacekeeping rather than forceful intervention to restore peace. In other words, they have been deployed when parties to the conflict have consented to their presence, for example to monitor a cease-fire. It is time, however, to provide the United Nations with both the personnel and equipment to handle full-scale peace-enforcement missions as well as peacekeeping missions. One way to achieve this goal would be to encourage the regional development of peacekeeping capacity to be placed at the disposal of the United Nations, so long as it is used to enhance and not detract from the pool of peacekeepers the UN already draws from to respond when its blue helmets are requested.

One of the Report's frank observations is that we have damaged the credibility of our current system of collective security by applying it inequitably. Too often the international community has discriminated in responding to threats to international security based on who the beneficiaries would be, their location, resources or relationship to great powers. One of the contrasts the High-Level Panel invites us to consider is that between the swift response to the 11 September 2001 attacks upon New York and Washington and the far deadlier events that occurred from April to mid-July 1994 in Rwanda. That country experienced the equivalent of three 11 September attacks *every day* for 100 days. Despite these horrors, the Security Council's reaction was to withdraw most of its peacekeepers from the country two weeks into the genocide. It then took almost another month for UN officials to call the horror by its true name, genocide. Further, when a new mission was eventually authorized, few states offered soldiers. By the time the mission was finally deployed, the genocide had ended of its own accord. Similarly, the response of our international institutions to the massive human rights violations in the Darfur region of the Sudan has been exceedingly slow.[32]

Interestingly, the Report also observed that the Security Council has become increasingly active and willing to use its powers under Chapter VII of the Charter after the end of the Cold War between the United States and the Soviet Union, dramatically shifting the balance from unilateral use of force towards collectively authorized force. This has led to a recent expectation and an emerging norm that the Security Council should be the arbiter of the use of force.[33] Warning against anarchy, however, the Report stresses the need for consensus on rules that govern the decision to go to war.[34] In other words, there has to be a common global understanding of when force is justified morally and legally and based on solid evidentiary grounds.[35] The Report rightly points out that a show of force, if deployed early enough while tensions are still mounting but before all-out conflict has broken out, will often deter would-be aggressors as well as reassure parties seeking peaceful resolution.[36]

In this vein, the Report also discusses how the new International Criminal Court can deter some breaches of the peace. It recommends that the Security Council use its authority under the Rome Statute which created the Court to refer cases to it.[37] Surprisingly, the Report does not recommend strengthening the International Court of Justice, in particular by extending its jurisdiction to make it compulsory over all disputes between nations. Nor does the Report address the importance of creating an international force to enforce the decisions of the International Court of Justice.

A critical area that the Report does touch upon is the role that fights over natural resources have played in destroying international peace and security. Examples can be found in the wars that have ravaged Sierra Leone, Angola and the Democratic Republic of the Congo. The Report makes a good recommendation to deal with this issue: it suggests that the International Law Commission (ILC) be asked to develop rules for the use of transboundary resources such as water, oil and gas.[38] It also suggests that the United Nations support weak states in managing their natural resources in order to avoid future conflicts.[39] The Report does not go so far as to recognize or address the need to put certain resources in the hands of a supranational institution.

Another key area that the Report addresses in some detail is the need to limit the proliferation of weapons of all kinds, starting with small arms and light weapons at one end of the spectrum to weapons of mass destruction, namely nuclear, biological and chemical weapons, at the other end. With respect to small arms, it recommends increasing transparency of member states' conventional weapons holdings and acquisitions using the UN Register of Conventional Arms established in 1991. Under this system, members make declarations every year about their sales and purchases of conventional weapons and their existing weapons holdings, as well as their defence strategies, policies and doctrines. Unfortunately, these annual declarations are purely voluntary. The declarations that have been made have been incomplete, untimely and inaccurate. As for the proliferation of nuclear weapons, the international treaty system that governs this is close to collapse, as reflected by the world community's surprise discovery that several nations, including Iraq, North Korea and Libya, each had a secret nuclear weapons programme they had been working on for years, by its continuing inability to deal with treaty violations by North Korea and Iran and by the recent willingness of the United States to begin cooperation in civilian nuclear technologies with India, which has steadfastly refused to join the nuclear non-proliferation treaties. It is critical to address both conventional weapons and weapons of mass destruction in crafting a new viable system for collective security. The Report recognizes that the international institutions involved, such as the International Atomic Energy Agency and the Organization for the Prohibition of Chemical Weapons, need to work more closely with the Security Council and that the inspection, monitoring and verification systems need to be substantially enhanced. There is also the problem of ensuring that the stockpiles of existing weapons are secured so that they do not fall into the hands of terrorists or others who might misuse them. The Report stops short of recommending that each nation be permitted to keep only a certain amount of weaponry that is necessary for it to maintain its internal order and no more. This is one of the key elements in the Bahá'í blueprint for crafting a workable system of collective security.

The work of the High-Level Panel on Threats, Challenges and Change represents a dramatic leap forward in collective thinking about a system of collective security that will ensure the peace of the planet at this stage in our history. It touches on many of the principles and elements identified in the Bahá'í writings as essential for a viable collective security system and clearly attempts to move the world, albeit unwittingly, further in the direction of the vision given to us by Bahá'u'lláh. Although it does not cover all of the elements to be found in the Bahá'í blueprint on collective security – such as the need to revisit the question of borders and to fix them anew, once and for all – it nevertheless represents a groundbreaking shift in thinking which nations would do well to embrace. The question that remains is how quickly the international community will implement the Panel's recommendations. Although the members of the Panel were all distinguished members of the international community, they were not acting on behalf of their governments but rather in their individual capacities. The Secretary-General of the United Nations was persuaded by much of the thinking in this Report and drew heavily on it in crafting a report of his own to the United Nations General Assembly.

'In Larger Freedom'

The Secretary-General's report, entitled 'In Larger Freedom' (ILF),[40] dated March 2005, reviewed the international community's progress in implementing the Millennium Declaration and proposed an ambitious agenda to reform the United Nations. The Secretary-General hoped that the leaders of the world would embrace his proposals at a world summit in September 2005 and create 'agile and effective regional and global intergovernmental institutions to mobilize and coordinate collective action'.[41] The Secretary-General believed that the recommendations were both vital and achievable in the coming months.

The ILF Report begins by reiterating the theme of global interdependence that has now become familiar in these reports. The Secretary-General writes, 'At no time in human history have the fates of every woman, man and child been so intertwined across the globe. We are united both by moral imperatives and by objective interests.'[42] He says that both 'the glue of common interest' and 'the impulses of our common humanity' should bind nations together in their attempt to reach consensus on a course of collective action, a consensus for which there is a 'yearning' in many quarters.[43] He goes on to articulate his belief that nations need to achieve broad, deep and sustained global cooperation of a kind that is only possible if every country's policies take into account not only the needs of its own citizens but also the needs of others.[44] A moment's reflection on these words and ideas makes it apparent that he is, in effect, talking about Bahá'u'lláh's principle of oneness, which requires that the nations of the world regard themselves as members of one body. That which redounds to the good of the whole will certainly serve the best interests of the individual parts.

The Secretary-General also talks about the need for shared principles and priorities.[45] He says we must reshape the UN, which was created in the radically different world of 1945, in ways not previously imagined and with a boldness and speed not previously shown so that it meets the needs and circumstances of the 21st century. He urges us by saying, 'At this defining moment in history, we must be ambitious.'[46]

In addressing the theme of collective security, the ILF Report notes that despite the deep threat that is felt by all, we lack even a basic consensus about how to face the threat and any attempts at action are fraught with disagreement and conflict. It concludes that collective security today depends on accepting that threats that each region of the world perceives as most urgent for itself are in fact equally urgent for all.[47] The Report also recognizes the need for better monitoring and firmer enforcement. To this end, the Report urges states to create strategic military reserves to be put at the disposal of the UN for rapid deployment when the need arises. It also applauds and encourages the development of regional organizations with reserve military capacities and suggests that a system be set up that allows the UN to work in partnership with such groups.[48] However, having enough troops is insufficient. There must also be agreement on when and how the international community may use force to defend international peace and security.[49] This has been a deeply divisive issue among states and will continue to be so unless it is resolved by agreement. To this end the Secretary-General recommends that the Security Council adopt a resolution setting out the principles and guidelines that it will look to when deciding whether to authorize or mandate the use of force.[50]

One of the principles that the Secretary-General advocates is that of 'a collective responsibility to protect'. This responsibility lies first and foremost with each state and requires it to protect the human rights and well-being of its citizens, especially in the face of genocide, ethnic cleansing, war crimes and crimes against humanity. Such responsibility shifts to the international community once it is clear that national authorities are either unable or unwilling to protect their citizens from such atrocities. The international community is then required to protect these civilian populations using all means at its disposal including, if need be, swift and decisive enforcement action by the Security Council using its Chapter VII powers.[51] Another principle that the Report briefly touches on is the need to apply the laws equally and consistently. The Secretary-General says that we must reduce arbitrary enforcement of our international laws and their selective application, which leads to breach without consequence.[52] Indeed, such uneven application of the laws has served to mar the credibility of the system as a whole. It is critical that our laws be implemented properly and even-handedly.

The ILF Report dwells at length on the need to revitalize our multilateral infrastructure for handling threats from nuclear, biological and chemical weapons. While acknowledging the role that such infrastructure has played to date in promoting disarmament and preventing proliferation among states, the Report recognizes that the infrastructure is fast eroding.[53] The Report makes several suggestions. The international community should resolve the tensions underlying the current problems relating to nuclear proliferation, especially the tension between the desire for cheap nuclear energy on the one hand and the desire to avoid nuclear proliferation on the other. The verification authority of the IAEA should be strengthened. Incentives should be created for states voluntarily to forgo the development of uranium enrichment and plutonium separation capacities while receiving a guaranteed supply of fuel necessary to develop peaceful uses of nuclear energy. It also recommends that the Security Council be

41

better informed on all matters related to nuclear, chemical and biological threats.[54] Nowhere, however, does the Report even hint at the possibility of limiting the number of arms that each state be allowed to maintain to a level sufficient to keep order within its borders but no more. This simple yet far-reaching recommendation made by Bahá'u'lláh is still to be broached by the international community.

The ILF Report recognizes the need to strengthen the rule of law by encouraging universal participation in multilateral conventions. Unlike the High-Level Panel's Report, the ILF Report also acknowledges the centrality of the International Court of Justice in the international system for adjudicating disputes among states and recommends that its work be strengthened. One way is to urge states to recognize the compulsory jurisdiction of the Court if they have not already done so. The ILF Report also recommends making greater use of the Court's advisory powers.[55] The ILF Report does not, however, go as far as to recommend that the jurisdiction of the Court be made compulsory upon all states or that the Court's decisions be backed by force if necessary, as envisioned in the Bahá'í proposals for collective security.

The ILF Report recognizes that many international treaty bodies have been compromised by the failure of a number of states to submit required reports on time. This, in turn, is caused partly by the duplication of reporting requirements. The ILF Report recommends that harmonized guidelines on reporting to all treaty bodies be put in place, allowing them to function as a unified system.[56] Moreover, multilateral agencies, funds and programmes which have significant overlapping or duplicate mandates and actions should be reorganized to eliminate those that are redundant while grouping the rest into tightly managed bodies.[57]

The ILF Report also deals with the question of institutional reform within the United Nations. It stresses the need for the General Assembly to deliberate on the substantive issues of the day rather than retreating into generalities and failing to take action.[58] It also urges that the Security Council become more representative and therefore credible. The Council should make its working methods more efficient and transparent.[59] However, the Report does not go as far as to recommend the elimination of the right of veto exercised by the five permanent members of the Security Council.

Millennium Summit Review and Outcome Document

In the interval between the release of the ILF Report and the world summit of leaders that occurred in September 2005, the international community wrangled over the Secretary-General's far-reaching proposals and agonized over how far it was willing to go. Many of the issues our leaders had before them proved to be contentious and fears ran high on all sides. Many nations were unwilling to look beyond their narrow national interests and to make necessary concessions that would benefit the collective inter-est. Rather, they dug their heels in, unwilling to give up positions they had staked out as critical to their self-interest. As the dead-line for the summit loomed, there was a fear that the international community would fail to agree on a final draft document that could be adopted by the summit. At the eleventh hour, however, a severely watered-down consensus was forged – a consensus that gave truth to the words of the Secretary-General in his ILF Report to the effect that the UN General Assembly tended to 'retreat into generalities' and that 'many so-called decisions simply reflect the lowest common denominator of widely different opinions.'[60]

The final Outcome Document[61] was hugely disappointing. World leaders failed to seize a historic opportunity to tackle thorny issues and make critical decisions towards the creation of a viable system of collective security. They chose to avoid many of the contentious issues raised by Secretary-General Kofi Annan. Foremost were the issues of nuclear non-proliferation and dis-armament. Not a word addresses these most critical concerns of our time. The failure was all the more acute in light of the failure in May of the same year of nations reviewing the Nuclear Non-Proliferation Treaty to agree on any matters of substance. The omission at the Millennium Summit displays the current paraly-sis of world leaders in the face of admittedly widespread concern about the proliferation of weapons of mass destruction and the danger that they might get into the hands of those who would use them unscrupulously to the detriment of all. The negotiators also failed to agree on several other critical issues. They failed to agree on an unambiguous definition of terrorism which would reflect the moral principle that killing civilians for any reason, political or otherwise, was unacceptable in the 21st century. Such a definition would have sent a strong message to communities worldwide. They failed to agree upon criteria for the legitimate use of force. They failed to agree on expanding the Security Council to make it more representative. The Secretary-General's response to the Outcome Document, particularly to its failure to address non-proliferation and disarmament issues, was simply, 'This is a real disgrace.'[62]

Perhaps the most significant agreement that did emerge from the Millennium Summit related to the international community's collective responsibility to intervene to protect civilian populations faced with genocide, ethnic cleansing, war crimes and crimes against humanity. Leaders agreed to intervene collectively when a state, as the front-line defender of its people, clearly has failed to protect its populations, and they agreed to use force if necessary. The acceptance of this principle of the responsibility to protect means that world leaders have also accepted the reality that state sovereignty is not unlimited or unfettered and that it carries with it responsibilities as well as rights. Another important agreement was to commit more readily available reserves, both military and civilian, for peacekeeping and peace enforcement operations. The world's leaders also agreed to create a new Human Rights Council to replace the discredited Human Rights Commission,[63] as well as a new Peacebuilding Commission that would focus on the needs of nations emerging from conflict.

Despite the hope of many that the World Summit of September 2005 would bring about a breakthrough in international relations and set the world on a course that would assure its peace and security, our leaders allowed the opportunity to slip by. They recognized the need for far-reaching change and had the Secretary-General's blueprint for action at hand. In the final analysis, however, they lacked the political will to embrace the changes necessary. One of the causes of the Summit's failure was the failure of enough of the world's leaders to engage in the critical debates and influence them. Despite the disappointment many feel because of this failure, we must not give up; indeed, we cannot afford to. We have no choice but to forge ahead. We must encourage our leaders to get more involved in the critical issues of the day and to exert every effort to ensure that our world is a safer place for this and future generations. History has taught us that if we do not have an international mechanism in place responsible for dealing with the peace and security of the planet, then we will have to create one. We learned this in the 1930s when the League of Nations, tasked with maintaining the peace of the world, fell apart. We had no choice but to build a new institution in the form of the United Nations to take its place. Rather than wait for a total breakdown again before we are forced to act, it behoves us to be bold and make the kind of changes that will secure our world.

Determining Final Boundaries

The 20th century's biggest conflicts, including the two world wars, the Korean War, the Vietnam War and the first Gulf War bear eloquent testament to the fact that boundary disputes, if left unresolved, can mire entire regions and even distant countries in war and conflict. There is no doubt, therefore, that this topic is of the greatest importance. Unfortunately, attempts to tackle the problem of border disputes worldwide have been haphazard, resulting in occasional success but leaving the bulk of the problems intact. So, for example, while international law has developed certain rules that govern the determination of territorial sovereignty, in other words, determination of the mass of land or water that may be said to lie within the territory of any given state, boundary disputes continue to flare up.

One of the problems we face is a historical one and stems from the fact that many regions of the world were occupied by external powers, be they western colonial powers or the Russian and Ottoman Empires, for instance. Once these empires collapsed, the Cold War froze these political structures as they were at the end of the Second World War. The balance of power maintained during the Cold War served to preserve the *status quo*. Once the Cold War ended, all the ethnic and religious divisions that lay smouldering beneath the surface began to heat up again. Disaffected peoples strove to break away from their states and set up their own dominions where they could exercise self-determination. To deal with this set of problems, international law developed a doctrine called '*uti possidetis*' with a view to ensuring the independence and stability of new states particularly after decolonization. This doctrine requires that territorial boundaries existing at the moment that independence is achieved must be respected.[64] However, despite the doctrine, many boundary disputes have continued to arise mainly because the independent peoples that emerged post-colonization had not had a say in the way their boundaries were drawn and were reluctant to accept wholesale a system of boundary demarcation agreed to among the colonial powers whose shackles they had broken. Moreover, the doctrine of *uti possidetis* often conflicts with another principle of international law, that of the self-determination of peoples.[65] An example of a boundary dispute arising in a post-independence situation but involving the principle of self-determination is Somalia, which claims those parts of Ethiopia and Kenya inhabited by Somali tribes.[66]

Despite frequent problems with boundary disputes, there has been no systematic effort on the part of the international community to tackle this issue effectively. There is no international system to identify in a timely fashion all of the flash points in the world resulting from such disputes. Nor is there a set of fair and consistent rules that can be applied methodically to resolve such disputes or a responsible international body with the authority to make such determinations. The approach we have taken to this problem has, again, been reactive rather than pro-active. Our usual procedure has been to wait for a border dispute to flare up, at which point one of two things will usually happen: either the parties involved voluntarily take the matter before the International Court of Justice and await its judgement, which they may or may not then implement, or the dispute takes a turn for the worse and conflict and violence ensue, forcing the international community to get involved and take some action.[67]

Both approaches leave much to chance and are inherently unsatisfactory because they do not guarantee an efficient, effective and systematic way to resolve problems in an equitable and timely manner. The first of the two approaches is risky as it depends on the parties' good will, which can be unreliable given the self-interest inherent in these situations. It requires the parties in a border conflict to do two things. First, they must be willing to submit to the jurisdiction of the International Court, because as things now stand, the Court does not have compulsory jurisdiction over all states regarding all disputes. This voluntary submission is generally made either by special agreement, called a *compromis*, or by virtue of the parties' prior submission to the Court's compulsory jurisdiction. Second, they must be willing to abide by any judgement rendered by the International Court given that the Court has no mechanism for enforcing its judgements.

There have been several instances where this approach has been successful but only because parties have chosen to take both of the requisite steps. One example involves Bahrain and Qatar, who both eventually agreed in 1991 to submit a longstanding series of border disputes to the International Court of Justice.[68] The disputes had been so fraught with difficulty that they had brought this internationally critical region to the brink of war in 1986. The Court resolved the disputes in March 2001 and awarded Bahrain the Hawar Islands and Qit'at Jaradah Island and gave Qatar Janan Island and the low-tide elevation of Fasht ad Dibal. The Court also drew a maritime boundary as requested by the parties. Almost immediately both countries praised the decision, even though the decision rejected some territorial claims each had long characterized as non-negotiable. There was a palpable sense of relief on both sides because the Court had managed to cut the Gordian knot that had long been the main point of contention between the two Gulf neighbours. The parties' reaction to this case illustrates that even persistent disputes can be set aside if resolved through an accepted medium – in this case the International Court of Justice. Another example involved a dispute between Belgium and the Netherlands over certain border plots surrounding the Belgian commune Baerle-Duc and the Dutch commune Baarle-

Nassau.[69] The countries submitted the dispute to the Court by a special agreement, asking the Court to decide which party had sovereignty. The Court held that the disputed plots were Belgian and the parties accepted the Court's decision.

The dispute between Cambodia and Thailand involving the Temple of Preah Vihear[70] demonstrates the persuasive power of a Court decision, even without formal, legal acceptance by the parties. Cambodia claimed that Thailand was infringing its territorial sovereignty over the land surrounding the ruins of the Temple of Preah Vihear, which is an ancient sanctuary and shrine of considerable artistic and archaeological interest. The Court found in favour of Cambodia. Thailand has overtly refused to accept the Court's decision, regarding which she continues to maintain a rather vague reservation.[71] Nonetheless, while formally refusing to accept the judgement, Thailand has in fact followed the Court's ruling ever since and there have been no disputes over the shrine by either state.

The land and maritime boundary disputes of Cameroon and Nigeria presented a more challenging example of dispute resolution. The Court was first seized of the dispute in 1994 when Cameroon brought it the question of sovereignty over the oil-rich Bakassi Peninsula.[72] Since both parties had accepted the Court's compulsory jurisdiction under Article 36(2) of the Court's Statute (also known as the 'optional clause'), the Court decided it had jurisdiction over the case. In 1996, before the Court could act, armed incidents occurred between the two countries, resulting in the occupation by Nigeria of the peninsula and Lake Chad. Cameroon subsequently widened its application to the Court by requesting that the Court determine the land boundary between the two states from Lake Chad to the sea and the maritime boundaries extending into the ocean. Cameroon also claimed reparations from Nigeria for damage suffered as a result of the occupation of Bakassi and Lake Chad. The Court rendered its judgement in October 2002. However, implementation of the Court-established boundaries proved troublesome. By May 2006, although most of the border had been demarcated and territories and villages had changed hands between Nigeria and Cameroon, the Bakassi peninsula remained in Nigerian hands, leaving the core dispute unresolved. After many interventions by the then Secretary-General of the United Nations, Kofi Annan, Nigerian President Olusegun Obasanjo finally promised in a May 2006 meeting in Geneva with his Cameroonian counterpart Paul Biya that Nigeria would withdraw her troops from the oil-rich Bakassi peninsula. Nigeria began her withdrawal on 1 August 2006. This was followed by a formal handover of the northern part of the peninsula in a ceremony on 14 August. The parties also reached an agreement that the rest of the peninsula was to stay under Nigerian civil authority for a further two years, until the end of 2008, when its residents would have to choose between staying and becoming Cameroonian subjects or being resettled in Nigeria.[73]

An even more challenging example involved armed conflict between Libya and Chad over the Aozou Strip,[74] a purported source for uranium in northern Chad. Libya set off the dispute by annexing the strip of land in 1973. With the assistance of the Organization of African Unity, Libya and Chad ultimately were persuaded to submit the dispute to the Court. The Court determined the boundaries of these vast disputed territories by ruling in favour of Chad. The parties accepted the judgement because it clearly demonstrated that the 1955 Treaty of Friendship and Good Neighbourliness between the two countries had left no boundaries undefined and because the background materials to the treaty showed that Libya understood that the boundaries were set. Troops withdrew under the surveillance of the Security Council and there has since been peace on the border.

In all the cases mentioned above the parties voluntarily agreed to submit their dispute to the Court for resolution and were willing to abide by the Court's judgement. All too often, however, countries have not been willing to accept the Court's jurisdiction or to abide by the Court's decision. For instance, Australia and East Timor have long disputed the maritime boundary between them. Underlying the dispute are substantial oil and gas deposits under the Timor Sea. Although East Timor proposed that the dispute be decided by the Court, Australia was unwilling to do this.[75] Indeed, in March 2002, two months shy of East Timor gaining its independence from Indonesia, Australia withdrew its previous, broad agreement to submit to the compulsory jurisdiction of the Court and replaced it with a more narrow declaration. Amongst other things, the new declaration excludes disputes involving maritime boundary delimitations or disputes concerning the exploitation of an area in dispute or adjacent to an area in dispute on the grounds that such disputes are best resolved through negotiation rather than by a Court or Tribunal.[76] In January 2006 the two countries entered into a treaty in which they agreed to defer the disputed issue of a permanent maritime boundary for 50 years and to evenly split revenues from extracting gas and oil from the Greater Sunrise field between them. This is a clear example of a case in which the parties have not submitted their dispute to the Court and are, rather, attempting to resolve the dispute by agreement amongst themselves.

Similarly, the People's Republic of China and Japan have long disputed sovereignty to certain islands (the Senkaku Islands) in the East China Sea. Moreover, the two countries disagree as to where the maritime boundary between them lies. Japan maintains that the median or equidistance line between the Ryukyu Islands and the Chinese mainland forms the boundary of its exclusive economic zone in the East China Sea. Beijing, on the other hand, insists that the continental shelf should be the basis for deciding this boundary. At stake are the potential oil and gas reserves that lie in the disputed areas which each side wants to have the right to develop. Talks between the two countries have not resulted in any agreement. Yet the countries have not submitted these disputes either to the International Court of Justice or to arbitration under the provisions of the United Nations Law of the Sea Convention.

When parties to a boundary dispute decline to rely upon the International Court of Justice, what often happens is that the dispute festers until it results in open conflict and violence. At that point the international community may decide to take action to ameliorate the situation or it may decide it is not worth the effort and resources and stand idly by in the hope that the situation will eventually resolve itself. The longstanding boundary dispute between Iraq and Kuwait provides an example of an instance in which the international community stood idly by for a long time but was finally compelled to act, albeit too late. The dispute stemmed from the days following World War I when the British divided Kuwait and Iraq into separate emirates. Iraq never recognized Kuwait's independent sovereignty. Indeed, in the 1960s the United Kingdom sent troops to Kuwait to prevent its annexation by Iraq. However, Iraq still did not recognize Kuwait's sovereignty. In August 1990 Iraq unlawfully invaded and attempted to annex Kuwait. In the face of this overt Iraqi aggression, the international community finally decided to respond. Coalition forces from 28 countries led by the United States acted under Security Council mandate to oust Iraq from Kuwait. Thereafter the Security Council, acting years too late, created the Iraq–Kuwait Boundary Demarcation Commission to resolve the dispute by demarcating the boundary between the two countries.[77] The Commission included one representative from Iraq, one from Kuwait and three independent experts appointed by the Secretary-General of the United Nations. Although Iraq stopped participating in 1992, the Commission concluded its work and set the boundary along the lines agreed by Iraq and Kuwait in 1932 and again in 1963. The Security Council then demanded that Iraq and Kuwait respect the inviolability of the boundary. In November 1994, while under pressure of international sanctions and continual monitoring by the Security Council, Iraq finally informed the Secretary-General of the United Nations that it acquiesced in the Commission's decision and recognized Kuwait's sovereignty, territorial integrity and international boundaries.[78]

Successful intervention by the international community represents the exception rather than the rule. In most cases the international community has opted to stand by and see what happens. This approach is evident in many parts of the world and includes some of the best-known regional conflicts of our time. For example, there is the question of the proper boundaries between Israel and Syria in the Golan Heights as well as the Israeli/Palestinian question involving disputed land in the West Bank and Gaza strip. Although members of the international community have been involved on and off in attempting to resolve these two disputes over decades, the interventions have not led to a successful resolution. Then there is the dispute between India and Pakistan over Kashmir, where the international community has been even less engaged, content to leave the parties to make their own way towards a solution.

What is clearly needed is a more pro-active approach that aims to identify potential trouble spots early on, to solicit input from all the parties involved, to craft a body of generally agreed-upon principles and rules which, by advance agreement of the international community, apply to all border disputes, and to appoint an international body, such as the United Nations Security Council or the World Court, with authority to apply the relevant principles and rules. Finally, there must be an enforcement mechanism to ensure that the parties will comply with the final decision of whatever international body is tasked with resolving these disputes. Bahá'u'lláh's vision inspires concrete recommendations for action, which will be discussed more in part 3 of this book.

Determining the Principles to Govern Our International Relations

Some careful thinkers, particularly in the field of collective security, have recently begun to recognize that to craft effective solutions to specific problems, be they genocide, amassing of weapons of mass destruction, terrorism and the like, we must begin by identifying some first principles and agreeing upon them. Gareth Evans, former Foreign Minister of Australia and President and CEO of the Brussels-based International Crisis Group, states this succinctly: 'There is no substitute for going back to first principles, getting consensus around them, and then applying them.'[79] He adds, 'Regrettably, none of the above is normal government practice, domestically or internationally.' His experience both as a cabinet minister in Australia for over a decade and as someone who has served on a number of high-profile international commissions and high-level panels has afforded him the opportunity to witness first-hand the inner workings of government at both the national and international levels. He is therefore well placed to make the sort of assessment articulated above. He does not stand alone, however.

Others have reached similar conclusions. They include former United Nations Secretary-General Kofi Annan, who said that the international community needs to work together 'on the basis of shared principles and priorities'.[80] Robert Kagan, a Senior Associate at the Carnegie Endowment for International Peace in Washington DC and an expert in US national security and foreign policy, has reached a similar conclusion. In a speech he gave in Melbourne in November 2004, he said that the differences that came to the fore between Europe and the United States over Iraq 'were not only about policy. They were also about first principles.'[81] He noted that polls taken before, during and after US military intervention in Iraq in March 2003 showed that some 80 per cent of Americans but less than 50 per cent of Europeans believed that war can sometimes bring about justice. Moreover, Europeans have a powerful aversion to military power, power politics and the very idea of the balance of power in international relations. Americans and Europeans also disagreed about the role of international law and institutions and the key question of what makes international action legitimate.[82] These differences, said Kagan, have led to a great 'philosophical schism' within the West which could have serious consequences given the proliferation of new dangers and threats.[83]

Fortunately, as a result of the nascent recognition of the need to identify first principles from which effective solutions can be extrapolated, we are beginning to see more discussion by leaders of thought as well as political leaders in an attempt to identify such principles. An example of a robust discussion that has given rise to what has been characterized by the former Secretary-General of the United Nations as an identifiable 'emerging norm'[84] is the discussion about our collective responsibility to protect civil populations from the threat of genocide, ethnic cleansing, war crimes and crimes against humanity. This discussion was initiated by the International Commission on Intervention and State Sovereignty and continued by the High-Level Panel on Threats, Challenges and Change. Over time this principle has won broad support among leaders of the international community, including that of the former Secretary-General of the United Nations as articulated in his ILF Report.[85] This principle accords with those urged in the Bahá'í writings. Other similar principles are emerging from discussions and writings, such as this book, around which we will hopefully build a solid consensus over time.

Principle of the Just War

A prominent example of an old, familiar principle that has seen a resurgence in recent times in the form of military interventions by the United Nations is that wars can be just if the reason for which they are fought and the way they are fought meet certain conditions. The principle of the 'just war' is closely associated with Christian philosophical tradition and is attributed by some to St Augustine. For a war to be just, it must be fought as a last resort, by a legitimate authority with the intention of redressing a wrong suffered and with the object of re-establishing a lasting peace. It must have a reasonable chance of success so as to avoid fruitless death and injury and the violence it wreaks must be proportional to the injury suffered. All efforts must be made to avoid killing civilians.

This principle finds its corollary in Bahá'u'lláh's principle that force must be made the servant of justice, that war fought for a righteous purpose can be a powerful basis of peace. The degree of consensus surrounding the principle of the just war is reflected in the report on security and geopolitics made by the World Economic Forum held in Davos in January 2003, which states that there was general acceptance of this principle by those attending the Forum's meeting.[86] Participants agreed that the wars in Bosnia and Kosovo were viewed as just and legitimate, as was the war by the United States against Afghanistan to punish it for the Taliban's harbouring of al-Qaeda terrorists.[87] They also generally acknowledged that countries could start a war of self-defence to prevent an attack if that threat were sufficiently real. The participants were even willing to acknowledge that taking pre-emptive or preventive military action against a non-imminent threat could be legitimate, so long as there was strong and ample evidence justifying such an attack and proper procedures were followed.[88] It appears that although many of us in the West have had a visceral discomfort with the use of military force, we are now relearning that war can be in some circumstances a progressive cause.[89]

Principle of Responsibility to Protect

A corollary of the principle of just war is the newly articulated principle of the 'responsibility to protect' that emerged from the groundbreaking work of the International Commission on Intervention and State Sovereignty (ICISS) sponsored by the Canadian government.[90] The Commission's report, presented to the Secretary-General of the United Nations in December 2001, asserted that the international community is responsible to protect those suffering from serious and irreparable harm, such as large-scale loss of life and gross human rights atrocities, and who are in dire need of protection. The report argued that this responsibility to protect is 'an emerging international norm or guiding principle of behaviour for the international community of states' which has the potential over time, if consolidated by state practice, to become customary international law.[91]

By using new language to frame the principle as one of a responsibility to protect, the report has been able in one stroke both to identify a principle that the international community could consider and to build consensus around while avoiding the age-old negative visceral responses that resulted when states talked about the principle of the 'right to intervene'. The latter has generally been associated with colonialist aspirations and trampling on what were considered the sacred rights enshrined in state sovereignty. By using new language evoking the noble human sentiments of responsibility and protection, rather than the more aggressive concepts of rights and intervention, the Commission calls for governments and leaders to rethink their previously entrenched stances and to consider the benefits of applying such a principle both in their capacity as individual nations and as a community of nations.

The Commission's formulation also broadened the scope of

international involvement. Whereas the disfavoured historical formulation of a right to intervene focused narrowly on acts during a crisis, the responsibility to protect connotes a continuum of obligations at various stages of a crisis, including the responsibility to prevent harm by addressing the root causes of internal conflict, the responsibility to intervene to cease human suffering and the responsibility to rebuild, especially after forceful intervention, by providing full assistance with recovery, reconstruction and reconciliation.

Since the articulation of this principle in this form, it has been endorsed both by the High-Level Panel on Threats, Challenges and Change in its report discussed earlier in this book, which stated that its members saw an 'emerging norm that there is a collective responsibility to protect'[92] and by the United Nations Secretary-General in his report 'In Larger Freedom'.[93] The Secretary-General explained that individual states have the primary responsibility to protect their own populations but if they are unwilling or unable to do so then the responsibility shifts to the international community to act using all means, including enforcement action if necessary.[94] Most importantly, the principle has recently been endorsed by the world leaders at their Summit in September 2005.[95]

The principle of responsibility to protect also has its corollary in the writings of Bahá'u'lláh over a century ago. In letters that He addressed to various kings and rulers of the world He called upon them to treat the people entrusted to their care with loving-kindness and mercy[96] and to protect and help their oppressed people.[97] He warned that failing to do so would lead to the destruction of the governments and rulers involved. The Bahá'í writings also clearly recognize not only the right but the duty of governments to use force for the maintenance of law and order and to protect their people.[98]

Principle of Collective Benefits and Curtailed State Sovereignty

Another related principle that is emerging as a result of the work of the ICISS concerns the concept of state sovereignty itself, focusing the discussion on what state sovereignty is meant to achieve and what it implies. The evolving thinking suggests that state sovereignty implies responsibility towards the people within the state rather than control over their destiny, which in turn implies that state sovereignty is not absolute but relative and limited. Indeed, the members of the ICISS Commission were intrigued to discover that even the most ardent supporters and defenders of traditional state sovereignty did not argue that a state had unlimited power to do what it wanted to its own people.[99] On the contrary, by and large the international community had moved away from the traditional notion of the respect owed to state sovereignty and had recognized the limits on such sovereignty dictated by other generally accepted principles such as human rights and human security, broadly understood as the protection of individuals and communities from any form of political violence such as civil war, genocide and the displacement of populations.[100]

Further evidence of the shift in thinking that is occurring with respect to the concept of state sovereignty can be found in a speech made by Dr Javier Solana in 1998 while he was still Secretary-General of NATO. In it he explains the limits of the principle of sovereignty that lies at the heart of the modern system of states, also known as the Westphalian system. This principle he asserts has 'produced the basis for rivalry, not community of states; exclusion, not integration'. He goes on to note that state sovereignty became associated with 'nationalistic fervour that degenerated into a destructive political force'. Consequently, he concludes, the system has been unable to guarantee peace or to prevent war. He then suggests an alternative approach saying, 'It is my general contention that humanity and democracy – two principles essentially irrelevant to the original Westphalian order – can serve as guideposts in crafting a new international order, better adapted to the security realities, and challenges, of today's Europe'.[101]

This emerging view of state sovereignty represents a huge paradigm shift from the framework upon which the UN Charter was crafted. It is an overdue and welcome breakthrough in world affairs. It is also entirely consonant with one of the cardinal principles inherent in the Bahá'í vision – that unfettered state sovereignty must be curtailed if we are to properly address the many problems of collective security that beset us. It is also a tangible example of the principle of timely change strongly advocated in the Bahá'í writings, which dictates that if our institutions, laws, concepts, ways of governance or policies no longer serve our best interests, then we should scrap them. To sacrifice humanity for the preservation of these outmoded ideas is insane and self-destructive. Finally, the emerging understanding of state sovereignty grows out of an even more fundamental principle expounded in the Bahá'í writings – that the good of the part can best be assured by ensuring the good of the whole.

Principle of Unity in Thought and Action

Another principle that is emerging as a result of the work done in several quarters (by the ICISS but also others) is that the international community must unite around general principles regarding collective military action when invoking the responsibility to protect. Indeed, the principles of international cooperation and collective action are becoming increasingly recognized and valued. Advocating that world leaders adopt his agenda to reform the United Nations at their 2005 Summit, the then Secretary-General of the United Nations stated, 'Declining confidence in the institution [of the UN] is matched by a growing belief in the importance of effective multilateralism.'[102] Noting that in today's world, no state, however powerful, can protect itself on its own,[103] he called for a 'broad, deep and sustained global cooperation among States'[104] and highlighted that 'there is a yearning in many quarters for a new consensus on which to base collective action.'[105]

The principle of cooperation parallels the call in the Bahá'í writings for the international community to bring unity of thought to bear on its deliberations and unity of action in implementing the fruits of those unified deliberations. The necessity for achieving this level of maturity within the international community was also articulated by 'Abdu'l-Bahá, authorized interpreter of the Bahá'í writings, in a passage concerning the 'seven candles of unity'. These represent the seven stages through which humanity must travel as it gropes towards its full maturity. One of these candles is 'unity of thought in world undertakings'[106] and reflects the recognition of the need to achieve consensus on criteria for collective action that affects our joint destiny.

We need only turn to our vast experience to see the perils and cost of disunity on the one hand and the benefits to be reaped from unified resolve on the other. Examples of problems stemming from disunity abound, such as the recent inability of the Security Council to agree on sanctions to impose on North Korea to deter it from further developing its nuclear capability. Fortunately, we also have some examples that demonstrate the power of unified action. For instance, when in February 2005 Faure Gnassingbé unlawfully seized power to become president of Togo in violation of the country's constitution, the unified action of the Economic Community of West African States (ECOWAS), which forms a large trading bloc to promote economic integration in West Africa, and other members of the African Union led him to step down to allow constitutional elections to take place, thereby averting a potential civil war in Togo and instability in the region. Another such example was the joint effort of diverse nations such as Russia, Germany, France, Saudi Arabia, the United States and Egypt, urging Syria to withdraw its troops from Lebanon after 29 years and abide by Security Council Resolution 1559 which called for all foreign troops to withdraw. In both instances, the immediate results sought by a unified community of nations were achieved in a short period (three weeks in the case of Togo and eight months in the case of Syria) and without the need for forceful intervention. We should take heart from these experiences.

Principle of Oneness

The international community is struggling to come to grips with the cornerstone of all principles, the principle of oneness. On the one hand, even a cursory examination of our key international institutions reveals that many nations and peoples view at least some others as not being on a par with them. On the contrary, certain nations view themselves as better than others because they believe they are stronger or smarter or wiser or more trustworthy. These feelings of superiority are reflected in some of our key institutional structures. Foremost among these is the Security Council, which is the prime international organ tasked with the critical responsibility of ensuring the peace and security of our planet. Yet the membership of this important organ of collective security is divided so that a mere handful of nations is considered permanent while the others serve for limited terms. The privileged five nations that led the effort to defeat Nazi Germany and fascist Japan in World War II have permanent seats on the Security Council, while all others rotate on and off. Moreover, the voting structure further entrenches the privileges of the World War II victors by granting them, and them alone, the power to prevent Security Council action by exercising a veto. Consequently, rather than basing decisions that affect the security of us all on the votes of a majority of members of the Council by according equal respect and weight to the considered views of each of the members, the five permanent members each enjoy the power to trump the collective views of their colleagues. Indeed, even if 14 out of 15 voting members of the Security Council decide that a certain course of action benefits the international community as a whole, any one permanent member nation, albeit acting in its own narrow self-interest, can block the action and thereby deprive the international community of the benefits of that decision.

However, there have been some glimmers of hope especially in the last couple of years. The idea of oneness is starting to gain credence amongst the leadership in the international community. The former UN Secretary-General's report 'In Larger Freedom' noted that international cooperation is possible if every country's policies take account not only of the needs of its own citizens but also the needs of others. This kind of cooperation both advances everyone's interests and recognizes our common humanity.[107] He further speaks of this being 'an era of global interdependence' and of the necessity for the 'glue of common interest' as well as 'the impulses of our common humanity' to bind all states together to make this world a more secure, prosperous and better place.[108]

Principle of Justice, Equity and Fairness

The UN Secretary-General's 2005 report 'In Larger Freedom' reminded world leaders that 'collective security today depends on accepting that the threats which each region of the world perceives as most urgent are in fact equally so for all'.[109] Indeed, he pointed out that in our globalized world, the threats we face are so interconnected that we are all vulnerable to the threats to other nations. Truly understanding this fact must lead us to address threats equally no matter where they arise. In a world where this reality is deeply understood, the kind of genocide we saw in Rwanda would be dealt with as effectively as a threat of weapons of mass destruction to the cities of Europe or America. If we all accept the reality of our interconnected world then we will deal with threats equally and thereby manifest justice, equity and fairness in our collective dealings with crises.

Principle of Timely Change

The world community is finally recognizing that age-old institutions, policies and laws must be reshaped to meet the current needs of humanity. The clearest evidence of this recognition may be found in the former UN Secretary-General's report advocating wide-sweeping reforms of the world's foremost international institution, the United Nations. In it, he acknowledges that the principles and purposes set out by the UN Charter remain as valid and relevant today as they were in 1945 but also admits that the practice and organization of the world body 'need to move with the times' and 'if the United Nations is to be a useful instrument for its Member States and for the world's peoples . . . it must be fully adapted to the needs and circumstances of the twenty-first century'.[110] He urges the international community to revamp 'our major intergovernmental institutions so that they reflect today's world' and to 'reshape the Organization [the UN] in ways not previously imagined and with a boldness and speed not previously shown'.[111] One of the critical ingredients that the Bahá'í writings identify for the kinds of organic changes in the structure of our society that will reflect the needs and requirements of the age is political will arrived at after collective consultation.[112] The need for this all-important ingredient is echoed by the Secretary-General in his report.[113]

Codifying International Agreements, Laws and Obligations

One of the salient features of international life as we know it today is the multiplicity of international agreements and obligations that regulate it. The United Nations has sponsored over 480 multilateral agreements.[114] They are part of the body of international law that exists to promote the economic and social welfare of the world as well as its international peace and security. These agreements cover a broad array of subjects and are legally binding for the states that ratify them. They govern and regulate activities ranging from the postal service and international transportation by air, rail and sea to trade, agriculture, the environment, nuclear non-proliferation and terrorism. These agreements tend to be complex and each one has its own unique composition of countries that are party to it. In addition to the body of international law that already exists, the International Law Commission (ILC) established by the General Assembly in 1947 to promote the progressive development of international law and its codification, meets annually and works on drafts of documents on a wide range of topics regulating relations among states for consideration by the world body. Given the number and complexity of existing international agreements and the continuous emergence of new law proposed by the ILC or others, one of the challenges facing the international community is to streamline these treaties and better integrate the institutional framework that supports and implements them. Fortunately, this fact was recently recognized by the Secretary-General of the United Nations.[115]

Arms Control and Reduction

Nowhere is the drama of a world community being pulled reluctantly and stubbornly towards Bahá'u'lláh's vision of collective security more apparent than in the areas of nuclear non-proliferation and arms reduction. On the one hand the proliferation of weapons of mass destruction (biological, chemical and nuclear) poses one of the most serious dangers to the world and in recognition of this danger the international community has created a system of multilateral treaties to hold such proliferation in check. On the other hand, this system of treaties suffers from some fundamental weaknesses which, if left unaddressed, threaten to undermine the entire system and lead to a cascade of proliferation with all its attendant dangers to the world at large.

Mass production of modern weaponry led to the recognition of the need to control them. However, it was not until poison gas was used during the First World War that a concerted effort was made, after the war, to discuss the prohibition of the use of certain weapons in times of war – namely, poisonous, asphyxiating and biological gases. This effort resulted in the Geneva Protocol, which was signed in June 1925 and entered into force in February 1928. The Protocol, however, confined itself to prohibiting the use of poison gas weapons and did not prohibit nations from producing and stockpiling them. Over the next several decades a number of international treaties were eventually concluded with the aim of controlling the proliferation of nuclear, biological and chemical weapons, in that order. This section focuses on three such treaties that have been particularly key to the attempt to rid our world of weapons of mass destruction.

The first was the Nuclear Non-Proliferation Treaty (NPT), which was signed in July 1968 and entered into force in 1970. The main aim was to ensure that civilian nuclear material would not be diverted for military purposes. This treaty was initially successful in checking the spread of nuclear weapons. It led several states such as South Korea, Taiwan, Brazil, Argentina, South Africa, Ukraine and Kazakhstan to abandon their nuclear weapons ambitions and made it more difficult for other non-nuclear-weapon states to acquire the material and technology needed to build such weapons or to avoid detection of a covert nuclear weapons programme. However, despite these successes, certain fundamental weaknesses in the system it established have become increasingly apparent over the last few years and now threaten to undermine the entire system. These weaknesses are discussed below. The International Atomic Energy Agency (IAEA), created in 1957 to promote the peaceful use of atomic energy under a system of international safeguards, was designated to serve as the primary mechanism for ensuring compliance with the NPT. The Agency has been only partially successful in achieving its mandate and needs to be considerably strengthened if the world community is serious about stemming the tide of nuclear proliferation.

The second international treaty to be concluded was the Biological Weapons Convention (BWC), which aimed to prevent the production and stockpiling of biological weapons. The BWC was signed in April 1972 and entered into force in March 1975. The treaty suffers from a number of serious flaws that have severely weakened its efficacy.

The third treaty is the Chemical Weapons Convention (CWC). It took the longest time to conclude. It was signed in 1993 and did not enter into force until 1997. This treaty completes the process begun by the Geneva Protocol which prohibited the use of poison gas weapons by additionally outlawing a further class of weapons of mass destruction such as those equipped with such chemical agents as mustard gas, soman, sarin and VX. The treaty also provides for an international oversight agency, the Organization for the Prohibition of Chemical Weapons (OPCW) to ensure compliance with the terms of the treaty.

Despite the laudable intent of these three international treaties, they each suffer, to a greater or lesser extent, from fundamental flaws. First, the treaties are not binding on all the members of the international community as a whole. States are free to accede to them or not whereas participation ought to be mandatory on the grounds of international security. Given the unprecedented dangers posed by weapons of mass destruction to the safety, peace, security and very existence of the peoples of the world, the international community must absolutely demand that all its member states be required to adhere to these treaties. This is one of those areas in which national sovereignty must be curtailed for the good of the world community of peoples and nations as a whole.

The second flaw is really a corollary to the first: all three treaties allow for a state party to withdraw. Moreover, the required conditions for withdrawal are very low and the minimum periods of notice required extremely short. So, for example, a member state may withdraw from the NPT on a mere three months' notice to the other parties and to the Security Council. It may do so 'if it decides that extraordinary events, related to the subject matter of this Treaty, have jeopardized the supreme interest of its country'.[116] In addition, withdrawal carries with it no consequences, even if the state is found to have been in breach of its obligations prior to withdrawal. It defies belief, given the dangers to our peace and security posed by weapons of mass destruction, that we would even entertain the notion of allowing a state party to one of these treaties so fundamental to the peace of the world to withdraw from it in the first place. But then to facilitate exit by allowing withdrawal to be based solely on a state's own decision justified on the basis of 'extraordinary events' (a term which is not defined in the NPT) in the name of honouring state sovereignty is to ensure that the treaties will unravel. These treaties should be binding on all states without exception, with no option for withdrawal.

The third fundamental flaw in these treaties is the absence of a reliable and shared system of intelligence coupled with robust monitoring and verification to ensure that states that have agreed actually comply with their obligations. The NPT does have a system of international safeguards in place to ensure that its provisions are complied with. The aim is to prevent nuclear energy being diverted from peaceful uses to nuclear weapons or explosive devices. These safeguards are embodied in agreements that are negotiated between the IAEA and states party to the NPT.[117] The IAEA's role is to serve as the world's international inspectorate verifying that the safeguards are adhered to. However, over time it has become apparent that both the safeguards and the scope of the IAEA's authority have been inadequate to bring breaches of the NPT to the attention of the international community in a timely manner. So, for example, the international community learned about Iran's recent undeclared nuclear activities from dissidents and not as a result of the safeguards system. The world learned about North Korea's undeclared activities when North Korea decided to divulge its secret and not because of the safeguards system. North Korea then proceeded to withdraw from the NPT altogether. And we learned about Iraq's clandestine pursuit of a programme to develop nuclear weapons after the Persian Gulf war in 1991, not because of the efficacy of the safeguards system.

As a result of these clear failures, the IAEA has set up a new programme to monitor and verify compliance with the NPT provisions prohibiting diversion of declared nuclear materials and to increase its capability to detect secret nuclear programmes. Known as Programme 93+2, or the 'Additional Protocol', the new programme was approved by the IAEA's Board of Governors in 1997. It relies on broader declaration requirements and expanded access to achieve its goals. However, as with the safeguards programme, the Additional Protocol is not mandatory; NPT member states may decide on their own whether to sign on to it. As of 2004, only one third of the states party to the NPT had ratified the Protocol. In addition, it suffers from its own inadequacies and limitations. One example of such an inadequacy is the national security exception that allows a member state, through its sole discretion, to exclude the application of the Protocol on the grounds that it has national security implications. A state that is secretly developing nuclear weapons could easily rely on this exclusion to hide such activities from the IAEA. It is interesting to note that the most successful monitoring and verification model adopted to date has been the United Nations Special Commission (UNSCOM), which was established by the Security Council with mandatory powers to find illegal weapons of mass destruction in Iraq and the power to conduct no-notice inspections. The IAEA was asked to undertake similar tasks in the nuclear area with UNSCOM's assistance.[118]

The CWC has the most stringent monitoring and verification procedures on paper. However, the CWC's watchdog agency, the OPCW, has been reluctant to use the most intrusive of these procedures for fear that it will not yield evidence of a suspected breach and will leave the OPCW with egg on its face and reduce its credibility in the eyes of all. The BWC is the weakest of the three treaties, as it has no monitoring or verification mechanism at all, leaving it to member states to discover and complain about non-compliance of other members.

The fourth flaw lies in the absence of effective penalties to deter member states from flouting the international nuclear non-proliferation rules and to bring them to heel when they are found to violate them. The best we have been able to do as a community of nations is to threaten a breaching party with referral to the Security Council but such referrals are not always successful. For instance, the threat to refer North Korea's nuclear activities to the Security Council for action went nowhere because China threatened to veto if the matter were raised at the Council. Moreover, even if a referral to the Security Council is successfully made, the consequences to the nation engaged in the breach are at worst the threat of economic and diplomatic sanctions, rather than coercive measures to enforce the rules or replace the recalcitrant government with one that is willing to abide by international rules. As a consequence of these two factors, over time, the threat of referral to the Security Council seems to have lost its deterrent effect and no longer appears to change the behaviour of recalcitrant nations.

This is amply demonstrated by press reports about Iran's reactions over time, first to warnings that it would be referred to the Security Council if it did not fully disclose the extent and purpose of its nuclear activities and scrap its nuclear programme, and later to the imposition of sanctions by the Security Council. When the issue of sanctions was first raised, the press quoted the secretary of Iran's Supreme National Security Council, Ali Larijani, as saying: 'Iran cannot be intimidated by the Security Council. We do not take such threats seriously'.[119] In December 2006 the Council proceeded to impose a first round of sanctions, banning trade with Iran of all sensitive nuclear-related technology and materials that could contribute to Tehran's uranium enrichment programme and imposing a freeze on the financial assets of certain individuals and entities listed.[120] In March 2007 the Security Council passed another resolution which slightly tightened these sanctions by banning arms exports from Iran and expanding the number of individuals and entities whose assets were subject to the financial freeze.[121] Yet both sets of sanctions proved ineffective. Iran continues steadfastly to refuse to suspend its enrichment-related and reprocessing activities. Indeed, as the Security Council was preparing to debate a third set of sanctions in June 2007, President Mahmoud Ahmadinejad was quoted as saying that it was 'too late' to stop Iran's nuclear programme. He went on to warn the US and its allies not to exert pressure on the United Nations to impose new sanctions, saying, 'We advise them not to play with the lion's tail.'[122] *The Economist* succinctly summed up Iran's attitude towards the Security Council in the following words: 'To ignore one unanimous United Nations Security Council resolution may be considered impudence; to defy a second looks like policy.'[123]

The lack of an effective enforcement mechanism has led certain countries to create new counter-proliferation mechanisms. An example of such an initiative is the 'Proliferation Security Initiative' (PSI), a voluntary effort of a group of nations aimed at preventing illicit trafficking in nuclear, chemical and biological weapons, by interdicting clandestine trade in such weapons, their delivery systems and related materials worldwide. States participate in this initiative entirely on a voluntary basis. As of April 2007, more than 80 nations were reported to support the initiative. Although the PSI reflects the growing recognition of a need for more effective enforcement mechanisms and of cooperation to achieve collective security, it is hampered by its non-universality and *ad hoc* nature.

The fifth flaw that applies particularly to the NPT lies in the unresolved tension between the need of nations, particularly developing nations, to have access to peaceful nuclear technology to meet their growing energy needs on the one hand, and the need of the international community to limit and control the creation of nuclear facilities for fear that they will be used to create fissile materials for non-peaceful use on the other. This tension is reflected in the wording of the treaty itself, especially in its preamble and in Article IV, which respectively provide that 'the benefits of peaceful applications of nuclear technology . . . which may be derived by nuclear-weapon States . . . should be available for peaceful purposes to all Parties of the Treaty' and that 'nothing in this Treaty shall be interpreted as affecting the inalienable right of all the Parties to the Treaty to develop research, production and use of nuclear energy for peaceful purposes without discrimination . . .' Such tension mirrors the realities of our world's seemingly dichotomous and competing needs. One of the unfortunate results of this lingering tension and the way the NPT has been interpreted to date is that countries can legally acquire technologies that bring them to the very brink of a nuclear weapons capability without explicitly violating the treaty. This means that nations bent on developing nuclear weapons can secretly acquire the materials and expertise to do so under cover of their membership of the NPT, albeit in clear contravention of their obligations under it. Then once they are ready to weaponize the technologies and materials, they can withdraw from the treaty without consequence.

The sixth flaw in these treaties is that they do not decisively and effectively deal with eliminating current stockpiles of weapons of mass destruction and related materials. For example, the NPT does no more than state the parties' undertaking to pursue negotiations in good faith on effective measures relating to the cessation of the nuclear arms race at an early date and to nuclear disarmament.[124] In practice, progress has been very slow: nuclear-weapons states have only grudgingly fulfilled their disarmament obligations and reduced their stockpiles. While there have been some successes resulting in the dismantlement of thousands of nuclear weapons, these have come about largely as a result of bilateral agreements between states, in particular the United States and the Union of Soviet Socialist Republics (USSR), now the Russian Federation. Examples of such agreements were the 1972 Treaty on the Limitation of Anti-Ballistic Missile Systems (ABM Treaty); the 1987 US–Soviet Union Intermediate- and Shorter-Range Nuclear Forces Treaty (INF Treaty); and the 1991 and 1993 Strategic Arms Limitation and Reduction Treaties (START I and START II).[125] However, there is yet much to be done. As of 2004, 1,300 kilograms of highly enriched uranium, which can be used for nuclear weapons, existed in research reactors in 27 countries and the total volume of such stockpiles was much greater.[126] Moreover, many nuclear storage sites worldwide are inadequately secured and there are many documented cases of illicit trafficking in nuclear materials. This means there is a real danger that terrorists will have access to these materials with potentially catastrophic results. Consequently, non-nuclear-weapons states are losing their incentive to forgo the pursuit of nuclear weapons either for prestige or for fear that they will need them to defend themselves. Then there is the further problem that nuclear states that are not party to the NPT are not covered by the treaty obligation to reduce their nuclear stockpiles and operate in a sphere of their own.

As for chemical and biological weapons, while the CWC calls for the complete elimination and destruction of chemical weapons by all states parties, chemical-weapons states are currently far behind in adhering to the schedule set out in the CWC for the destruction of their declared stockpiles. By June 2007, of the approximately 71,000 metric tons of declared weapons agents, the OPCW had verified the destruction of only 23,125, roughly a third.[127] At this rate, it is highly unlikely that the CWC's goal of the complete destruction of chemical weapons agents will be met by the extended deadline of 2012. With respect to biological weapons, although the BWC requires states to destroy or divert to peaceful purposes all the weapons, toxins, agents and equipment covered by the treaty no later than nine months after its entry into force in 1975,[128] this has not yet been done, as there is no verification or enforcement mechanism to ensure that the obligation will be met.

The seventh flaw lies in the uneven manner in which these treaties, particularly the NPT, have been applied vis-à-vis different nations. One example of this unequal treatment can be seen in the United States's current dealings with India regarding nuclear issues as compared to its treatment of Iran and North Korea. Unlike Iran and North Korea, India never signed the NPT and went ahead to develop nuclear weapons on its own, testing them in 1976 and again in 1998. Despite India's flouting of the entire nuclear non-proliferation system for decades, in early March 2006 the United States agreed to provide India civilian nuclear technology in exchange for India's opening some 14 of its 22 nuclear facilities to a form of international inspection. The explanation for this cooperation was that India's energy needs depend on expanded use of nuclear power. France had entered a similar agreement shortly before, for similar reasons.[129] In contrast, Iran and North Korea, both of which did accede to the NPT but have since been found secretly dabbling with plutonium and highly-enriched uranium, possibly useful for nuclear weapons, have been subject to intense pressure from the United States and several other members of the international community, particularly European states, even though they, too, have argued that their purpose in developing nuclear power is to satisfy their current and growing energy needs. The message being sent is that, as a nation, you are better off ignoring the nuclear non-proliferation system. You may be snubbed by the 'nuclear club' for a while and subjected to intense pressure if the club deems you untrustworthy, but if you succeed in developing nuclear capabilities, the international community will ultimately deal with you and may even support your nuclear energy needs.

The proliferation of nuclear weapons is one of the biggest threats that currently faces us. Over the last two decades or so, the international community has been faced with example after example of the breakdown of the treaty regime that was designed to safeguard it from such proliferation. Not only have Iraq, North Korea and Iran each been shown to have engaged in clandestine activities in breach of their international obligations, Libya admitted to doing the same but has now come clean. One of Pakistan's top nuclear experts was found to have been at the centre of an elaborate clandestine system for disseminating know-how and equipment for the creation of nuclear material. The discovery of these activities, successfully hidden from the anti-proliferation monitoring system, has served to heighten tensions within the international community, raise suspicion, erode trust and engender fear and counter-reactions. These events, coming in quick succession during the past decade, have tested the mettle of our world leaders to deal decisively and effectively with this problem. Each event represented an opportunity to tackle the problem head-on. If experience itself were not enough, information and ideas have been forthcoming from thinkers and academics who have studied this issue at length.

There is no doubt that it is time for our leaders to overhaul the system significantly. Despite the glaring need for effective action, our leaders seem utterly paralysed. In May 2005 leaders of 188 nations gathered at the NPT review conference to consult and make critical decisions about strengthening and revamping the nuclear non-proliferation system, which all acknowledge is in danger of unravelling. Unfortunately, the conference was a complete flop. Despite the need to address some critical issues such as nuclear testing, new weapons programmes and the production of fissile material, no agreement could be reached on anything. The extent of the debacle was evident in the inability of the conference even to produce a final statement, as there was nothing positive to report. This failure was further compounded in September 2005 when the leaders of the world's nations attending a World Summit in New York failed to mention the glaring problems of nuclear proliferation and arms reduction in its final Outcome Document. These twin failures were summed up by Secretary-General Kofi Annan in the wake of the summit: 'Our biggest challenge, and our biggest failing, is on nuclear non-proliferation and disarmament. Twice this year – at the NPT review conference, and now at this Summit – we have allowed posturing to get in the way of results. This is inexcusable. Weapons of mass destruction pose a grave danger to us all, particularly in a world threatened by terrorists with global ambitions and no inhibitions . . .'[130] The Director-General of the IAEA also expressed disappointment that neither of the two events reached any agreement to curb the spread of atomic weapons or to promote disarmament: 'The current challenges to international peace and security, including those related to nuclear non-proliferation and nuclear arms control, cannot be wished away . . . It is urgent and indispensable that we continue to build a global security system that is both equitable and inclusive.'[131]

Until the world's leaders overcome their paralysis in this area of international life as in others (such as the prevention of genocide), the challenges will continue to recur with increasing frequency and intensity. It is evident that the problem of weapons proliferation is not going away anytime soon. On the contrary, all signs indicate that the problem will simply escalate, as recent world events have demonstrated. These birth pangs that will come more frequently and intensify with each event will eventually force us to create an effective and comprehensive system for controlling the spread and reducing the volumes of arms, as part of an effective system of collective security that will properly safeguard the peace of our planet.

Committing to the Principle of Collective Security

After the Second World War, with all its attendant horrors and atrocities, the international community was determined to take steps to ensure that it would never again experience human tragedy on such a scale. It was to this end that the United Nations Charter was crafted and the United Nations, comprising 51 member states, was born. One of the pivotal principles upon which this agreement between nations was constructed was the principle of collective security, which dictated that in the future nations would act collectively to protect a wronged state and nations would similarly act collectively to bring to heel an errant one, thereby restoring or maintaining the peace. The Security Council was the organ of this newly-founded international organization charged with the primary responsibility for maintaining peace and security.[132] It was given the power to determine when collective action was to be taken by the world community. This it would do by deciding whether certain actions or conditions were grave enough to amount to a 'threat to the peace', a 'breach of the peace' or an 'act of aggression'.[133] Once the Council had made such a determination, the Charter provided it with a range of options for action. These included, at the mild end of the spectrum, recommendations (under Article 39 of the Charter) and certain provisional actions (Article 40) such as the declaration of a cease-fire. More severe actions range from measures that do not involve the use of force (Article 41), such as the imposition of sanctions and the severance of diplomatic relations, to the use of whatever force is necessary by land, sea and air – the most draconian of all actions – to maintain peace and security (Article 42). It was clear to the framers of the Charter as long ago as 1945 that there would be circumstances in which nothing short of the use of force would work.

At first blush it would seem that, after going through intense suffering, the world had embraced the major elements of Bahá'u'lláh's vision of collective security. His principle that all nations should arise collectively to bring to heel any recalcitrant nation appeared to be at the core of the UN Charter. Moreover, there appeared to be an acceptance that force was sometimes a necessary tool for the achievement of justice. What went wrong? Why has this system not been effective in securing the peace of the planet?

The answer is several-fold. First, the Security Council has been hamstrung in its ability to threaten action by force or to effectively wield force when necessary owing to the inability or unwillingness of the international community to provide it with the properly manned and equipped UN military forces foreseen by the Charter. This failure will be discussed in greater detail in part 3 of this book. Second, the failure of the international community to commit to the principle of the oneness of humanity and nations has led to paralysis within the Security Council, the very organ charged with maintaining peace and security. This manifested itself in the superpower rivalry between the US and the former USSR during the Cold War in the decades following World War II and the misuse of the veto power by those wielding it. Third, the unwillingness to act has been exacerbated by the lack of specificity regarding circumstances in which the Security Council could declare a threat to the peace, a breach of peace or an act of aggression. The vagueness inherent in these terms, coupled with the festering suspicions caused by superpower rivalry, has severely retarded the work of the Security Council in protecting the peace and security of the planet.

Despite these problems, the Security Council did make some progress over the years in the direction of collective action as envisioned both in the Bahá'í writings and by the framers of the UN Charter. This progress can be seen in the increased willingness of the Council to broaden its application of the concept of a 'threat to the peace' to encompass situations that were previously considered purely internal and therefore outside the scope of intervention by the Council according to Article 2(7) of the UN Charter. For example, Security Council Resolution 221 passed in 1966 found that the actions of the white minority government of Ian Smith in Rhodesia in issuing a Unilateral Declaration of Independence from the United Kingdom constituted a threat to the peace. Then in 1991 Security Council Resolution 713 determined that the circumstances of civil unrest in the former Yugoslavia constituted a threat to the peace and imposed an arms embargo. The following year the Council made a similar determination in Resolution 788 (1992) with respect to the civil war in Liberia. Two years thereafter the Council in Resolution 955 (1994) decided that the genocide in Rwanda amounted to a threat to international peace. The Council has continued to expand its application of the concept of a 'threat to the peace' to cover situations other than civil unrest or civil war. These include violations of international humanitarian law as reflected in Resolution 733 passed in 1992 regarding the situation in Somalia, which made it very difficult for the international community to provide much needed humanitarian assistance to the civilian population. They also include international terrorism as clearly articulated by the Council both in Resolution 748 passed in 1992, in which it cited the Libyan government's failure to concretely demonstrate its renunciation of terrorism by complying with a previous Council resolution, and in Resolution 1070 passed in 1996, in which the Council cited Sudan's failure to extradite suspects wanted in connection with an assassination attempt on the President of Egypt while he was in Ethiopia.

By contrast, the Council has been more skittish about declaring a 'breach of the peace', limiting such declaration to four instances: in 1950 after North Korea invaded South Korea;[134] in 1982 after the Argentine invasion of the Falkland Islands;[135] in 1987 during the Iran–Iraq war;[136] and in 1990 after Iraq's invasion of Kuwait.[137] The Council has been even slower to declare an 'act of aggression' and has only done so twice: in 1976 (Resolution 387) in response to South African aggression in sending invading forces into Angola, where they wreaked destruction and seized Angolan equipment and materials; and in 1990 (Resolution 667) in response to acts of violence committed by Iraq against diplomatic missions and their personnel in Kuwait, including abduction of the latter.

In addition it should be said on the positive side that since the end of the Cold War the Security Council has become increasingly active in addressing international threats. The average number of resolutions it passed each year increased from one resolution a month to one a week (from 15 a year to 60).[138] It has also imposed sanctions 14 times for an increasingly diverse range of stated purposes including to reverse aggression, restore democratic governments, protect human rights, end wars, combat terrorism and support peace agreements. This is in contrast with its meagre application of sanctions only twice before 1989.[139]

Despite its increased willingness to flex its muscles and intervene in various circumstances that threaten international peace and security, there have been some problems that the Council has been unable to deal with, including long-standing regional conflicts such as Kashmir and Korea, or to deal with successfully, as in the case of the Palestinian/Israeli conflict. It has also failed to act decisively in the face of ethnic cleansing and genocide in Rwanda, Bosnia and Darfur. These problems are likely to persist until the kind of collective security system envisioned by the Bahá'í writings, with all its components, is put into effect, including a standing international force at the disposal of the Security Council.

Creating a Standing International Force

One of the most critical components of a viable system of collective security is enforcement capability. Inability to enforce its decisions has rendered the Security Council toothless and its interventions in some of the world's most pressing and long-standing crises ineffectual. The Council's stated powers under Article 42 of the Charter to use whatever force is necessary to maintain or restore international peace and security have been crippled because Articles 43 to 46 of the UN Charter, designed to give the Council the tools it requires, were never implemented.

Looked at from the vantage point of Bahá'u'lláh's blueprint for a system of collective security, Article 43 is at once heartening and frustrating. It provides that all members of the United Nations shall 'undertake to make available to the Security Council, on its call . . . armed forces, assistance, and facilities, including rights of passage, necessary for the purpose of maintaining international peace and security'. This is to be done in accordance with 'a special agreement or agreements' between the Council and the member states. These agreements are to 'govern the numbers and types of forces, their degree of readiness and general location and the nature of the facilities and assistance to be provided'. The following Articles 44 through 46 then provide further details regarding these arrangements and how they are to come about. That such provisions already exist in the Charter is heartening because it demonstrates that the world has moved, at least at a conceptual level, closer to Bahá'u'lláh's vision of a system of collective security.

The international community's failure to implement any of these Articles reflects a failure to follow through on what the Charter's drafters and the world community in 1944 knew is sorely needed to help ensure our peace and security. The reasons for this frustrating failure lie in our countries' unwillingness to cede national sovereignty in areas involving the use of military power, including those relating to the composition, maintenance and location of forces. In February 1946 the Security Council directed the Military Staff Committee, a body created by Article 47 of the UN Charter to 'advise and assist the Council on all questions relating to [its] military requirements for the maintenance of international peace and security' including 'the employment and command of forces placed at its disposal', to begin work. After spending the next two years and five months working on an arrangement for standby forces, the committee reported to the Security Council in early July 1948 that it was unable to fulfil its mandate.[140] The members of the Committee comprising representatives of the air forces, navies and armies of the five permanent members of the Security Council had failed to reach final agreement owing to squabbles over certain issues such as time limits for the withdrawal of forces after action, whether forces should be based only on a nation's home territory or elsewhere, the right to withdraw forces in the event of national emergency and the all-important issues of command and control.[141] It is clear that clinging to outworn ideas of absolute state sovereignty has hindered us from doing what is necessary for our own security.

Because of the crippling blow dealt to Article 42 and, by extension, to the Security Council's ability to maintain international peace and security, the Council has been forced to rely on its more limited powers under Article 41 of the Charter (see above). Although it has used these powers liberally to craft a wide range of measures short of the use of force, these measures have often proved insufficient. To compensate for this handicap the Security Council has, over time, been creative in devising new strategies.

One strategy has been delegating its enforcement powers under Article 42 to member states. For instance, when North Korea invaded South Korea in 1950, the Security Council condemned the act as a breach of the peace[142] then called on all member states to assist in repelling the invasion. Sixteen states acted under the United Nations flag with the United States at the helm, in command of the forces. This strategy worked only once during the polarized period of the Cold War between Security Council members the United States and the Union of Soviet Socialist Republics owing to an unusual confluence of circumstances: the Soviet Union was boycotting Council meetings in protest at the inclusion of the Chinese delegation and mistakenly believed that its abstention during the Council vote to delegate authority was equal to a veto.

Another strategy resorted to by the Security Council has been to authorize military action by a coalition of member states, generally justified in part under Article 51's preservation of countries' right to individual or collective self-defence. The Council resorted to this strategy after Iraq's invasion and annexation of Kuwait in 1990. Following a series of resolutions condemning certain of Iraq's actions as a breach of the peace[143] and other actions as acts of aggression[144] and imposing trade embargoes that failed to dislodge Iraq, the Security Council issued Resolution 678[145] setting 15 January 1991 as the deadline for withdrawal and authorizing 'all necessary means to uphold and implement' prior resolutions requiring withdrawal. A few days after the deadline passed approximately 27 states,[146] including the Government of Kuwait, acted in concert to attack Iraq.

Yet another mechanism has been the use of peacekeeping forces whose mission has shifted over time to include self-defence and then de facto enforcement. In Somalia, for example, civil war leading to a massive humanitarian crisis led the Council to authorize a series of UN missions with ever-increasing authority to establish enough peace and security in the country to allow delivery of humanitarian supplies. These missions came to include forces from some 20 nations, yet ultimately failed and were driven out of the country after a series of attacks on UN mission forces. As reflected by this example as well as by the failed UN peacekeeping missions in Palestine, Cambodia, Congo, Rwanda and Bosnia, the attempt to use peacekeeping as an enforcement mechanism has never worked, often for lack of political commitment and adequate resources from UN member states. There is also a more fundamental problem with this approach which contributed to the failures in Somalia. Peacekeeping implies that the parties involved have voluntarily consented to having a force there. Peacekeeping forces are unsuited to intervening in a situation against the will of some or all of the fighting parties to restore and/or maintain peace and security. Therefore, when the latter is what is really required and yet peacekeeping forces are sent, the strategy ultimately fails, leaving a bad taste in everyone's mouth.

Recent events, however, indicate that the tide may be turning with respect to the use of peacekeepers. The repeated failures seem to have led to a growing recognition on the part of the Council that it needs to act more decisively. Thus the UN force in Congo, known as MONUC, has traditionally been referred to by the locals as 'butterflies' because, although pretty to look at, the 'blue helmet' soldiers are useless at keeping the peace. Indeed, they have developed a reputation for standing idly by as civilians are slaughtered or enslaved by one militia or another. MONUC's excuse has always been that it lacks both the arms and the troops to respond to the militias' actions. However, the Council has now raised their numbers from 10,800 to 16,700 and has provided them with air cover. There is hope that they will now be able to disarm the militias and free slaves.[147]

Another strategy that the Council has increasingly used is to ratify the actions of regional forces. Examples of this action can be seen in its resolution welcoming NATO's intervention in the conflicts in Kosovo and Bosnia and the intervention of ECOWAS in Sierra Leone. Although military intervention by any nation or organization arguably should be authorized in advance by the Security Council, a practice has developed by which regional forces intervene first and obtain the Council's blessings after the fact. Often the intervening nations invoke their right to collective self-defence under Article 51 of the Charter. The Security Council has increasingly also relied upon pre-existing forces assembled by another, usually regional, multinational organization – a welcome source of troops and equipment, especially when international resources are lacking. There has been quite a bit of cooperation between the UN and regional security arrangements with respect to peacekeeping, for example in Haiti, where the Organization of American States and the Council have been cooperating, or in Liberia, where ECOWAS and the Council cooperated, and in Bosnia where NATO and the Council cooperated.

On the whole, the good news is that the Security Council has, over time, become increasingly active and willing to use its powers under Chapter VII, even without the standing forces and other tools of Articles 43 through 46. The Anand Report, discussed earlier in this part of the book, reporting on the needs of collective security to the Secretary-General, concluded that the Council has dramatically shifted the balance between unilateral use of force and collectively authorized force.[148] The Panel also observed a rising expectation and emerging norm that the Council be the arbiter of the use of force, although this norm appears 'precious but not yet deep-rooted'.[149]

It has become increasingly apparent that the Security Council has stretched its Article 42 powers to their farthest limit and beyond. As a mechanism to enforce international peace, however, it is no longer viable. The situation in Iraq since its original invasion of Kuwait provides a stark example. Over the course of 12 years the Security Council used every tool at its disposal short of the direct use of a UN force under Article 43 to deal with the threat from Iraq. These tools included the imposition of economic sanctions in various forms including banning imports and exports, forbidding the transfer of funds into and out of the country, banning aircraft from flying into or out of the country and imposing naval blockades; the reduction of diplomatic staff; the imposition of legal responsibility on Iraq for direct damages to individuals, governments, corporations and international organizations caused by its unlawful invasion of Kuwait; the assertion of Iraq's liability for its foreign debt; guaranteeing the international boundary between Iraq and Kuwait (a milestone that is discussed later); requiring that all proceeds from the sale of oil be held in escrow by the United Nations for use in accordance with the international community's dictates; requiring the destruction of all weapons of mass destruction; and establishing an international inspection regime to ensure that this was done.

However, all of these actions short of the use of force were insufficient to allay the fears of the international community that Iraq still posed a threat to the peace of the world. Moreover, despite general consensus within the international community that Iraq posed a continuing threat to the peace of its neighbours, the world was paralysed. The Security Council was not willing to delegate its enforcement power to any state or group of states, nor was it willing to lend its seal of approval to the actions of a military coalition. Also, since military action before the use of any weapons of mass destruction would have been pre-emptive, it did not neatly fit into the self-defence model of Article 51, which requires that a threat be imminent. Peacekeeping, forceful or otherwise, was not an option as Iraq's consent was lacking. Furthermore, there was no Arab regional force to rely upon to intervene militarily with Council blessing either before or after the fact. Although the Iraqi crisis is now behind us, there was no resolution of the situation that could serve as a model for the future. The question remains: what would happen if the world community faced similar situations in the future? What if next time around there is incontrovertible and clear evidence of the existence of weapons of mass destruction? What action would or could the Council take? What would happen if it were unable or unwilling to preserve the peace of the planet? As the Secretary-General of the UN said in September 2003, 'History is a harsh judge: it will not forgive us if we let this moment pass.'[150]

Fortunately, some effort has been made in thinking how to craft a viable system of collective security. The report of the ICISS is a good example. It proposes certain criteria that should be satisfied before resorting to the ultimate sanction of collective force. Some criteria must be established to ensure that war is reserved for the very worst cases. The Security Council should not invoke military force too often, otherwise the international will to support it will evaporate.

The ICISS Report suggested the following criteria.[151] First, military intervention for humanitarian purposes should be an exceptional and extraordinary measure. Serious and irreparable harm, such as large scale loss of life or 'ethnic cleansing', must occur or be imminently likely owing to deliberate governmental action, governmental neglect or governmental inability to act. Second, it is important that the purpose of the use of force be to halt or avert human suffering. This can better be assured with multilateral operations, clearly supported by regional opinion and by the victims concerned. Third, every non-military option for peaceful prevention or resolution of the crisis must have been explored before military intervention. Fourth, the force used should be proportional and in any event involve the smallest scale, shortest duration and least intensity necessary to achieve the objective of human protection. Fifth, there must be a reasonable prospect of successfully halting or averting the suffering targeted by the intervention. Finally, the right international authority must authorize military intervention for human protection purposes. The most appropriate authority for this is the Security Council. The ICISS recognized, however, that the Security Council might sometimes fail to act, in which case it acknowledged that individual states might step into the breach to avert suffering. The report also recognized that the danger of unilateral action would be quite real in the event of such an abdication of responsibility. It would therefore be necessary for the international community to come to terms with its failure and the ensuing consequences in such circumstances.

The principles for the use of force set out in the Bahá'í writings are crafted in broader terms than those in the ICISS Report. However, the approach of the ICISS appears to be consonant with both the fundamental spirit and the letter of the Baháʼí teachings. First, Baháʼuʼlláh's approach to collective security is firmly grounded in the principle that the international community must forgo force as a general instrument of international relations and, instead, must seek to settle disputes through peaceful means. Although the international community recognized and acknowledged this principle, especially after the Second World War, as critical to maintaining collective security and embodied it in the United Nations Charter, as a practical matter, the international community has yet to apply the principle universally.

Second, under the Baháʼí approach to collective security the leaders of the world must come together – independently of any particular crisis – and agree upon a set of principles they will follow and a mechanism they will use for ensuring peace in our world. In other words, the first requirement is that leaders agree on how they will respond in situations that threaten to or do disturb the peace of the planet. Despite the United Nations Charter and its application over some 60 years of international crises, clear rules delineating what constitutes a disturbance of the peace calling for and justifying international action are yet to be determined. Similarly, rules on precisely what actions the international community will take in response to what kinds of disturbances of the peace have also not yet been worked out in any detail. Baháʼuʼlláh tells the world's leaders that they should all arise as one to bring to heel any nation disturbing the peace, including through the use of collective force as needed. Although the Baháʼí writings do not set out any specific rules for what constitutes disturbing international peace or what actions to take, the principles espoused in them do inspire concrete recommendations, which will be discussed in part 3 of this book.

Creating an Effective International Tribunal

Although the idea of an international tribunal was urged upon humanity by Baháʼuʼlláh as early as the 19th century, it was only after the world had suffered the torment and anguish of a ruinous and violent first world war that a world court was established under the Covenant of the League of Nations. This first modern attempt at a world court was known as the Permanent Court of International Justice (PCIJ). The hope of the nations that crafted the Covenant was to ensure that humanity would never again have to endure a nightmare akin to the World War I. Unfortunately, when put to the test during the politically turbulent years of the 1930s, the nations' commitment to the League and the PCIJ faltered. The remains of the PCIJ were salvaged but only after humanity had been through the crucible of a second world war. During the final stages and immediate aftermath of World War II, the victors of that conflict and many other nations crafted a new Charter of the United Nations. Under the terms of the Charter, the World Court was reincarnated and named the International Court of Justice (ICJ). Once again the world hoped that nations would turn first to the Court to resolve their disputes rather than resort to armed conflict and violence. Embodying the founders' vision of peace through law, the words '*Pacis tutela apud judicem*', which mean 'the judge is the guardian of peace', are inscribed on the main facade of the ICJ's Hague Peace Palace.

Reality, as it unfolded, proved to be rather different. The high hopes that the framers of the UN Charter had for the World Court have been battered, if not completely dashed. Over the years it has become evident that the World Court suffers from some significant shortcomings that will continue to hinder it from attaining its original purpose. The problems inherent in its structure and mode of operation are several-fold and unless each of these is properly addressed and rectified, the World Court will be unlikely to function as the instrument of peace it was designed to be.

The first problem lies in the limits of what the Court can do, what in legal circles is called the 'competence' of the Court. While designed to serve as the world's highest judicial organ in its capacity as the 'principal judicial organ of the United Nations',[152] the World Court's role is limited to judicial settlement, which is generally the last phase of dispute resolution. In other words, its proceedings are confined to formal presentations of evidence and legal arguments both written and oral, made by the parties to judges who consult among themselves and render a final decision in the case.

In many parts of the world, judicial settlement is not the most preferred or practised of a whole range of options, such as negotiation, consultation, mediation, conciliation and arbitration. In addition, the Court's jurisdiction is restricted to legal disputes between states. In other words, only states may be parties in cases before the Court.[153] Consequently, although all UN member states automatically have access to the Court, private persons and international organizations cannot bring a case to it.[154]

One of the consequences of the Court's limited competence has been the proliferation of judicial bodies at both the international and regional levels. For example, we now have two separate War Crimes Tribunals for the former Yugoslavia and for Rwanda that were established to prosecute individuals for war crimes that had taken place in those specific geographical regions during specific periods of time. We also have a newly created International Criminal Court which is designed to bring to justice those individuals who are accused of committing war crimes, crimes against humanity or acts of aggression no matter where these crimes occur. Then there are several international tribunals or similar dispute-resolution organizations associated with multilateral treaties on limited topics, such as the International Tribunal for the Law of the Sea and the World Trade Organization. The European Court of Justice, the European Court of Human Rights and the Inter-American Court of Human Rights are examples of international courts that address a wide range of issues but only in the context of a specific geographic region. This proliferation of international courts can lead to inconsistent decisions in certain cases or inconsistent interpretations of legal principles in separate but factually similar cases. For example, international disputes about maritime resources may be resolved by the International Tribunal on the Law of the Sea but also by the World Court. Inconsistent results in the same dispute obviously pose problems. Inconsistent development of legal principles is more insidious but also a much bigger problem because it makes future disputes more likely, not less, as countries in a dispute choose the interpretation that best suits them at the time. The world needs a hierarchy or system of international courts in which the precise relationship between them is well-defined and, perhaps, with the ICJ standing at the pinnacle, as the supreme court.

Second, even within the limited sphere of inter-state disputes to which it is confined, the World Court lacks the fundamental power of compulsory jurisdiction. Without it the Court is severely weakened because it can only assert jurisdiction over a dispute if all of the disputing states voluntarily submit the dispute to it for decision. This can be done in a number of ways, most commonly by a special agreement of the parties, called a *compromis*, which specifies the terms of the dispute and the framework within which the Court is to operate.[156] States usually take this approach when they conclude they are better off compromising on fixed parameters rather than prolonging any conflict between them. Several other mechanisms are also available but have been relied upon less often. The history of the case may allow the Court to infer consent to jurisdiction from the conduct of the parties. Such inferences are, of course, controversial if a state tries to deny consent. Article 36(2) of the Statute of the Court also allows states to accept the jurisdiction of the Court in advance, regardless of the issue involved. Perhaps not surprisingly, the majority of UN member states have not agreed to bind themselves under this clause or have done so conditionally. These so-called 'reservations' vary substantially from state to state but usually attempt to prevent the Court from becoming involved in a dispute which the state asserts concerns vital interests.[156] For instance, many reservations say that matters within the domestic jurisdiction 'as determined by' that particular state are automatically excluded from the Court's jurisdiction. This type of reservation clearly undermines any notion of compulsory jurisdiction and turns the whole process into a shell game. Moreover, over time, many of those states that originally signed up to compulsory jurisdiction have withdrawn their acceptance for different reasons. Yet another way of invoking the Court's jurisdiction is under a 'compromissory clause' included in some other international treaty that compels signatories of that treaty to resolve disputes before the World Court. Fortunately, a large number of international treaties, including both bilateral and multilateral ones such as the 1948 Genocide Convention and the 1965 International Convention on the Elimination of All Forms of Racial Discrimination, include such a clause granting the ICJ jurisdiction to interpret and apply the agreements.[157] All these mechanisms for achieving voluntary jurisdiction suffer from another flaw of any voluntary scheme: they depend upon reciprocity for the Court's jurisdiction to be activated. In other words, the Court will only have jurisdiction under Article 36(2) if both disputing parties have accepted jurisdiction on the same terms. Incredibly, even if the Security Council recommends that a dispute be referred to the Court, a 'decision' that is binding upon all member states of the UN in accordance with Article 25 of the Charter, the ICJ does not have power over the case without the clear consent of the parties.[158]

How can we rely upon such a system to preserve the peace in a world plagued by crises and conflict? Only when the stakes are low or the outcome seemingly assured would states that believe they have violated international law or who might suffer humiliation as a result of an adverse ruling by the Court willingly submit to its jurisdiction. We would never dream of setting up a national court system in which criminals or civil litigants could choose whether to submit to a court's jurisdiction if, for example, they were accused of murder or breach of contract. Such a system would be a sham and would leave our societies dangerously unprotected, subject to the whim of lawless individuals. Why then are we so willing to establish an international judicial system that so obviously lacks viability?

However, even when the Court has jurisdiction over the parties in a particular dispute there is a third problem, relating to the enforcement of judgements rendered by the Court. Although the Court's judgements are final and cannot be appealed, one of the curious features of the system is that the Court itself is not concerned with compliance. On the contrary, it takes the view that 'once the Court has found that a state has entered into a commitment concerning its future conduct it is not the Court's function to contemplate that it will not comply with it'.[159] The Court appears content to rely on the provision in Article 94 of the Charter by which each member state undertakes to comply with the decision of the Court in a case in which it is a party. In other words, the Court is happy to assume that once a party loses a case, it will properly and voluntarily comply with the adverse judgement. Yet this policy leave parties to their own devices to wilfully disregard the Court's judgements. By enabling non-compliance, the system effectively encourages impunity and undermines the stature and viability of the Court. After all, what incentive is there for a nation that does not care about international law or how it is perceived by its fellow nations to abide by a ruling that it deems antithetical to its interests? To draw again on the analogy with domestic judicial systems, we would never countenance a system in which criminal or civil law judgements were not enforced. Imagine saying to a criminal, 'You have been found guilty of murder, now please take yourself to some prison and ensure that you stay there for the requisite number of years.' Or to a civil litigant, 'You must compensate Mr X for damages to the tune of $1 million. Please make prompt payment,' without any attempt to monitor or enforce compliance with the judgement. It should be noted that if one party to a case before the Court fails to comply with the Court's decision, then the other party may complain to the Security Council which may make recommendations or take binding decisions.[160] However, as a practical matter this has not proved an adequate means of enforcement. The Security Council, like the Court, lacks enforcement power of its own. Nonetheless, it is no wonder that the record of compliance with the Court's judgements is, to quote an international law scholar, 'only marginally satisfactory'.[161] Examples of non-compliance include Albania in the Corfu Channel case,[162] Iceland in the Fisheries Jurisdiction case[163] and Iran in the case concerning the Tehran hostages.[164]

A fourth problem is that defendant governments that accept jurisdiction sometimes fail to appear before the Court at all. In such a situation Article 53 of the Court's Statute provides that the appearing party may ask the Court to decide in favour of its claim. To avoid arguments later by the defaulting party that its side of the argument was not properly taken into account, the Court is forced to act on behalf of the absent defendant government by providing legal arguments to support its case. This policy requires the Court to strike a fine balance that, itself, could be challenged by either party after the fact. Examples of cases in which this issue has arisen can be seen in the Fisheries Jurisdiction case,[165] the Nuclear Tests case,[166] the Aegean Sea Continental Shelf case[167] and the Iran case.[168]

Then there is a fifth problem, regarding how judges are elected to the World Court and the need to ensure that they discharge their duties impartially, independent of political and national pressures, in a way that inspires trust among peoples and nations. At present, the ICJ is composed of 15 members who are elected as follows. First the national groups of an international body called the Permanent Court of Arbitration (PCA), or specially appointed national groups in the case of UN members that are not represented in the PCA, draw up a list of qualified persons. Next the UN General Assembly and Security Council vote separately for individuals on this list. Successful candidates must obtain an absolute majority of votes in both bodies. In practice, there is close coordination between the Assembly and Security Council in electing judges. Also, the reality is that political factors do play a role in the election. The members of the Court are elected for nine years and may be reelected. Their election is staggered and takes place once every three years for five judges each time. This ensures some element of continuity on the Court.[169]

Although the election procedures aim to produce a judicial body of independent members rather than state representatives, this aim has been somewhat compromised by Article 31 of the Statute of the Court which provides that where parties to a dispute do not have a judge of their nationality already sitting on a case, they are entitled to choose a person to sit as an *ad hoc* judge for the duration of that case. Although intended to make parties comfortable with the Court, many observers believe this provision undermines the independence of the Court, especially given the overwhelming statistics that show that *ad hoc* judges support the state that has nominated them. Another factor that tends to undermine the Court's apparent independence is that when the Court sits in chambers of three or more members, as it may do under Article 26 for a particular case or categories of cases, 'it is inevitable . . . that its composition must result from a consensus between the parties and the Court'.[170] This was evident in the Gulf of Maine case in which it was alleged that Canada and the US threatened to withdraw the case if their wishes as to composition were not carried out.[171]

Although the decisions and advisory opinions of the Court have played a crucial role in the evolution of international law, as far as the maintenance of peace and security is concerned, the Court 'has indeed played a very minor part'.[172] This is largely due to the fact that the system is founded on close to two hundred sovereign states who cling tenaciously to their sovereignty and are therefore extremely cautious about permitting a third party to determine what they deem to be their vital interests. This tendency, combined with the flaws discussed above, are largely responsible for the current state of affairs. A serious effort to counteract and override the natural tendency towards excessive nationalism must be initiated.

Working Towards a World Federation of States and Equitable Distribution of Critical Resources

The idea of a world government or a worldwide federation of states still evokes visceral fears in many of us. At a very basic level it implies some loss of sovereign control that, given our present conditioning, is too uncomfortable to imagine. And yet some developments in our international community indicate movement towards an international federation. These developments have been driven not by any one factor alone but by a curious blend of idealism, practical necessity and collective self-interest.

The Creation of the League of Nations and the United Nations

The first notable development towards a world federation was the creation of the League of Nations in 1919, in the aftermath of World War I. Its creation was an attempt to establish a system of international cooperation and collective security that would safeguard future generations from the scourge of war. Its chief architect and proponent was President Woodrow Wilson of the United States who was inspired by lofty moral ideals. Unfortunately, the League was defunct a mere 17 years after its creation. This failure was due to several fundamental weaknesses in its structure and procedures. These included relying too much on moral condemnation as a remedy for armed aggression, requiring that collective action in response to external aggression have the unanimous agreement of members of the Council as well as the parties to a dispute, and ultimately the refusal of the United States to either join or effectively support the League of Nations. As a result of these weaknesses the League failed in its fundamental purpose of safeguarding the peace and preventing war. This became apparent in a series of incidents beginning with the Japanese invasion of Manchuria in 1931–2 followed by Mussolini's invasion of Abyssinia in 1935–6 and Hitler's occupation of the Rhineland in 1936, leading to the horrors of a second world-encompassing war. Despite the League's failure, the world community recognized the imperative of having an international body that would provide a forum for states to cooperate on matters of peace and security and that would implement a system of collective security. In recognition of this need, the international community created a new international organization known as the United Nations in 1945.

The moral and political foundation upon which the United Nations was built was first laid out in a document known as the Atlantic Charter made by President Franklin D. Roosevelt of the United States and Prime Minister Winston Churchill of the United Kingdom in August 1941. The two leaders met secretly aboard warships in Argentia Bay, off the coast of Newfoundland. Their primary goal was to rally support to win the war against the Axis powers of Germany, Italy and Japan by declaring 'certain common principles . . . on which they based their hopes for a better future for the world'.[173] One of the most important principles was 'that all of the nations of the world, for realistic as well as spiritual reasons, must come to the abandonment of the use of force'.[174] They also believed that the 'disarmament of such nations' which threatened or may threaten aggression outside their frontiers was essential 'pending the establishment of a wider and permanent system of general security'.[175] A prior American revision of the original British draft of the Charter included some language expressing the 'hope' that world governments would arrest the 'continued expenditures for armaments' except for 'purely defensive' weapons,[176] an idea that Bahá'u'lláh had advocated in the middle of the 19th century. Unfortunately, only a less explicit version of this principle made its way into the final document.[177]

On the whole, this approach of identifying and articulating first principles upon which nations agree to establish peace was entirely consonant with the approach advocated by the Bahá'í writings. Once the principles and values were firmly agreed upon, practical solutions to specific problems could be extrapolated. The leaders of two of the world's most powerful and influential nations, then and now, acknowledged the need to abandon the use of force both for practical and spiritual reasons. They clearly believed in according equal weight to the moral imperative as well as to the practical necessity. Within six months, on 1 January 1942, 26 nations signed the Declaration by the United Nations in Washington. In it they promised to wage war against the Axis powers with everything they had and to accept the principles of the Atlantic Charter as 'a common programme of purposes'.[178]

As the war continued, leading academics, opinion-makers and members of government, particularly in America, spent a lot of time thinking about and debating the kind of collective security system that would be established to ensure the peace once the war was over. A central issue in these debates was the conflict between the recognition of what was needed to safeguard the world community, on the one hand, and the attachment to outmoded ideas and policies and the fear of losing control, on the other. Thus many recognized the need for collective use of force but those in power still denied any intention to establish an international police force. A similar tension existed between recognizing that traditional national sovereignty was no longer consonant with either peace or justice and needed to be curtailed to secure world order and strongly resisting the creation of a world superstate.[179] (This conflict continued even to the naming of the United Nations. Although the Soviets first suggested calling it the 'International

Security Organization' and then 'World Union', the US leaders were uncomfortable, considering that these suggested some sort of supranational federation.[180])

Yet, at the same time, the debates led to some very forward-thinking ideas that were in line with Bahá'u'lláh's vision of collective security. Among them was a book entitled *Union Now*, written in 1939 by former *New York Times* journalist Clarence K. Streit, who compared the Covenant of the League of Nations to the Articles of Confederation that bound together the American colonies in the 1770s and 1780s before the US constitution was adopted. He argued that just as the Articles of Confederation had proved inadequate and needed to be superseded by a federal union with a central government and a constitution defining its powers, so too the League must become a federal union with a single defence force, a single currency, a single postal system, a single communications system and a customs-free economy.[181] Another example of ideas that were in line with the spirit of the times were those that were proposed by the Commission to Study the Bases of Just and Durable Peace headed by John Foster Dulles and presented to Franklin D. Roosevelt in 1943. The Commission produced a document entitled 'Federation of the World', which called for a world government complete with a parliament, an international court and other necessary agencies.[172] Apart from the proposal that this government be given the power to settle disputes between member states and regulate international trade, it also advocated that the government be given control of all military forces except those needed to maintain domestic order, an idea that is critical to the scheme of collective security envisioned by Bahá'u'lláh. Another example of the global thinking going on at the time was a resolution sponsored by a small group of US senators led by Joseph H. Ball of Minnesota calling for a new world organization which, amongst other tasks, would create a postwar world police force to suppress 'any future attempt at military aggression by any nation'.[183]

One of the ideas discussed before the creation of the United Nations was to form regional blocs headed by regional councils, with a Supreme Council of the three major powers – Britain, the United States and the Soviet Union – forming an umbrella organization above them. Winston Churchill was the chief proponent of this approach. However, President Roosevelt was not in favour of a system of interlinking regional blocs and pushed hard for a central global organization. Having been a member of Woodrow Wilson's administration, Roosevelt truly believed in a world governed by a democratic process with an international organization playing the role of arbiter of the peace. He eventually prevailed on Churchill and Stalin to accept this idea.

The charter of a new international organization tasked with maintaining the peace and security of our world was eventually agreed in a historic conference held in San Francisco in April 1945 at which 46 nations were represented. The new organization was initially called the United Nations Organization. In the end, the new United Nations was not intended to be a world federation of states or a world super-state. It can probably best be described as a loose confederation of states each insisting on its sovereign rights. Although advocates of world government or a supranational federation very much opposed the traditional system of sovereign nations, which they argued was a chief cause of anarchy and war, the reality was that none of the nations, large or small, was prepared to forgo any meaningful sovereignty. Consequently, the new organization was built on the traditional basis of unfettered national sovereignty. This decision had ramifications for its ability to discharge its responsibility to maintain peace. Even though the UN was to emphasize enforcement power, in contrast to the League of Nations, clinging to outmoded notions of absolute national sovereignty meant that the organization, its founders and member states struggled to create an effective peacekeeping mechanism. They wrestled with difficult questions, such as how decisions would be made about the use of force and how the UN could ensure the availability of adequate forces to back its decisions. Unfortunately, the solutions they crafted, premised as they were on a strong attachment to unfettered national sovereignty, quickly proved inadequate. So, for example, decision-making was seriously hampered by the veto power accorded to the permanent five members of the Security Council, none of whom was willing to relinquish ultimate control over decisions that might affect their self-interest. There was also an unwillingness to create a permanent international force because of the prickly sovereignty issues it raised, as discussed above. Instead, the framers of the Charter opted to create a system of national contingents which would be placed at the disposal of the Security Council by prior agreement between the UN and each member state – a system that has not worked in practice.

Although the UN has functioned as a much-needed forum where the member states, now totalling 192, have been able to air their diverse views and grievances, consult and decide on issues of international importance impacting the welfare, peace and security of the planet, it was ultimately not intended to be and is not a world government of the kind envisioned in the Bahá'í writings. Consequently, the UN General Assembly, albeit diverse in its membership, does not function as a world parliament would. Indeed, its members are not even elected by the citizens of their respective countries. Rather, they are appointed by and represent their governments. And while the Assembly's decisions carry the weight of world opinion on major international issues, they have no legislative authority. The General Assembly is unable to legislate on matters of global significance in the sense that its decisions do not have the force of law. Moreover, it lacks important powers including control over the planet's resources and the authority to ensure their equitable distribution, as well as the power to levy taxes. As for the Security Council, while it functions to some degree like the executive branch of a world government, with the power to take decisions which member states are obligated under the UN Charter to carry out, it also suffers from the serious handicaps discussed above – its composition, which reflects the world as it was in 1945 rather than the world today, the veto power of its five permanent members and the absence of standing forces to enforce its decisions. And while we have an International Court of Justice in name, it too has significant weaknesses, discussed above, that make it considerably less effective than it should be.

Most importantly, perhaps, there are no international legal provisions limiting the amount of arms that each nation can maintain for purposes of safeguarding internal order as envisioned in

Bahá'u'lláh's blueprint for collective security. Although the League Covenant contained a provision in Article 8 to the effect that the Council would 'taking account of the geographical situation and circumstances of each State . . . formulate plans for such reduction [of national arms] and action of several Governments', this provision was never implemented and subsequently was not even included in the UN Charter.

The reality is that at the end of World War II all nations, small, medium-sized and large, were unwilling to forgo their sovereign right to make decisions or to subordinate their interests sufficiently to create anything remotely akin to a world government or world federation. This reality was expressed well in a US State Department postwar planning draft statement of 15 March 1944 which said that a 'federal form' of organization was not feasible because 'nations should retain, and will insist on retaining, a large degree of freedom of action; no international super-government is feasible at this time, even if it were desirable'.[184] Even to this day, despite the fact that any concept of absolute national sovereignty has been significantly eroded by developments in the spheres of economics, technology and social relations, nationalism continues to be a deeply-rooted and powerful force in world affairs.

The Evolution of the European Union

Apart from the creation of the United Nations, the 20th century marked another important development in the gradual but unmistakable move towards a world federation, namely the establishment of the European Union (EU). The evolution of the EU from the European Coal and Steel Community (ECSC) into a multinational organization with strong federal attributes is a story of progressive economic, social and political integration among a group of disparate European nations that had often fought bitter wars against each other. At the core stood France and Germany, two countries that had suffered nearly a century of wars and enmity. It is a story of success born of a combination of idealism, self-interest and practical necessity and worthy of close examination and emulation at an international level. If implacable hatred among nations such as France and Germany and a desire for domination culminating in the horrors of the First and Second World Wars could be overcome by the creation of an economic and political union, should it not be possible for the larger community of nations to overcome similar obstacles?

The EU has been described as 'the triumph of voluntarily shared sovereignty over excessive nationalism, ideological division, and imperial ambition'.[185] In that sense it is tangible proof that intelligently applying Bahá'u'lláh's foundational principle of curtailing national sovereignty redounds to the success, security and happiness of peoples. Yet the success of the EU was not driven by idealism alone but also by calculated national self-interest and the recognition that something needed to be done to break with the destructive patterns of the past. The roots of this understanding can be seen at the outset, in the creation of the European Coal and Steel Community. In the aftermath of the two world wars that had originated in the heart of Europe and had resulted in the wanton destruction of human life and economic ruin, the people of western Europe – outside the sphere of the Soviet Union's dominance – craved military security, economic recovery and political stability. Over time they came to recognize that if they were serious about achieving these goals there was only one way to do so and that was to curtail their own national sovereignty in favour of some form of supranational governance, albeit limited.

They arrived at this understanding thanks in large part to the unflagging work and vision of one individual, Jean Monnet, Planning Commissioner for France who was charged with modernizing his country. Recognizing the central importance of coal and steel to the economic and military power of European nations and wishing to avoid further ruinous wars in Europe over these critical resources, Monnet proposed placing the coal and steel production of France, Germany and any other European country that wished to participate under the management of a jointly agreed High Authority. A customs union and common market for these products would also be created, within which the High Authority was to ensure the supply of coal on equal terms to participating nations.[186]

Monnet wisely recognized that the nations of Europe were not yet ready to cede sovereignty in large policy areas. European federalists had been calling for the creation of a United States of Europe for some time without success. Among them were Philip Kerr and Richard Coudenhove-Kalergi, who wrote a book in 1923 entitled *Pan-Europa* which called for a federal union of European states with France and Germany at its core. Then there were political leaders, such as French Prime Minister Edouard Herriot, who publicly spoke about a United States of Europe as early as 1925; Aristide Briand, another French Prime Minister, who had called for the creation of a federation of European nations and who shared the 1926 Nobel Peace Prize with German Gustav Stresemann for their work on the Locarno Treaties to normalize relations between their two countries after the First World War; and Winston Churchill, who joined many others to support such ideas. Alas, the Great Depression, the rise of fascism and the outbreak of the Second World War ended any hopes for such cooperation. Soon after the end of the Second World War Churchill again took up the call, describing the 'quivering mass of tormented, hungry, careworn and bewildered human beings' in war-torn Europe 'who wait in the ruins of their cities and homes and scan the dark horizons for the approach of some new form of tyranny or terror'. He called again for the construction of 'a kind of United States of Europe'[187] and then devoted many postwar years to creating such a union on the European continent.[188]

Monnet calculated that, practically, the only hope for success in integrating Europe lay in creating a supranational institution that was limited in its sphere of operation.[189] Eventually, he hoped that success in integrating a narrow sector of the economy would encourage the Europeans to integrate their economies in ever-expanding areas, creating links in the chain of European integration that would evolve by degrees. It turned out that Monnet was right.

Monnet's proposal for the creation of a European Coal and Steel Community was wholeheartedly embraced both by French Foreign Minister Robert Schuman and by German Chancellor Adenauer. Their decision to establish the ECSC was announced publicly by Schuman in a radio broadcast in May 1950. The Schuman Declaration, as the public statement has come to be known, proposed that the coal and steel sectors of France, Germany and any other European state caring to join be pooled under joint management of a supranational High Authority. Doing so would remove one of the main irritants in the relationship between France and Germany, namely Germany's possession of an abundance of coking coal used to produce steel, which France lacked to the detriment of France's steel production. Having suffered through yet another world war as a result of German aggression, many in France could not bear the thought that Germany's coal and steel production would put it on a faster road to economic recovery. The Coal and Steel Community would ensure the supply of these critical commodities on equal terms to both the French and German markets by integrating them. Thus the proposal addressed the practical needs of security through limited economic integration.

It was not long before six European nations were found willing to cede control over a small measure of their sovereignty because they perceived that they had certain common interests and believed that together they could achieve more than they could alone.[190] Ultimately, it was a sober calculation of national advantage coupled with the desire for a better life and the vision of the idealists that led these nations to the belief that some sacrifice of their sovereignty was well worth the benefits. Thus was established the European Coal and Steel Community which became the foundation of the future development of the European Economic Community and the European Union.

The ECSC came into being in 1951. Scholars see in it two successes. On the one hand it represented the first step on the road to a united Europe and on the other it brought to an end almost a century of war and antagonism 'that had come absurdly to be called hereditary', giving way to 'a will to cooperate on completely equal terms'.[191] However, while the ECSC represented a practical solution to the question of what to do with a rebuilding (West) Germany, for some it was also an expression of a higher ideal. The Schuman Declaration itself linked it to a greater goal of European integration and said it would 'lead to the realization of the first concrete foundation of a European Federation indispensable to the preservation of peace.'[192]

The drivers of changing historical circumstances and national advantage are evident at different junctures in the history of European integration since the creation of the ECSC. Examples include the impulse towards deeper integration prompted by the fall of the Berlin Wall and the consequent rise of a stronger, reunified Germany. The latter made France nervous and prompted it to push for deeper economic integration to ensure that Germany was so embedded in Europe that it would not yet again pose a threat to France or Europe. The war in the former Yugoslavia and the ethnic conflagration in Kosovo provide further examples of events that drove the European Community to integrate even further in response to new realities. More specifically, these events led the European Community to recognize that it needed to forge a more effective common foreign and security policy and to form a Rapid Reaction Force to enable military solutions to such problems, if necessary.

Another recurring theme in the story of European integration starting with the Coal and Steel Community has been the ever-present tension between supranationalist and intergovernmentalist visions. The supranationalist vision willingly cedes absolute national sovereignty in certain areas of activity to a supranational body whose decisions govern in those areas. In contrast, the intergovernmentalist vision rests on the belief that national sovereignty is absolute and national self-interest trumps all other interests, such that a body constituted by a group of states can only make decisions that are perceived to be in the self-interest of all participating states. The constant tug-of-war between these two visions of European integration has meant that integration has proceeded in fits and starts depending on which vision has prevailed at any given phase in the unfolding history of the EU.

For example, while Charles de Gaulle was President of France in the 1960s, his firm intergovernmental beliefs led him to resist the use of qualified majority voting within what was then the EEC's highest body, known informally as the Council of Ministers. The qualified majority vote enshrined in the governing EU treaties grants each country a fixed number of votes determined by its population and weighted in favour of smaller nations. A proposal could pass if supported in the Council by votes representing a majority of member states and a certain percentage of the population of the EU. Believing in a 'Europe of the states' rather than a federal Europe, de Gaulle insisted on unanimity in the Council on important questions and, in 1965, withdrew French representation from the Council, creating a constitutional crisis for the European Community. As he hoped, the crisis resulted in an agreement, known as the 'Luxembourg Agreement' to forgo voting whenever a member state claimed that important national interests were at stake. This effectively created a power of veto within the Council of Ministers, which hampered the work of European integration for a number of years. By contrast, Hallstein, who was President of the Commission during de Gaulle's presidency of France, had a distinctly federalist vision of Europe. His view is best summed up in a speech he made in New York in which he compared the histories of US federalism and European integration, saying: 'By its very nature . . . the Community must be an ever-growing, ever-developing organism . . . Essentially, [it] may be described as a federation in the making . . .'[193]

Despite initial resistance by intergovernmentalists like de Gaulle, however, the history of ever-tighter cooperation within the European Union has led inevitably to greater supranationalism. Time and again the tensions between supranationalism and intergovernmentalism have been resolved in the context of European integration in favour of the former because it eventually became apparent that supranationalism benefits the Union as a whole and assures that most or all member states benefit. By contrast, clinging to intergovernmentalism has simply delayed the inevitable and prolonged Europe's growing pains.

A study of the history of the EU teaches us that there is power in acting on principle, even if the first step is reluctant and without a full understanding of where it might lead. Indeed, it is not even necessary to have a complete understanding of where an action will take us as a community of nations as long as it is firmly rooted in a foundational principle such as the oneness of humanity or international cooperation. The story of the EU demonstrates that a step thus taken sets in motion organic changes in the structure of our institutions and societies that we could never have envisioned and which ultimately redound to our benefit. One example of such a powerful step can be found in a proclamation by European Community leaders after their summit in Paris in October 1972. In the final paragraph of the proclamation they 'set themselves the major objective of transforming, before the end of the present decade . . . the whole complex of the relations of [the] member states into a European Union'. At the time, these words were appended as an afterthought to the communiqué and none of those present at the summit seriously believed that there would be a European Union by 1980. Yet those words set in motion a chain of events that in fact led to such a Union in 1992. Another example of the power of first steps based on principle is the Solemn Declaration on European Union that was agreed by the member states meeting at the Stuttgart summit in June 1983. The Declaration called for closer cooperation on foreign policy and security and deeper European integration. British Prime Minister Margaret Thatcher reluctantly agreed to the Declaration on the theory that it had no legal force and could therefore not have that much effect. She would later regret her acquiescence and complain that she could not have foreseen that the Declaration would turn into 'the linguistic skeleton on which so much institutional flesh would grow'.[194]

The story of the EU also teaches that integration may involve a series of steps in a variety of fields, such as peacekeeping, military security, economic recovery and political stability, some of which may end up being successful and others unsuccessful. What stands out about the EU, however, is the willingness and courage to persevere in the face of repeated failures. For example, at the same time that the European Coal and Steel Community was formed, France also led an attempt to form a European Defence Community (EDC) that would have established a pan-European military defence force to control the re-arming of the (West) German military. The EDC would also have joined the ECSC in a broader European Political Community. These early attempts to unify military and political activities ended in failure at the time, ironically over French concerns about losing too much national sovereignty. However, these failures did not deter the Europeans from forging ahead in other fields of cooperation to create the European Economic Community and the European Atomic Energy Community in 1958, eventually establishing procedures in 1989 for European Monetary Union and, in 1993, the European Union, which now encompasses a broad range of areas including human rights, labour rights, the environment and a common foreign and security policy. Also worthy of emulation is the European habit of building upon successes, such as the creation of the European Commission, the first and most important supranational body of the European Economic Community. The Commission was modelled after the High Authority of the Coal and Steel Community, which was institutionally innovative in its time but not as powerful as its successor.

Another important lesson we can draw from the story of the European Union is that supranational institutions can initially be created with modest federal-like powers that are not threatening to member states. In time, those powers can incrementally be expanded as trust in the institution and its capabilities grows. In addition to the European Commission, the European Parliament is a good model for such an approach. It began as a benign organ of the European Community that neither truly represented the people of Europe nor possessed real legislative or oversight powers. Yet, over time, its members came to be directly elected by the citizens of the member states and its legislative powers have gradually increased. Whereas at first the European Council of Ministers was merely required to consult the Parliament about proposed legislation, later the Council was required to seek the Parliament's cooperation and ultimately to include the Parliament as a co-decider.

Incremental accretion of federal powers within the institutions of the EU is also evident in the voting procedures that have evolved over time within the Council of Ministers, the intergovernmental body that gives direction to the European Union as a whole. The Council began life as an entity in which most voting required unanimity on significant issues. The Council was able to act by qualified majority vote in only very few spheres of activity. Indeed, even those limited spheres subject to qualified majority voting were constrained by de Gaulle's Luxembourg Compromise mentioned above, which effectively created a veto power in the Council. It was a long time before the Council was able to get out of that rut of intergovernmentalism and to broaden the areas in which a qualified majority of members could act. With the passage of time, however, the areas subject to qualified majority voting have expanded incrementally and now cover many of the EU's subject matters.

Similarly, the European experience demonstrates that supranational institutions can begin life with limited spheres of jurisdiction that can gradually be expanded over time. While the European experiment was initially confined to a narrow economic sector, namely coal and steel, it gradually expanded to include the atomic energy sector, a customs union, a common commercial policy, transport policy, limited cooperation on monetary policy and other features of an economic community. In time, these spheres were further expanded to include all sorts of areas, including human rights, labour rights, the environment, common foreign and security policy, and so on.

The story of EU integration also teaches us that when the timing is right, new and innovative institutional capacity can be added to federal-like infrastructure as was done with the creation in 2004 of the Rapid Reaction Force in response to the ineffectualness of the European Union in Bosnia and its inability to prevent Serb atrocities both there and later in Kosovo in 1998 and early 1999. In both cases atrocities ended only after US military intervention while the EU stood by ineffectually.

Despite positive developments in the direction of world federation exemplified by the creation of the United Nations Organization and the gradually evolving European Union, there does not yet exist a world federation of states with the attributes envisioned by Bahá'u'lláh. Our nations still need to renounce the right to possess armaments except in a predetermined number deemed necessary for each state to maintain internal order within its borders. Our nations still need to cede to a world federal system some national rights to impose taxes so as to ensure that international bodies and agencies can function effectively. We also have yet to organize a system, like the European Coal and Steel Community, in which all the world's critical resources will be in the hands of a supranational institution that will ensure their effective and equitable distribution. Even within the European Union these issues have not yet been successfully tackled and overcome. Although the European Union provides an exciting model, both for what might work and what should be avoided to create a successful international federation of states, there is further work to be done to create and refine a system that it is truly viable and free of the weaknesses inherent in the European experiment.

Part 3

What We Should Build Next

What We Should Build Next

The first part of this book set out the blueprint for a comprehensive, effective and efficient system of collective security offered to humanity in the Bahá'í writings more than a century ago and discussed the elements comprising this system. The second part sought to demonstrate that our world has in fact been moving, unbeknownst to itself and albeit unevenly and reluctantly, towards the vision of collective security enunciated by Bahá'u'lláh. The aim of this third part is to offer a realistic way to bridge the remaining gap between the confused state of international cooperation and conflict in which we still find ourselves and the comprehensive vision of Bahá'u'lláh. Henry Kissinger, a master of 'realpolitik' in international affairs, once said that even if you have a great idea you must be able to break it down into a series of stages that are capable of implementation.[1] Accordingly, this part proposes next steps inspired by the Bahá'í writings for consideration by our governments, steps that are practicable in the short term and have a high impact. Although these steps require our leaders to stretch themselves in new ways, the intent is not to stretch them so far that they dismiss these ideas out of hand. Nonetheless, if taken courageously and swiftly, these steps should set us firmly on the road towards lasting peace and security.

Core Group of World's Leaders to Meet

To resolve the problems of international insecurity that face us all, it is essential that our leaders take collective and unified action. Before this can happen, however, these leaders must first agree on the priority of concerns to be addressed, the principles to be applied in resolving them and the strategies to pursue. This, in turn, will only occur if they are willing to engage in constructive consultation. Fruitful consultation is difficult even when there are only a few people involved. It would be vastly more difficult for the leaders of over 190 nations. As a practical matter, therefore, it makes more sense for a small group of the world's leaders to come together initially. Their first order of business should be to identify and agree upon a core set of first principles that will constitute the bedrock upon which a strong system of collective security can be built. Their second order of business should be to draw up an agenda of items critical to the establishment of international peace and security for in-depth consultation amongst them. The third order of business should be for them to commit to resolving each of the items on the agenda within a certain time period. Once these three objectives have been satisfied and agreement reached both on core principles and the solutions to the items identified as chief impediments to peace, the core group must then present them to the rest of the world's leaders and must work untiringly to build universal consensus around them.

For this endeavour to be successful, the core group of leaders must be imbued with certain qualities. They must be distinguished, trusted and well-regarded both by their fellow leaders and by their people. They must be high-minded and motivated only by what is best for the peoples of the world and will conduce to their peace, security and happiness. They must be determined and must not give up at the first sign of difficulty or resistance. Moreover, they must gather together in a spirit of sincere open-mindedness and humility, willing to listen to each others' point of view and concerns, to consider new ideas and to engage in creative consultation, spurred by their recognition of the reality that we live in a highly interconnected world in which we have no choice but to act collectively to find solutions to common problems. At the same time they must be frank and willing to share their concerns openly with their colleagues. They must be aware that the old ways of tackling our problems have failed us and that it is time to think out of the box and begin working on the long-term task of consciously and systematically creating intelligent and lasting solutions.

The sooner such a group of core leaders forms, gathers and

begins its deliberations, the better. To this end, this book proposes that the Secretary-General of the United Nations invite a number of leaders he deems to possess the qualities articulated above to begin this important work.

Agree Upon Shared Principles and Priorities Governing International Relations

Identifying a set of first principles is a critical foundational step in building a new and viable system of collective security. These principles are necessary guideposts and can be used to extrapolate solutions to specific problems and responses to individual crises. They will also be essential to shaping international institutions to reflect moral values that will serve us well in the 21st century and beyond.

The need to agree on first principles was clearly articulated by the international governing body of the Bahá'í community in a message addressed to the peoples of the world in 1985 entitled 'The Promise of World Peace'. In it, the Universal House of Justice said: 'Leaders of governments and all in authority would be well served in their efforts to solve problems if they would first seek to identify the principles involved and then be guided by them.'[2] Since then some of the leading thinkers of our times, including academic and think-tank scholars, former government officials and even the Secretary-General of the United Nations, have begun to talk and write about the importance of identifying such a core set of first principles. As mentioned earlier in this book, Gareth Evans, President and CEO of the highly respected International Crisis Group, has said, 'There is no substitute for going back to first principles, getting consensus around them, and then applying them.'[3] Kofi Annan, former Secretary-General of the United Nations wrote in a recently published report about the need to act 'on the basis of shared principles and priorities'.[4] In his recently published book entitled *Lawless World*, international law professor Philippe Sands expressed the view that some of our conflicts arise because of the tension between political values and legal rules and between competing conceptions of the hierarchy of moral choices.[5] Wouldn't it make sense to start by agreeing on a hierarchy of shared principles and values and then basing our laws upon them so that there is no incongruence between the two?

One of the many benefits that would flow from agreeing upon a set of shared first principles is that the members of our international institutions would operate with a greater degree of comfort and confidence as they approached complex and knotty problems, making them more decisive in crafting solutions and more effective in their actions. They would no longer shirk making decisions or avoid action, nor would they feel that they were shooting in the dark. Rather, they would have the strength and determination that flow from knowing that they are following the spirit and letter of a clear mandate conferred upon them by the world's citizens, stamping their actions with unquestionable legitimacy.

Just as the entire United Nations system was built upon a few principles articulated and agreed upon by Prime Minister Churchill and President Roosevelt in the Atlantic Charter, so too can a new international security system be created on the basis of shared principles. Therefore, it is proposed that the core group of leaders draw up a statement of such principles and labour untiringly to obtain the wholehearted commitment of their fellow leaders to it. This statement should include the principles set out below.

Principle of the Oneness of Nations and Peoples

This principle is the foundation of all others and should be made the chief operating principle of international relations. All other core values must be tested against and found congruent with it. It serves as the glue that binds all other principles and values the leaders agree upon and ensures the integrity of the foundation as a whole. It must be the chief driving moral force that influences and shapes all other values, policies, laws and the institutional infrastructure that are crafted to ensure our collective security. Starting from the premise that we are all one would alone would give us the clarity to identify organic changes that we need to make to our current laws, policies, procedures and institutions. So, for example, it would be unthinkable to continue to have the international organ primarily tasked with maintaining the world's peace and security operating on the basis that a handful of nations possess the power to veto decisions that would conduce to the long-term peace and security of all. It would also be unthinkable that a few nations should have the privilege of permanent membership on the Security Council while others were somehow considered second-class citizens and deprived of such a privilege.

Principle of Justice and Equity

All nations and peoples must be treated justly and fairly, without favour or discrimination. Several things follow from this. One is that certain key resources must be shared fairly. So, for example, provisions must be made and international mechanisms set up to allow all nations and peoples equal and fair access to critical sources of energy such as oil, water and nuclear power. Another consequence that should flow from the application of these principles is that crises and threats that affect different peoples and nations should be accorded the same importance regardless of whether they involve rich or poor nations, powerful or weak ones. So, for example, the international community should respond to the types of human rights atrocities that occurred in Rwanda and Darfur with the same alacrity that it did to the 11 September 2001 attacks in New York City. This sense of fairness can only stem from an understanding of our oneness. If one part of the international body politic is suffering then the entire body must rally to its protection and defence.

One of the consequences of applying the principles of justice and equity will be that rules embodying what behaviours are acceptable and unacceptable by nations must be clearly spelled out in advance and made known to all, along with the specific punishments that will result from their breach. These rules must then be applied consistently and equally with respect to all nations regardless of the identity of the offending nation. Similarly, punishments must be meted out even-handedly to all offenders. In other words, we can no longer condone or tolerate the practice of double standards. It follows that breaches of the rules on the non-proliferation of nuclear weapons must be punished equally whether the offender is a nation that is powerful and well liked in the international community or weak and unpopular. Similarly, all nations should be required to open their doors for unlimited international inspection if called upon to do so regardless of their status as friend or perceived foe of states serving on decision-making institutions. Illegal occupation of territory must be dealt with equally, regardless of the nation engaging in the unlawful behaviour or the perceived importance of the victim nation to others in the international community. All borders must be sacrosanct, protected from wilful violation by the collective might of the world community. Finally, rules affecting international peace and security should apply to all nations if a critical majority (to be defined by our leaders) of the world's nations support their creation. So, for example, all treaties involving human rights issues such as torture or the status of women, or the civil and political rights of people, as well as treaties involving non-proliferation issues and treaties creating international organizations such as the International Criminal Court should be binding upon all nations without exception. No nation should be given the choice of opting out, as this compromises the integrity of the system's fabric and eventually causes it to unravel.

The importance of the principles of justice and equity cannot be overstated. Their faithful and widespread application will eventually dissipate suspicion and feelings of injustice among nations and peoples of the world. They will also be a central element of a transparent system in which all players are held equally accountable. As a consequence, an atmosphere of trust amongst nations and peoples will be engendered which is essential for building a credible system of collective security. Over the long term, implementing these principles will play a major role in unifying nations as promised by Bahá'u'lláh in the following words: 'The purpose of justice is the appearance of unity among men.'[6]

Principle of Rooting Out Expediency

Expediency is a deep-rooted problem that needs to be openly and honestly addressed by our leaders. By *expediency* I mean the problem of acting in the perceived short-term interest at the expense of long-term interests, which generally involves compromising fundamental principles in the process. These short-term interests can range from friendship to commercial relationships to strategic considerations. Expediency is endemic to how governments currently work both at the national and international levels and is a root cause of many of our serious international problems.

One of the problems of expediency is that it generally comes back to haunt us. In the misguided belief that we are acting to solve the problem at hand, we often end up spawning myriad new problems, which tend to be more severe than the original one. Examples of misguided expediency in international relations abound. For instance, during the 1980s the United States encouraged Islamist fundamentalists gathering in Afghanistan to resist first occupying military forces of the Soviet Union and then a government widely viewed as a Soviet puppet. Unfortunately, once the Soviet-installed government dissolved, those same fundamentalists spawned the Taliban movement that ultimately led to the need for military intervention by the United States in 2001 to oust them. Iraq provides us with another example. For years the world allowed Saddam Hussein's government to get away with murder and human rights violations within its own country. This served the perceived commercial interests of some nations and the strategic interests of others that saw in Iraq a counterbalance to Iran, whose influence they feared. Ultimately, two wars were fought and much blood was shed to address the problems caused by Hussein, including his invasion of neighbouring Kuwait.

Our leaders should discuss frankly the problem of expediency and root it out from international relations. Fortunately, political leaders and scholars alike are beginning to acknowledge this problem. For example, in his speech made before the Summit of World Leaders began its meetings in September 2005, Kofi Annan said that we must not give up the rule of law or other basic principles for the sake of expediency.[7] Similarly, the Canadian representative to the May 2005 Review Conference on the Non-Proliferation Treaty said: 'We have let the pursuit of short-term, parochial interest override the collective long-term interest in sustaining this treaty's authority and integrity.'[8] He went on to say, 'If governments simply ignore or discard commitments whenever they prove inconvenient, we will never be able to build an edifice of international cooperation.' Similarly, at a recent meeting of the American Society of International Law in Washington DC, Professor Harold Koh, Dean of Yale Law School, explained that international law plays the role of facilitating and legitimizing action in the global environment. He went on to say that it was important that we not only follow the rules when it serves our short-term interest. Rather, he urged us to think long-term.[9]

Principle of Using Reward and Punishment to Preserve Peace and Order

One of the principles that our leaders should espouse is that international order is based on the two pillars of reward and punishment. Any system of collective security must ensure that actions that disturb the peace are swiftly punished and, by contrast, actions that promote the peace are encouraged and rewarded. For instance, facing a country that is illegally developing nuclear weapons, the world community might make clear to it that if that country gives up its illegal nuclear programme and accepts a comprehensive inspection regime, then the world community will ensure that all of its energy needs are met. But if that country insists on continuing its illegal activities, then the international community will impose comprehensive sanctions for three months, followed by the use of military force to replace the country's government.

Principle of Using Force in the Service of Justice

This principle requires accepting that force is not always to be shunned and avoided at all costs. This was forcefully and clearly expounded by 'Abdu'l-Bahá in His work *The Secret of Divine*

Civilization. There he stated that there are times when war becomes the powerful basis of peace, and ruin the very means of construction.[10] He went on to say that if war is waged for a righteous purpose, then this seeming wrath is mercy itself, and this apparent tyranny the very substance of justice and this warfare the cornerstone of peace.[11] This idea that 'war can be a progressive cause' and that military intervention is in certain circumstances 'not merely defensible, but a compelling obligation' is one that the international community had to relearn in the 1990s, according to Gareth Evans.[12] Michael Levi and Michael O'Hanlon, two scholars at the Brookings Institute, support this principle as well. In their book *The Future of Arms Control* they say that 'there may now be situations in which, paradoxically, war in the near term is preferable to an illusory peace.'[13]

The ability to use timely and adequate force is a critical element in the creation of a strong and effective system of collective security. Such a system demands both strength and elasticity. Its strength depends on having at the international community's beck and call the military and police forces necessary to quell disturbances to international peace and security. However, the system will only work if the threat of the use of force is a credible one. One example of how a nation can be induced to comply with an edict of the Security Council by assembling military forces and putting them on alert is afforded by Iraq. Despite Security Council resolutions requiring inspections of its facilities, Iraq had kicked the inspectors out. Once the United States began to build up a military force against Iraq in the summer of 2002, Iraq agreed to allow international inspectors to return. According to Hans Blix, former Director General of the International Atomic Energy Agency and later the Executive Director of the United Nations Monitoring, Verification and Inspection Commission (known as UNMOVIC), the build-up of military force that summer in anticipation of possible action against Iraq constituted the 'essential reason' why Iraq accepted the inspectors back.[14]

The exercise of flexibility and restraint in deciding when to use force lends the system some elasticity and should be reflected both in the rules that specify the circumstances in which action is to be taken and in the judgement of the institutions tasked with applying those rules. The recent growing acceptance by the international community of an obligation to protect those within a country's boundaries, which falls initially on the shoulders of each state and only by default upon the international community itself, is an example of the exercise of such flexibility and restraint when crafting rules for the protection of the peoples of the world.

Principle of Curtailing National Sovereignty

National sovereignty must be limited to the extent necessary to protect the citizens of the world as a whole. The willingness to adopt this principle will depend in large part on a deep understanding that the advantage of the part is assured if we bend all our energies to ensuring the advantage of the whole. Fortunately, this understanding is starting to take hold amongst some political leaders as well as leaders of thought. So, for example, Kofi Annan in his March 2005 report entitled 'In Larger Freedom' said that it was through hard experience that we learned that 'no legal principle – not even sovereignty – should ever be allowed to shield genocide, crimes against humanity and mass human suffering'.[15] A more striking example of the corrosion of unfettered sovereignty was the United States's decision reported by the media in March 2005 to invite some foreign nations to participate in its hitherto purely domestic and closed internal defence review. According to Pentagon officials, this was done 'as a sign of the heightened importance being given to international cooperation'.[16] The purpose of the defence review was to determine how to translate into action the new national defence strategy that had recently been issued by the Pentagon. In this strategy the United States apparently sought to take preventive steps to stop internal problems within other countries (including terrorism, insurgency, drugs and organized crime) from mushrooming into crises that would require US military intervention.[17] The growing recognition of our international connectedness is leading us, in some instances, to loosen our hold on dearly cherished notions of sovereignty.

Principle of Acting Collectively and in Unity

Finally, our leaders must recognize that for action to be most effective, especially when it comes to countering threats to the peace of the international community, it must be collective. They must commit themselves to speaking with one voice when faced with such a threat. They must be firm in applying the core principles and the rules of collective security that they agree to and must exercise their utmost to prevent expediency from prevailing in critical moments of decision-making. The world may gradually be learning this lesson as it addresses the challenge of the development of Iran's nuclear capacity. First we witnessed the closing of the gap between the positions of France, Germany and Britain on the one hand and the United States on the other. Then we began to see the gradual coalescence of the positions of this group of countries with the positions of Russia and China. Unity of thought is manifesting itself in increased unity of action which alone will yield effective results. As *The Economist* stated in a June 2005 article, 'The best hope for a peaceful outcome would be for all these countries to deliver the same tough message to Iran.'[18]

Strengthen the Security Council's Ability to Act Swiftly, Effectively, Equitably and Decisively

For a well-functioning, viable system of collective security to exist, three things must happen. First, it is critical to identify exactly who is responsible for doing what and the circumstances in which they can act. Our international institutions charged with maintaining the peace must be given clear and comprehensive mandates. Second, procedures must be crafted for these institutions to ensure that decisions and actions are taken efficiently, effectively and equitably. Finally, the institutions must have a set of first principles that they fall back on and apply when the answer to a problem is not clearly covered in their mandate or is not immediately apparent and when they have to consult and be creative about a solution. In the section above entitled 'Agree Upon Shared Principles and Priorities Governing International

Relations', concrete recommendations were made regarding a set of core principles to be embodied in a statement adopted by world leaders. The present section offers proposals to create a proper mandate for the Security Council and to craft adequate procedures and guidelines it should follow before it resorts to the use of force.

Provide the Security Council with a Clear Mandate for Action

Identifying from the start exactly who is responsible for doing what, especially when it comes to the use of force, avoids confusion and the possibility that potential institutional players will duck their responsibility to act. Somebody must be clearly in charge. Otherwise, in times of crisis, instead of decisive, swift action we will end up with indecision, delayed action or bungling. The Security Council currently is the international organ tasked with maintaining and restoring the peace and security of our world. Its authority to act must be clearly determined. It is especially important to delineate in advance the particular circumstances in which the Council is empowered to use force or to authorize its use, yet members of the United Nations have long disagreed on this critical point. As the former UN Secretary-General Kofi Annan said in his report 'In Larger Freedom', our leaders need to develop consensus on when and how force can be used to defend international peace and security.[19]

This sort of clarity serves a number of useful purposes. Most importantly, it reduces the opportunities for various nations to game the system. Once all nations and leaders know and are on notice as to when the Security Council may properly use force, recalcitrant leaders and nations who threaten the peace of the world will find it more difficult for them to play other nations off against each other, thereby delaying or completely avoiding the consequences they would otherwise suffer for their behaviour. It also makes it harder for politicians of nations whose narrow self-interest is at stake to play on the emotions of their domestic societies as a means to justify inaction or obstruction of the Council's broader purposes of maintaining international peace and security. A clear mandate also serves to reduce fear and suspicion of member nations of the international community that the Council will act beyond the scope of its authority and in the event that the Security Council does overstep the bounds of its authority, it can more easily be held accountable against clear terms of reference.

As our system of collective security currently stands, the Security Council has not only been tasked with preserving the peace but has also been given a broad range of powers to discharge this responsibility. As described above, these powers are set out in the Charter of the United Nations and include the use of force. What is lacking, however, is a clear, unambiguous, simple and definitive delineation of the circumstances in which the Security Council may use the weightiest of its powers – force. By its terms, the Charter provides that the Security Council may use force if non-forceful measures have not or would not work to address a 'threat to the peace', a 'breach of the peace' or 'an act of aggression'. The Charter does not explain any of these terms or what circumstances they might cover. This unfortunate gap has often caused the Security Council not to act early and decisively when facing situations that might threaten international peace and security. When the Security Council has eventually taken decisions, particularly regarding the use of force, the decisions have tended to come too late and often with enough public debate and disagreement among its members to allow offending nations to take advantage of the delay or to play one member against another. What is needed in many situations is more forceful action taken sooner rather than little action taken too late. Providing the Council with more detailed guidance of the circumstances that are covered by the above terms should help us achieve this end.

What we need is for our international community leaders to flesh out what is meant by the terms 'threat to the peace', 'breach of the peace' and 'act of aggression' used in the Charter. They should be willing to specify at the very least the categories of circumstances that fall under these headings and in which the Security Council can use force without undue hesitation. There are those who argue that to do so would merely encourage the use of force.[20] However, the reality is that problems endangering the peace, if left to fester, generally become more complicated and end up requiring the use of a greater of amount of force than would have been necessary had action been taken earlier. Sometimes a credible threat of the use of force by the Security Council alone will suffice to avoid a problem from deteriorating further. Thus Kofi Annan suggested that '[Security Council] members may need to begin a discussion on the criteria for an early authorization of coercive measures to address certain types of threats . . .'[21] Moreover, as repeated experience has taught us, in the absence of previously agreed rules, it is much more tempting, and therefore likely, for expediency to rule and for self-interest to prevail.

One useful way that the Charter's terms can be fleshed out is to say that specific categories of circumstances will be construed by the Security Council as amounting to either a 'threat to the peace' or a 'breach of the peace', triggering its authority to use force. Given recent history, threats to the peace should include, at the very least, the following: genocide and ethnic cleansing as defined by international law as it has evolved either through customary use or by treaty; flagrant human rights abuses and gross human rights violations of all kinds, such as large-scale torture (all these terms will need to be agreed upon by our leaders and clearly defined); state support of terrorism; verified production and build-up of weapons of mass destruction in contravention of arms control treaties; civil unrest that threatens to create a state incapable of maintaining internal order and of preventing internal instability from affecting other states (for instance, by enabling international terrorists or roving militias to operate from within the state); and substantial infiltration or take-over of state government by organized crime. Circumstances that amount to an act of aggression should similarly be clearly identified. These should include the obvious, such as the invasion, in contravention of international law, of the territory of one state by the other. They should also include the less obvious, such as statements by government officials that are so provocative as to incite acts of hate, war and violence against other nations.

In identifying the circumstances that fall under each heading, our leaders should be guided by two signposts. The first is a set of core principles that they have universally agreed upon, with which any action should always be congruent. For example, in addressing a threat to the peace caused by a government's actions within its country's borders, such as genocide, our leaders, relying on the core principles of oneness, justice and equity and the curtailment of national sovereignty, should make it clear that no nation may rely on Article 2.7 of the United Nations Charter, which prohibits intervention 'in matters which are essentially within the jurisdiction of any state', to shield itself from the consequences of its breaches of international law. The second is a constellation of international rules found in a number of treaties that outlaw specific behaviours worldwide because they are so inimical to the interests of the international community. These behaviours include terrorism, organized crime, torture and genocide.

To make the second signpost as effective as possible, our leaders need to do two things. The first is to clarify many existing international treaties, such as the various human rights treaties. Very often there is a clause in such treaties allowing signatories to refer violations of provisions of the treaty to the United Nations but the treaty is ambiguous about the action that is to be taken and the entity that should take it. An example of this is the Genocide Convention, which provides first that parties to it are required to 'undertake to prevent and to punish' genocide. Then Article VIII provides that signatories may call on the United Nations to 'take such action . . . for the prevention and suppression' of genocide. But the treaty does not make clear what 'undertaking to prevent' and 'suppressing' genocide mean. It is also unclear who is to carry out such measures.[22] These treaty defects need to be remedied as quickly as possible.

The second is to create new treaties or extend existing ones to cover actions by state or non-state actors that may not yet be clearly illegal under international law but which our leaders identify, in the course of their consultations, as threats to the peace of the international community. New treaties or treaty amendments should expressly make those behaviours illegal and actionable by the Security Council under Chapter VII of the UN Charter. An example of the kind of behaviour that could be thus criminalized is the very possession of nuclear, chemical or biological weapons by non-state actors, as proposed by scholar Ashton B. Carter.[23]

Using these two guideposts to identify circumstances that fall under the headings 'threat to the peace' and 'breach of the peace' will yield two main benefits. First, members of the international community will be on notice that certain behaviours are unacceptable and will have specified consequences that could include the use of force by the international community. Second, the Security Council will have detailed guidelines regarding what constitutes a violation of these laws and will have an easier task of making any decisions necessary regarding the possible use of force.

In addition to identifying the precise circumstances in which the Security Council can act forcefully to preserve international peace and security, the revised mandate should also include those powers that the Security Council needs to restore peace. An example is the power to disarm and demobilize combatants. Disarming and demobilizing combatants' military forces is often critical in ensuring that violence does not break out again after peacekeeping or enforcement forces have left a region. It is crucial to eliminating suspicion and to reintegrating the combatants into society, so that peace can take root and flourish. Examples of the positive impact of such disarmament can be seen in two cases. First is Aceh where a 30-year war was fought between insurgents of the Free Aceh Movement (known as GAM) fighting for the independence of the Aceh province and the Indonesian government. Shortly after a devastating tsunami hit Indonesia in late 2004, the two sides of the conflict came together and by August 2005 had hashed out a detailed peace agreement. The insurgents agreed to hand in 840 weapons and by late December that year had not only followed through on their promise but also announced that they would disband.[24] Second is Northern Ireland where partial disarmaments in 2001, 2002 and 2003 were followed by declarations in mid-2005 that the Irish Republican Army (IRA) was ready to dispose of its stockpiled arms. In September 2005 General John de Chastelain, one of three commissioners of the Independent International Commission on Decommissioning (IICD), an independent body whose job it was to oversee the decommissioning of paramilitary arms in Northern Ireland, reported that the IRA had 'put beyond use' what the IICD believed to include all the arms in the IRA's possession.[25] He was also reported as saying, 'We are satisfied that the arms decommissioning represents the totality of the IRA's arsenal.' This success was followed by further positive developments in Northern Ireland, culminating in a historic agreement made in March 2007 between the Rev. Ian Paisley, leader of the Democratic Unionist Party (DUP), and Gerry Adams, leader of Sinn Fein, to share power between these hitherto rival groups, beginning on 8 May 2007.[26] In accordance with their agreement, the two former enemies, the Rev. Ian Paisley and Martin McGuinness (of the republican and mainly Catholic Sinn Fein party) were sworn in as leader and deputy leader respectively of Northern Ireland's executive government in May 2007.[27]

In contrast, the Palestinians are still struggling with the refusal of Hamas to lay down its arms even though the quartet of governments and institutions involved in the Middle East peace process have long urged them to dismantle militias.[28] In a joint statement after meeting at UN headquarters following Israel's withdrawal from Gaza in September 2005, the quartet (comprising the European Union, Russia, the United States and the United Nations) called for the Palestinians to 'dismantle terrorist capabilities and infrastructure' and said: 'Ultimately, those who want to be part of the political process should not engage in armed group or militia activities, for there is a fundamental contradiction between such activities and the building of a democratic state.'[29] By the summer of 2006 the failure to disarm militias active in Palestinian territories has led to armed conflict between competing factions, despite recent democratic elections in those territories. Indeed, a bitter and violent power struggle between Hamas and Fatah ensued after the surprise election victory by Hamas in early 2006. The conflict between the two rival groups continued to escalate, culminating in June 2007 with Hamas seizing power over the whole of Gaza.[30] President Mahmoud Abbas of the Fatah group responded by dissolving the Hamas-led Palestinian unity government, dismissing Prime Minister Ismail Haniya of Hamas and announcing the creation of an interim emergency government staffed by his Fatah party to govern the West Bank.[31] As of June 2007, this has left Gaza and the West Bank under the control of warring Palestinian groups, Hamas and Fatah respectively. With pressure being exerted on these groups and their leaders from nations in the region and beyond, it remains to be seen how the tension and conflict will eventually be resolved.[32]

Another power that the Security Council should be given in the revised mandate is the power to place under a temporary trusteeship a nation that is found to be a threat to international peace and security but whose domestic government structures are so incompetent or weak that they cannot govern responsibly. In other words the international community would temporarily take over the reins of governance while assisting the nation to strengthen its domestic government infrastructure. Similarly, there should be rules about what to do if an offending country's government collapses after the Security Council has intervened militarily. There must be provisions for post-conflict building and strengthening of that country.

WHEN CAN A NATION OR A GROUP OF NATIONS ACT IN SELF-DEFENCE, PROTECTIVELY OR PREVENTIVELY?

Although a viable system of collective security will be at its most robust when our leaders recognize the powerful effect of collective and unified action, we must face the reality that it might take us a while to achieve the ideal of consistently unified action. Consequently, no revision of the mandate granting the Security Council authority to use force would be complete without addressing the critical question of who has the right (or even obligation) to take pre-emptive, preventive or protective action. This question is in turn intimately interwoven with another question that must be honestly and openly addressed by our leaders, namely, what should happen when the Security Council abdicates its responsibility to the international community and fails to take appropriate collective action including the use of force if necessary, for instance, to halt genocide or the unlawful build-up of weapons of mass destruction or a particular state's support of international terrorism?

Under Article 51 of the UN Charter, as interpreted by state practice, an individual nation or a group of nations may act in self-defence or pre-emptively if they face an imminent threat from another nation and the Security Council has not yet acted. However, the Charter does not address what to do when the imminent attack comes not from a state actor but from a non-state actor, such as a terrorist group. This question has cropped up repeatedly over the last few years, especially since the 11 September 2001 terrorist attacks in the United States. The International Court of Justice has ruled that there is no right to self-defensive action against a non-state actor. Does this mean that only the Security Council may act in this situation? What happens if it fails to act? One interpretation of the Court's ruling is that, absent robust collective action by the Security Council, the state that is the target of the attack is left completely vulnerable, with its hands legally tied until the attack occurs. This is clearly an issue that must be consulted upon and for which a solution must be agreed by our leaders.

Another critical question that needs to be openly and honestly addressed is what happens when a state or group of states faces a threat that is not imminent but latent and potentially devastating. Such a situation, which requires preventive action (as distinguished from pre-emptive self-defensive action), is not presently covered by the self-defence provision in the United Nations Charter. The question for our leaders is, should the Charter and international rules be expanded to allow a nation to act unilaterally or a group of nations to act as a self-appointed coalition in response to such a threat? As the rules presently stand, such threats may not be acted upon unilaterally but can be effectively acted upon by the Security Council under its current mandate because the threat can clearly be construed as a threat to the peace. Indeed, this book proposes that such situations of high-risk and non-imminent threats be specifically included in the list of situations in which the Security Council is authorized to act under its proposed newly clarified mandate. The bigger question is, what happens if the Security Council fails to act quickly enough or fails to act at all? Should unilateral preventive action or action by self-appointed state actors ever be allowed and, if so, when?

A related question that also needs to be addressed and clarified once and for all is whether it is ever lawful for a nation or a group of nations to act protectively to address a threat directed by a third nation against its own people. Indeed, do states have an *obligation* to act protectively and should they be required to do so by international law? For example, when genocide is being committed in a third country and the Security Council delays action or fails to act, can a single nation acting unilaterally or a group of nations acting in coalition step in to protect the people of that country from genocide? Must they? This has been an evolving area of international law known as humanitarian intervention, one in which nations are increasingly willing to condone action outside the Security Council to prevent egregious and flagrant human rights abuses and to alleviate extreme humanitarian distress.[33] It is an area in which tensions have arisen between the security of the state and the security of its citizens and between the rights of the state and those of its citizens.[34] Again, this is a situation in which the Security Council may, under its current mandate, choose to step in and use force if necessary on the grounds that it constitutes a threat to the peace. However, thanks to the groundbreaking work of the International Commission on Intervention and State Sovereignty (ICISS) in framing the new principle of the responsibility to protect discussed in part 2 of this book, the Security Council is now more likely to step in and take action because this principle recognizes the international community's collective fallback responsibility to protect the citizens of a nation if that nation fails in its primary duty to protect them. Indeed, there is a strong argument to be made that this principle has emerged as a new norm of customary international law, especially in light of the fact that the world's nations gathered at the Summit of World Leaders in September 2005 endorsed it in the Summit's final Outcome Document.[35] But the critical question that remains is, what happens in the event that the Security Council abdicates its responsibility to act?

One way to deal with these issues about the rights and obligations of nations to act unilaterally or in coalition with other individual nations pre-emptively, preventively or protectively is to broaden the terms of Article 51 of the Charter. The revised Article would include not only the present right of states to act pre-emptively but also the right of an individual nation or group of nations to act both to protect the citizens of a third country from flagrant human rights abuses and to prevent non-imminent but potentially very destructive threats directed either against themselves or against the citizens of a third country. It does not make sense to continue to distinguish, as we have been doing, between threats arising because of egregious human rights abuses and threats to security arising, for example, because of a dangerous build-up of weapons of mass destruction or as a result of state-sponsored terrorism. However, if we are to permit protective or preventive actions, the following conditions must first be satisfied. First, the types of threat that can be responded to must fall within the categories of threats in which the Security Council has authority to act, as discussed above. Second, the Security Council must have been notified of the situation first, given the opportunity to act and failed to do so within a period of time specified in the rule (for example, one month). Third, there must be strong and reliable evidence supporting the existence and severity of the threat, as discussed in more detail below. The country or countries wishing to act outside the Security Council must, before they act, assume the burden of presenting such proof to a standing committee of either the General Assembly or the International Court of Justice. Such a peace and security committee must be established and tasked with the sole responsibility of deciding whether the burden of proof has been met by individual nations seeking to act protectively or preventively, in the absence of an affirmative decision by the Security Council within the specified time. The reason for vesting this responsibility in a body other than the Security Council is to ensure that paralysis within the Council caused, for instance, by maintaining the veto system, will not hinder effective action. What the standard of proof should be is another critical question that our leaders must decide ahead of time and embody in the agreement that covers the issues discussed in this section.

Fourth, once an individual nation or group of nations satisfies the criteria for acting unilaterally or in coalition, they may continue to so act only until the Security Council steps in and assumes the international community's responsibility to act collectively.

INTERNAL GUIDELINES FOR SECURITY COUNCIL DECISIONS ON THE
USE OF FORCE

In addition to clarifying when the Security Council may use force, it is also important to set in place certain internal guidelines that the Security Council must follow when deciding whether it should use force. Some good work has recently been accomplished on this front, as embodied in the recommendations made by the High-Level Panel on Threats, Challenges and Change.[36] These recommendations pose several questions that clarify issues which, if not addressed in advance, might lead to hesitation by the Security Council when making decisions. First, how serious is the threat? And second, would force be used for a proper purpose? A catalogue of serious threats included in a new mandate, as proposed above, would automatically answer these two questions for many categories of threats. Third, should the Security Council try all other measures before resorting to the use of force? Article 42 of the Charter contemplates the use of force if the Security Council considers that other measures 'would be inadequate or have proved to be inadequate'. There may be circumstances in which this requirement is sensible, particularly when the danger to human life is not imminent, but not where the international community is facing an imminent danger or one that is potentially very destructive. For instance if intelligence shows that a state is about to use biological weapons against another, it might not make sense to shackle the Council's freedom to use force by requiring it to try other measures first. There may simply not be the luxury of time. In any event, this question must be seriously addressed by our leaders and detailed guidance provided as part of a revised Security Council mandate. Fourth, should the Security Council be required to consult with other states, such as those neighbouring the troubled area, before it acts? Although it might make sense to do so as part of its investigation of the facts of the case and the likely impact of the trouble on the surrounding region, it might not make sense to condition Security Council action upon the approval of neighbouring states where, for instance, genocide is involved and the neighbouring states are not terribly concerned about it. It is time that we begin to trust our international organs to act for the benefit of us all. Fifth, the Security Council should ask itself what kind of force and how much is proportionate to the danger? The answer to this will depend on the circumstances of the case. It is only fair and just that the punishment fit the crime and that only enough force be used to avert even greater suffering than the use of force itself would inflict. To these five questions, a sixth should be added: must the Security Council pass a resolution requiring the offending state to correct its actions by a given time and warning that if it fails to do so the Council will use force? Again, although in most circumstances such a requirement would make sense and be fair, there are likely to be exceptional cases, such as the kind of genocide we witnessed in Rwanda, in which time is short and action must be taken immediately.

WHERE SHOULD A REVISED MANDATE AND GUIDELINES BE EMBODIED?

What is the best mechanism to embody a newly-amplified and clarified mandate and decision-making guidelines for the Security Council? The ideal is to add them to the UN Charter by amendment. This would put the mandate and guidelines where they belong: in the document that created and established the United Nations and its primary organ, the Security Council. As a practical matter, however, this would probably prove rather difficult because such an amendment would require the agreement of two-thirds of the members of the General Assembly, including all the permanent members of the Security Council. Since it came into being, the Charter has only been amended twice.[37] A more practical and suitably effective mechanism would be to embody the mandate and guidelines in a new international treaty.

Create Streamlined Procedures for Security Council Action

For the Security Council to discharge its mandate, it is essential that its internal procedures be streamlined. It is time to move beyond the 'provisional' rules of procedure that the Security Council currently follows and to establish permanent standing rules.[38] This should be done with a view to maximizing the potential for unified and collective action. It is much easier to act collectively when the rules of procedure are well defined in advance and it is simply a question of following them as the Security Council seeks to apply the requirements of its mandate to any given situation. Following certain procedural rules also makes it less likely to fall into the trap of expediency. Previously agreed rules have the additional benefit of making it harder for countries to play members of the Security Council against each other. Once the rules of procedure have been revised, they should be consistently followed.

Past mistakes suggest several areas in which we can change, to great effect, the way the Council does business. The first is to ensure that the language of Security Council resolutions is clear and unambiguous and unequivocally conveys the Council's intent. The language must leave no room for misinterpretation and misunderstanding by either Council members or third parties. Ironically, the reason for the equivocal language that characterizes so many resolutions is the Security Council's practice of seeking consensus in its decisions, even though it is empowered to take decisions by majority vote. Building consensus requires compromises, which are often made at the expense of specificity.[39] The resulting ambiguity temporarily masks differences among the members of the Security Council. These differences tend to emerge later in the heat of the crisis, however, and often paralyse the Council regarding further action.

A recent, well-known example of this problem arose in late 2002 when international inspectors of Iraq's disarmament, mandated by the Security Council, had been denied entry into Iraq for four years. On 8 November 2002 the Security Council voted unanimously in favour of Resolution 1441 giving Iraq one last opportunity to comply with the Council's demands despite the fact that it continued to be in 'material breach' of previous Council resolutions. The resolution provided that if Iraq failed to comply with this latest resolution it would be in 'further material breach' of its obligations and the failure to comply would be reported to the Council for assessment. The Council would then convene 'in order to consider the situation and the need for full compliance with all the relevant Council resolutions in order to secure international peace and security'.[40] According to lead inspector Hans Blix, France and the United States had different interpretations of what constituted a 'material breach' by Iraq of its disarmament obligations and what would happen if such material breach continued. The French interpreted the language of the resolution to mean that before any serious enforcement action would be considered or taken there would have to be a report by the inspectors that Iraq had failed to comply with the Council's resolution. They also believed that the use of armed force required a further Council decision. By contrast, the Americans interpreted the resolution to mean that if they concluded that Iraq had failed to comply with its terms, they could proceed with armed action without coming back to the Council for further approval.[41] This fundamental difference in interpretation resulted in disunity between long-time allies and an ultimate failure to take collective action.

The problem of ambiguity has surfaced again in the negotiations among six nations – Russia, China, the United States, France, Britain and Germany – acting in partnership on the one hand, and Iran on the other, aimed at curbing Iran's nuclear activities. Although the six partners have demanded that Iran suspend all activities related to uranium enrichment before talks can begin, there is a difference in understanding amongst them as to what constitutes 'suspension' and 'enrichment'. While some of the six believe there is room to allow Iran to conduct low-level enrichment activity for research purposes so long as it suspends enrichment on an industrial scale, others insist that Iran halt all enrichment. According to media reports, diplomats involved in the negotiations have intimated that the six negotiating partners deliberately left the definition of suspension vague to maintain unity amongst themselves and to lure Iran back to the negotiating table.[42]

The issue of making Security Council resolutions clear and unambiguous is intimately linked with the question of voting rights within the Council and the problem of the veto. Before we can have a properly functioning system of collective security, we will need to deal with the anomaly that a handful of nations alone have the right to veto a decision of the Council. Why should such a small group of nations be given such disproportionate power in an increasingly democratic age? Why should we continue to embrace the right of veto when it has demonstrably been the major cause of the failure of the Security Council in its task of preserving international peace and security?[43] Once our leaders make the principle of the oneness of peoples and nations the ruling principle in international life and accept the principles of justice and equitable treatment as core principles of international relations, the concept of permanent membership on the Security Council as well as the right to veto will have to be abandoned.

The rules regarding the Council's composition must also be revised to make the Council more broadly representative of the international community as a whole, for instance by ensuring that every region has a permanent representative thereby vesting it with more legitimacy and credibility in the eyes of the world. As an interim step, it might be worth trying to gradually expand the number of permanent members to broaden representation, while eliminating the power of veto.

Another problem that the rules of procedure must address is ensuring that members of the Security Council are able to vote without undue pressure from other member states. The practice of bringing intense economic and diplomatic pressures to bear on certain countries for the purpose of gathering votes should be discontinued and made illegal under revamped rules of procedure to be agreed upon by our leaders. The rules must prohibit attempts to influence voting by threats of economic or political punishment or by promising financial or political rewards. This would prohibit current egregious practices of attempting to influence voting on the Council such as conditioning the provision of aid upon a state's vote or threatening to withhold military assistance.

With respect to voting, the Council's rules should also allow any decision regarding the preservation of peace and security to be taken by majority vote of the members. Also, once a vote has been taken, only the resulting decision should be made public and not the way different states voted. This will allow members of the Security Council to vote in accordance with international law and, in the absence of clear laws, in reliance on the core principles without undue pressure from external forces. Moreover, the rules of procedure should provide that once a vote has been cast and a decision taken, the Security Council must be required whole-heartedly to support it and set out unitedly to implement it swiftly and effectively.

Another matter that must be covered by the procedural rules is the obligation of the Security Council to act swiftly and decisively to maintain or restore peace and security when they are threatened. To this end the rules must specify a time line for Security Council action once a security problem has been brought before it. As we have seen, often violators of the peace do not fear verbal condemnation by the Security Council, which makes it even more essential to act quickly. Early action is also critical to avoid deterioration in circumstances that lead either to a narrowing of options, as happened in North Korea according to the director of the IAEA,[44] or to unnecessary suffering, as in the case of Rwanda where an estimated one million people were massacred in the course of just over three months. In either case rectification of the situation becomes all the more arduous, costly and difficult. A rare example of timely action and its effectiveness can be seen in the case of East Timor, where the Security Council worked together with national governments and regional players to rapidly apply consistent pressure to stop large-scale killing.[45]

Early collective action also has the benefit of forestalling the secondary problems that flow from unilateral action or the action of coalitions that step in to fill the void left by Security Council inaction. These secondary problems are many and varied and include suspicions and charges of colonial aspiration on the part of the unilateral actors, charges of regional destabilization and charges of unscrupulous motives such as ethnic or religious hatred or the desire for control of natural resources.

Another procedural issue that must be properly addressed concerns how the Security Council conveys to a recalcitrant state the sequence of steps that it must take to resolve the problem it has caused. Once the Security Council decides that there has been a threat to the peace, a breach of the peace or an act of aggression, it must act quickly to issue a resolution to the offending state. This resolution must specify the precise steps that the offender must take to satisfy the Council's demands, along with clear and measurable benchmarks to gauge compliance. It must also specify the exact time line within which these measures must occur, including a firm deadline. Finally, it must clearly set out the consequences (including forceful action) that will be triggered by failure either to implement the measures or to achieve them within the time allotted.

Iraq offers another example of the consequences of not having such a system in place. The idea of creating a specific list of remaining disarmament tasks for Iraq appears to have come very late, after over a decade of inspections in which some nations had lost patience with the country. For years the international community had effectively looked for signs that Iraq had undergone a 'change of heart' and had decided to comply fully with the Security Council resolutions terminating the first Gulf War. Mohammed ElBaradei, the head of the International Atomic Energy Agency, noted that whereas 'change of heart' was a subjective criterion, identifying compliance with key tasks provided an objective one.[46] In his book Hans Blix says that the idea of measuring Iraq's actions against precise requirements rather than judging whether it had had a 'change of heart' was the right approach.[47] It is clearly easier to take decisive action, especially collective action, in the face of failure to comply with measurable benchmarks than it is to do so based on an amorphous, subjective concept like a 'change of heart'.

Interestingly, this idea of setting clear benchmarks to be reached within specified time periods seems to be taking hold among policy thinkers. Recently, two eminent think-tank scholars in the field of foreign policy suggested that in dealing with Iran, the United States and its allies should define clear benchmarks to measure Iran's compliance with their joint demands and

specify the consequences that will flow, both positive and negative, if it does or does not comply.[48] Despite some progress in this
area, however, the lesson is yet to be learned. As of 13 July 2007
Iran had failed to comply with the Security Council's demand that
it suspend all of its nuclear activities, especially its production
of uranium and plutonium useable to create a nuclear weapon.
This failure occurred despite the Security Council's imposition of
two rounds of sanctions on Iran which although weak, imposed
increasingly stiff sanctions in an attempt to elicit Iran's compliance. However, as *The Economist* points out, Iran responded to
this stepping up of sanctions by speeding up its installation of
centrifuge machines at Natanz, its nuclear enrichment facil-
ity, and reducing its cooperation with the International Atomic
Energy Agency.[49] Now, just as the United States is pushing for
further tough Security Council sanctions against Iran, the latter
has reportedly offered to allow international inspectors to visit
its heavy-water research reactor at Arak by the end of July 2007
and has apparently agreed with the International Atomic Energy
Agency on ways 'to resolve remaining issues regarding Iran's past
plutonium experiments'. In addition, an early August 2007 meeting is reportedly being planned to finalize the manner in which
inspection and monitoring is to be undertaken at Natanz, the site
of Iran's uranium enrichment programme.[50] Whether Iran's offer
of cooperation is a first measurable step in the direction of total
compliance with the demands of the Security Council or is simply
a ruse to buy time and avoid referral to the Security Council for
a third round of sanctions – a ruse it used in 2006[51] – remains to
be seen. It also remains to be seen whether the international community will maintain a resolute and united front in specifying the
consequences that flow from Iran's actions, whether positive or
negative.

Once an offending state has received clear demands from the
Council as the agent of the international community, if it demonstrates bad faith in complying with them, the rules should
require that adverse consequences attach. Deliberately lying to or
misleading the Council should qualify as instances of behaviour
demonstrating bad faith. The games of deception that Iraqi offi-

cials played with the UN inspectors charged with ensuring that
Iraq destroyed its weapons of mass destruction are a recent example of such deception. Videotapes taken by the inspectors show
how the Iraqis moved files and burned documents while forcing
the inspectors to wait outside the gates of the site to be searched.[52]
These games resulted in further raising the suspicions of members of the Security Council rather than allaying them and were
ultimately detrimental both to Iraq, which suffered a war, and the
international community, which continues to expend human life
and financial resources.

The Security Council's procedural rules must also ensure that
it will not vacillate when nations miss compliance deadlines.
Once the Security Council has detailed its demands and specified
a compliance deadline, it must not procrastinate in implementing the consequences it has specified for failure to act. Failure to
implement the penalties provided by Security Council resolutions undermines and eventually destroys the credibility of the
Security Council as a body whose job it is to preserve the peace.
How much time is enough? This will depend on the specific case
and is a matter for the Security Council to decide in each situation. However, once set, time lines must be adhered to. In this
regard, the decade-long disarmament effort in Iraq provides yet
another lesson. Time and again members of the Security Council
and UN agency staff excused less-than-full compliance by pointing to partial compliance and accepting pleas for additional time.
Ultimately, as observed by Hans Blix in one of the final Security
Council meetings to decide what to do with Iraq, British Foreign
Minister Jack Straw reminded the Council that in 1991 Iraq had
been given 90 days to disarm. What had it done in 11 years, seven
months and 12 days? He concluded that the diplomatic process
had to be backed with a credible threat of force. Shying away from
using force and giving unlimited time for little cooperation would
make disarmament in Iraq and elsewhere much harder.[53]

The lesson has remained unlearned, however, as the Security
Council's recent handling of the widespread human rights viola-
tions in the Darfur region of Sudan unfortunately demonstrates.
The Security Council issued a resolution in late July 2004 requir-

ing Sudan, by one month later, to reign in militias responsible for the large-scale human rights atrocities that are estimated by the International Crisis Group to include more than 200,000 deaths caused by violence or by war-caused disease and starvation, the forced displacement of 2.6 million villagers, with another two million dependant on international assistance, the rape of untold numbers of women and grievous injury to countless adults and children. Moreover, the violence has spilt over the border into Chad and threatens to spread across the Central African Republic as well.[54] As in Iraq, the Council allowed the deadline to pass without taking any action. Eventually, in late 2004, the Council passed another resolution asking the Secretary-General to establish a five-member commission to investigate the charge made by US Secretary of State Colin Powell that what was happening in Darfur was genocide. The Council also made a vague threat to impose economic sanctions against Sudan's oil industry but gave no deadline for when this would occur. In November 2004 the Council held an extraordinary meeting in Nairobi to discuss Sudan. Yet, once again, all the Council managed to do was pass another weak resolution expressing 'serious concern'.[55] On 1 February 2005 the UN Commission of Inquiry on Darfur finally produced its report accusing the government of crimes against humanity and war crimes – though unwilling to accuse it of genocide – and recommended that the situation be referred to the International Criminal Court. In March 2005 the Council passed three resolutions relating to Darfur. The first provided that those individuals accused of crimes against humanity be referred to the ICC for prosecution. Although the US had opposed such a referral because of its refusal to recognize the ICC based on its fears that the Court would be misused to target American servicemen, it agreed to abstain from voting and let the resolution pass. The second resolution provided for the imposition of limited sanctions in the form of travel bans and asset freezes on those individuals guilty of offences in Darfur. The Council did not, however, impose an oil embargo on Sudan because of China's interest in Sudan as a source of oil and the likelihood that it would therefore veto a proposed embargo; nor did the Council impose an effective arms embargo because of Russia's interest in Sudan as a market for its arms and the likelihood that it would veto a resolution proposing such an embargo. The Council has also grappled with the question of providing peacekeepers to Darfur. In March 2005 it managed to pass a resolution establishing a 10,000 strong peacekeeping force to monitor the peace in the south of Sudan and assist in Darfur without, however, allocating Darfur its own peacekeeping forces. The African Union had, alone, been willing to assume the responsibility of providing peacekeepers for Darfur. However, it quickly realized that its 2,200 troops were insufficient to achieve this task. Consequently it increased the number of its troops to somewhere between 6,000 and 7,000 by the autumn of 2005. That, too, proved insufficient. In addition to suffering from inadequate training and equipment, the Union announced that it was running out of funds to support the peacekeepers and asked that the UN send in its own peacekeeping force to replace the AU's troops. It was only in May 2006 that the Security Council was willing to consider such a replacement. In August 2006 the Council passed resolution 1706[56] extending to Darfur the mandate of the UN peacekeeping mission in Sudan (UNMIS). The resolution asked the government of Sudan to consent to the deployment of 20,000 UN peacekeepers to the region. The government refused to consent. Eventually in November 2006 a compromise was reached which provided for three phases of UN assistance to the African Union's African peacekeeping mission in Sudan (AMIS): a light support package, a heavy support package and ultimately an AU-UN hybrid force. On 16 April 2007 the government agreed to accept the heavy support package which finally allowed up to 3,000 UN personnel in Darfur to assist the African Union troops and provided certain necessary equipment. On 12 June 2007 the government accepted the proposal for the AU-UN hybrid force. It remains to be seen whether these agreements will now be implemented in a timely manner.[57]

Three years have now elapsed since the Security Council first passed its July 2004 resolution requiring Sudan to reign in its militias and yet the killing, rape, pillage and displacement of the residents of Darfur continues. A report to the Security Council by UK Ambassador Emyr Parry Jones about the Council's mission to the Sudan had already concluded in 2005 that 'The situation in Darfur has deteriorated this year'.[58] How much longer shall we wait? Is it not time that our leaders agree on procedural rules for the Security Council that ensure that it will not vacillate or procrastinate in imposing consequences upon recalcitrant nations that fail to meet their deadlines for compliance with the Council's demands?

Finally, in the interests of justice, the rules should also provide for judicial review of any decision of the Security Council to use force. The rules would have to specify the grounds upon which such an appeal could be based. Such grounds should include that the Security Council has failed to follow its own mandate, the core principles or its procedural rules and that it is consequently either about to use force in an unjust manner or is failing to take action that is necessary to avoid such injustice or a breach of the peace. A nation or a group of nations could apply for review of the Council's decision when it has proof to support any of these grounds. Responsibility for the review should probably be given to a standing committee of the World Court that would expedite it.

Provide the Security Council with the Tools to Make It Effective

Once the international community through its leaders has clarified and fleshed out the mandate of the Security Council to preserve peace, it is essential that it also provide the Council with the tools it needs to adequately discharge this weighty responsibility. There are two tools that are particularly critical to the Council's ability to maintain and restore the peace. They are complementary in function. The first is reliable and timely intelligence. The second is a properly trained military force that can enforce the decisions of the Council when necessary.

INTERNATIONAL INTELLIGENCE AND INSPECTIONS AGENCY

This book proposes the creation of an International Intelligence and Inspections Agency composed of two arms that have complementary functions. The first is the intelligence arm responsible for providing accurate, timely and reliable intelligence. The second is the inspections arm responsible for monitoring and verifying compliance with international non-proliferation rules. The agency would operate as a subsidiary organ of the Security Council. It would be subject to oversight by the Security Council, a committee of the UN General Assembly (which should eventually become a World Parliament as discussed later in this part of the book) and the International Court of Justice. The nature and specifics of the oversight powers will need to be decided and agreed upon by our leaders.

Supranational Intelligence Gathering Arm of the Agency

The lack of timely and accurate intelligence from an independent and reliable source has hampered the Security Council's ability to take appropriate action including the use of force to maintain or restore international peace and security. In the lead-up to the 2003 Iraq war, the members of the Security Council were unable to agree on whether Iraq still possessed weapons of mass destruction, despite four months of resumed international inspections. They disagreed because they were relying on different intelligence sources that arrived at conflicting conclusions. In the end, the war in Iraq was fought by a coalition of countries relying largely on intelligence provided by one country's national intelligence service, which appeared to point strongly to the existence of weapons of mass destruction in Iraq. Yet, in the aftermath of the war that intelligence was found to have been inaccurate and faulty.

The intelligence problem has yet to be solved. The lack of accurate and reliable intelligence continues to hamper the Security Council's ability to take decisive and swift action, as we currently see regarding Iran's nuclear activities. Although the United States and Russia agree that Iran should not have nuclear weapons, they have had very different views about whether Iran is in fact trying to build a nuclear weapon: the Americans think they are, while the Russians say they are not.[59] As *The Economist* pointed out in an article on the issue, what is needed, but missing, to resolve the factual difference is credible and shared intelligence on what Iran has been doing in its nuclear development programme. Moreover, acting without such intelligence could lead to a series of missteps that would further erode relations between nations ranked on both sides of the argument.[60]

The lack of reliable intelligence is similarly apparent regarding North Korea. In the absence of independent and shared intelligence, the true extent of North Korea's nuclear activities appears to be unclear. For example, in February 2005, even after North Korea announced that it now had nuclear weapons, Mr Zoellick during his Senate confirmation hearing for the position of Deputy Secretary of State cautioned about reading too much into North Korea's statement.[61] As a Senior Scholar at the Woodrow Wilson International Center for Scholars points out, it is hard to determine whether North Korea is enriching uranium for military purposes as one needs to distinguish between civilian and military uranium-enrichment capabilities and that can only be done with proper intelligence which is currently lacking.[62] Indeed, other countries including China, Japan and South Korea have also been uncertain to what extent North Korea may be bluffing. In the absence of reliable intelligence, they have had to rely upon overt actions on the part of Pyonyang to surmise how far along North Korea may be on the nuclear path. On 5 July 2006 North Korea test-fired seven missiles in the direction of Japan. However, it was its test of a nuclear device later in October of the same year that came as a shock to the international community, leading to near universal condemnation and the rapid passage by the Security Council of resolution 1718 demanding that North Korea suspend all activities relating to its ballistic missile programme, that it abandon all nuclear weapons and nuclear programmes in a complete, verifiable and irreversible manner and that it retract its withdrawal from the Nuclear Non-Proliferation Treaty.[63]

For the Security Council to take swift, decisive, equitable and effective action to preserve the peace, it must first be convinced that there is a genuine threat to the peace, breach of the peace or act of aggression. This is particularly true if the Council is to take preventive action using its powers under Chapter VII of the Charter, including the power to use force. To be convinced, the

Council must have access to reliable evidence that such a threat is real. Such evidence usually comes from intelligence sources. It is critical that the intelligence that forms the basis for decisions by the Council on the use of force be credible. Intelligence is more likely to be credible if it comes from an independent source, as opposed to one or two national intelligence agencies. All the members of the body charged with making a decision to use force in reliance on intelligence must also have equal access to that intelligence. No one nation or group of nations should have preferential treatment, as this is likely to lead to suspicion on the part of other states. To achieve these dual ends of providing the Council with credible and shared intelligence, the international community needs to find ways for its member states to cooperate on intelligence matters. Both international political leaders and scholars have begun to support the need for sharing intelligence between states. They have concluded that such sharing is essential for stopping terrorism.[64] It is also crucial to detecting clandestine nuclear programmes.[65]

To this end, this book proposes that our leaders set up a formalized, supranational system integrating national intelligence capabilities and responsible for gathering credible and timely intelligence for the Security Council. It would exist solely to serve the Security Council. It must operate under the Council's direction and supervision, and the information gathered must be used for the sole purpose of preserving the peace and security of the planet. One way we can achieve this result is to establish a supranational intelligence and inspections organization with an intelligence arm that is independent and owes its allegiance solely to the Security Council. Its personnel would be international civil servants trained at an international intelligence university established for this purpose. The independence of such an agency would alleviate one of the problems with the current system, which is that the Council relies on intelligence produced by individual governments. This, according to Hans Blix, who led the UN Inspection Commission for uncovering weapons of mass destruction in Iraq, leads to 'a good deal of disinformation'.[66]

At present there is no trusted entity that gathers intelligence to

be shared with all members of the Security Council and is responsible solely to the Council. Although the Brahimi Report talked
about the need for a new entity to gather information, particularly
about conflict situations, analyse it, generate policy and formulate long-term strategies for the Secretary-General of the United
Nations, it did not address the even greater need of the Security
Council to have an international intelligence agency at its disposal
so it can faithfully discharge its mandate. Even the International
Atomic Energy Agency, which functions as the world's nuclear
watchdog, lacks an intelligence arm. All it has is a department
for gathering open data.[67] The idea of a supranational intelligence
agency is not as far-fetched as it may seem at first blush. In the
aftermath of the terrorist attacks committed in London in July
2005, the well-respected non-partisan think-tank the Oxford
Council on Good Governance issued a press release calling for
the establishment of a European Intelligence and Security Service.
It proposed merging all the existing national intelligence and
security agencies of the European Union into one strong supranational security service. If this can be contemplated and done at
the regional level, why not at the international level where it is so
clearly needed?

The benefits of a supranational intelligence agency cannot be
overstated. First, it will make available to the Security Council
intelligence that is not tainted or skewed by any single national
intelligence agency. It will therefore not be viewed suspiciously by
the membership of the Council at large as serving the expedient
interests of a single or small group of nations. This, in turn, will
make it easier for the members of the Council to trust the intelligence and to feel comfortable relying and acting upon it. Second,
since all the members would have equal access to the intelligence,
they would be able to base their decisions on a shared knowledge-
base resulting in more equitable decisions. This sort of equal access
to intelligence that forms the basis of critical decisions like the
use of force is an example of how the principle of oneness can be
applied to enhance the quality of our international institutions.

Another benefit would be greater unity in the Council's decisions. One of the Council's current problems is that its members

view threats differently, as discussed above. These differences stem in part from the member governments' access to different pools of intelligence. Also, the Security Council would probably act more swiftly and decisively if it felt it had a reliable set of shared facts before it.

Despite the compelling arguments for establishing an International Intelligence and Inspections Agency, our leaders may be unprepared to cede enough sovereignty to establish such an agency at this stage of their collective development. If so, a possible intermediate step could be to set up a UN office to coordinate efforts by national intelligence agencies of all UN member states regarding a regularly agreed-upon list of the world's trouble spots. The office would pool, integrate and analyse intelligence gathered by the national agencies and provide the resulting intelligence reports to the Security Council. Trouble spots could be identified regularly, say on a six-monthly basis, by a network of early warning offices, as discussed in the next section.

Early Warning System for the Security Council

An effective International Intelligence and Inspections Agency requires a comprehensive early warning system to alert the Security Council to emerging problems and threats to the peace, such as genocide, ethnic cleansing and the unlawful build-up of weapons of mass destruction. Many nations and non-governmental agencies compile and regularly update similar lists for their own planning purposes. For instance, at one time the United States reportedly had identified some 25 countries it deemed unstable enough potentially to require US military intervention in some form.[68] Similarly, the International Crisis Group compiles its own assessment of potential trouble spots around the world. Early warning would allow the Council to take steps early enough to intervene effectively and avoid bloodshed. The information compiled by the early warning system would also allow the international coordinated intelligence office to update its list of the world's trouble spots.

Had we had such a system in place, we might have been able to prevent the genocide that occurred in Rwanda, especially in view of the findings of the High-Level Panel on Threats, Challenges and Change that Secretariat officials failed to provide the Council with early warning of extremist plans to kill thousands of Tutsis and moderate Hutus.[69] We might also have been able to avoid the escalation of the nuclear proliferation threat in North Korea, a large part of which occurred after North Korea dismissed the IAEA's inspectors. A well-rooted early warning system would have continued to provide information on the ground.

An early warning system could incorporate issues other than strict threats to international peace. For instance, including famine, natural hazards, outbreaks of infectious diseases and humanitarian crises could help avoid wasting human and financial resources and spare the world community the problems that flow from spreading ourselves too thinly. A single early warning system could cover all these threats, so long as local or national offices house experts on each of the topics mentioned above.

An early warning system should encompass a network of national field offices located in all nations around the globe. Each national office should receive regular objective and impartial input from field agents based in local communities around the country it serves. These national offices should in turn provide regular input to a regional office, which should then report the findings to the international intelligence agency. Since it will take some time to set up an infrastructure within the nations and regions of the world, it might be useful, in the interim, to encourage existing regional organizations like the African Union and the Organization of American States to establish their own early warning systems or to improve existing ones and to feed that information to the Security Council's international intelligence agency.

Some countries will oppose establishing within their territory early warning offices tasked with fact-finding and transmitting results to an international organization, on the grounds that it is too much of an intrusion upon their national sovereignty. However, if the system is worldwide and comprehensive then all nations will be treated equally. Also, the gradual emergence of a new norm in international law and relations that the international community has a responsibility to protect vulnerable populations against humanitarian atrocities reflects the recognition by states that national sovereignty is limited and not absolute and that they can never hide behind it to excuse human rights violations.

No early warning system would be sufficient if the Council failed to act on the information it yielded. Bitter experience has shown that the international community can fail to agree on what to do, even when an early warning system exists and functions as it ought. This occurred in the case of the famine that afflicted Niger. Despite the existence of the Famine Early Warning Systems Network (FEWS Net), which alerted the international community to the danger of famine in Niger in both 1997 and 2005, relief agencies and donors failed to agree on an assessment of need each time. Their failure resulted in the people of Niger suffering hunger, disease and death, all of which could have been prevented.[70] To reduce the chances of this sort of dilatory action, our leaders should, in crafting the statement of principles suggested earlier in this part of the book, include a commitment to respond swiftly and decisively to all early warnings of large-scale human suffering regardless of where they occur.

Inspections, Verification and Monitoring

In addition to providing timely and reliable intelligence to the Security Council, the International Intelligence and Inspections Agency must, through its inspection arm, provide another important function: to verify and monitor proper compliance by states with international rules and with the demands made upon them by the Security Council.

The need for verification and monitoring is most pressing in the area of nuclear, chemical and biological non-proliferation. The Security Council cannot effectively implement and enforce the international rules on non-proliferation without proper inspections and monitoring to verify compliance. Moreover, such inspections and monitoring cannot be erratic, otherwise they are is ineffective. Indeed, for the Council to act decisively, swiftly and equitably, the monitoring and verification system must yield accurate and comprehensive information. Unfortunately, the system currently in place relies on states to declare their own compliance, followed by verification, occasional destruction of the illegal weapons and continued monitoring. While recent attempts have been made to improve the system by asking nations to sign on to the International Atomic Energy Agency's Additional Protocol, which provides broader and more intrusive inspection and verification authority, the system still suffers from the fundamental flaw that countries may decline to sign up for these more ambitious inspections.

The system of inspections is in dire need of being overhauled. What is needed is a system in which international inspectors function as independent international civil servants representing the international community and owing their allegiance to it alone, free of pressures from any state. Like the personnel of the international intelligence arm of the agency, they should be trained at an international university for intelligence and inspections. They must have intrusive powers to search, inspect and monitor. This means that they must have the authority to enter any country at will and to search at any time and in any place, without notice. Indeed, experience has shown that the most effective inspections regimes are those special ones set up with intrusive powers of search. Examples of this were the special inspections programmes set up under the auspices of UNSCOM and the IAEA. These programmes were far more intrusive than that provided for under the Additional Protocol and were specifically set up to ferret out information about Iraq's clandestine programmes concerning weapons of mass destruction. Without such powers, countries being monitored can play cat and mouse games with the inspectors. This is precisely what Iraq did throughout the 1990s regarding its obligation to disarm after being forced out of Kuwait.

Detailed guidance on what events would trigger the right to intrusive inspections vis-à-vis a country should be decided upon in advance by the international community and set out in the mandate of the newly-formed inspections arm of the International Intelligence and Inspections Agency. Trigger events should include a country engaging in suspicious behaviour to be defined, repeatedly flouting the demands of the Security Council or engaging in deceitful behaviour such as cheating and lying, particularly with respect to activities related to the production or proliferation of weapons of mass destruction. Intrusive no-notice inspections should also be triggered when there is a certain threshold of intelligence from the coordinated international intelligence group or the international intelligence agency indicating activity that is a threat to the peace.

If the creation of an international verification and monitoring arm with intrusive powers of inspections is too threatening to the sovereignty of nation states at this stage in their development, this book proposes that an interim solution be found in the form of a regional inspection regime. Indeed, some scholars have argued that such a regime focused narrowly on verifying the absence of weapons of mass destruction would be more effective than a broader, international inspection and verification regime. One of the reasons for this, according to scholar Chen Zak (who served both as an officer in the Israel Defence Forces and later in the external affairs division of the Israeli Atomic Energy Commission and subsequently was a visiting fellow at the Washington Institute for Near East Policy and then the Center for Strategic and International Studies), is that at the regional level requests for special inspections tend to be viewed more as 'fact-finding missions' than as political tools. To support this argument she cites the example of the Conventional Forces in Europe.[71] She also contends that regional organizations are more likely to use no-notice, short-notice or random inspections, something that she says the IAEA has been afraid to do.[72] Regional organizations would do this because the only purpose of the regional verification regime would be to ensure that there were no weapons of mass destruction. Moreover, a regional verification regime would not have conflicting missions, such as the IAEA's mission to ensure that states get access to nuclear technology for civilian use.[73] A third argument Zak makes in favour of a narrow regional verification regime is that member states are more likely to conduct intrusive inspections quickly to stop a state from getting weapons because they would be the first and closest to suffer the consequences of

WHAT WE SHOULD BUILD NEXT

proliferation.[74] By contrast, she argues, states participating in a global regime have a hard time agreeing on what constitutes 'cheating' because their interests are not directly affected, either because of geographic remoteness or for strategic reasons. She cites as an example that Asia has generally not been worried about problems in the Middle East and that the Middle East has not been very concerned about what is going on in North Korea.[75]

POLICE FORCE TO EXECUTE THE DECISIONS OF THE SECURITY
COUNCIL

The international community has the responsibility to provide the Security Council with adequate tools and resources to implement its mandate to maintain and restore peace and security. We cannot ignore the current reality that the Security Council may decide to authorize force but lack the capacity to implement its decision. The Council needs troops for a variety of operations. These include conflict prevention, peacekeeping and peacebuilding in the aftermath of conflicts. The Security Council must have at its immediate disposal troops and equipment ready to deploy rapidly and effectively when it needs them. The Brahimi Report recommended that troops be able to deploy 30 days from the time the Council passes a resolution to prevent or intervene in a conflict and from six to 12 weeks after the end of a conflict to maintain peace.[76]

The absence of a readily deployable UN force undermines the Security Council's authority. Without a standing army at its disposal, what the Security Council has actually done in many cases, particularly when coercive enforcement action has been required, is delegate forceful action to coalitions of willing states, authorizing them to act under Chapter VII of the UN Charter. The United Nations thus has not acted as a collective whole and, more importantly, has not been seen to act in complete unity. The lack of visible, worldwide unity detracts significantly from the deterrent value of the action taken by authorized coalitions. The message sent to rogue nations would be much more powerful if the entire world body were seen to act as one, using an international standing army that was beyond national control. In contrast to situations where coercive intervention is needed, when the military intervention of the Security Council is based on the consent of the parties who have invited the Security Council to send troops, the Security Council has generally used troops that are under direct UN command and in UN uniform. These are commonly referred to as 'blue helmets'. They operate under Chapter VI of the UN Charter as opposed to Chapter VII and generally help implement a peace agreement or monitor cease-fire lines after a conflict is over.

Providing the Council with a strong and properly equipped army able to act immediately at the Council's command to enforce peace is long overdue. The Security Council's credibility and authority have already been severely compromised by its patent helplessness to act effectively in the face of severe breaches of international law and peace. Political science academic Paul Diehl makes this point most forcefully when he says that just as Joseph Stalin once asked how many armed divisions the pope had, today's dictators probably ask themselves how many divisions the Secretary-General of the UN has. Given that the answer is none, he concludes that it is unlikely that any dictator contemplating genocide, for instance, would be quaking in his boots at the mention of the UN's special adviser on the prevention of genocide.[77]

There are those who argue that the costs involved in establishing a UN army are prohibitive. However, they should compare the costs of a UN army to the costs of maintaining the *status quo*. The cost of continuing to rely on *ad hoc* 'coalitions of the willing' far exceeds the cost of establishing a UN army, in human lives lost, misery suffered, the collapse of states and resulting regional instability, and the financial costs of ensuing wars not prevented, not to mention the cost of reconstruction after those wars. As the Secretary-General's High-Level Panel on Threats, Challenges and Change pointed out in its report, our unwillingness to invest time and resources early to prevent the outbreak and escalation of conflicts ends up leading to much larger and deadlier conflagrations that are much costlier to handle later.[78] Paul Diehl noted that the monetary costs of creating a UN force 10,000–15,000 strong would be approximately one billion dollars a year after start-up costs. This, he argues, is a modest sum relative to the military expenditures of most major nations.[79]

The establishment of a standing UN army would bolster international peace and security in a number of ways. For one, it would deter countries that would now have to think carefully about committing international crimes such as genocide or flouting international rules on non-proliferation with impunity. They would have to ask themselves whether it was really worth their while to incur the wrath of the international community, which would now have an effective tool with which to enforce its collective will, as published in pre-agreed rules and laws known to all. Rogue nations would no longer be able to argue that military intervention in their affairs was the work of only a handful of nations driven by nefarious motives, such as a desire for energy resources or out of hatred for their peoples or their religion or out of colonial aspirations.

The existence of a UN army would free any one country from the burden of being the world's policeman. No one nation really wants to tackle alone the many problems leading to a breach of the peace, no matter how powerful it is. Experience has taught us that the cost is too high in both lives and money. Moreover, it has become evident that acting as the world's policeman is a thankless task. It tends to incite the enmity of many and spawns new acts of violence and terrorism that then have to be dealt with. In contrast, intervention by forces under the command of a supranational body would reflect the collective will acting for the common good rather than appear to be the whim or self-interest of a single country.[80] Exercising the international community's collective will in this way would send a very forceful and effective message that certain types of behaviour specified in the Council's mandate will not be tolerated and will be acted upon by the international community, forcefully if necessary, using the standing army as the Council's tool.

Another way in which the very creation of an international army would be a boon to international security is that its existence would allow the Council to move quickly to quell emerging problems, thereby saving millions of lives and avoiding unnecessary escalations that would end up being costlier to fix. It would also make it more likely that the Council would intervene early rather than procrastinate, vacillate and wait for someone else to do the job, as happened during the genocide in Rwanda. Romeo Dallaire, the Canadian lieutenant general who commanded the UN peacekeeping contingent in Rwanda at the start of the Rwandan genocide, explains in his book about his experience that 'while most nations seemed to agree that something had to be done, every nation seemed to have a reason why some other nation should do it. So there we sat, waiting for a promise to be kept, reduced to the role of accountants keeping track of how many were being killed.'[81]

Most importantly, perhaps, the army would function as a focal point around which political will could be marshalled. As Mark Schneider, senior vice president of the International Crisis Group, has said, political will needs to have 'an institutional focal point' that is able to deploy force. He also notes that we spend more time lamenting the absence of political will than we do 'organizing its presence'.[82]

A standing UN army, once in place, could be used as an effective tool to tackle a number of different problems that impact the international community. These include, first and foremost, undertaking enforcement actions at the bidding of the Security Council, especially in cases where there is hard evidence that a country is flouting the demands of the Security Council to restore peace or in instances where a country has committed serious violations of international law, for example in the area of genocide or non-proliferation. Second, the army can be used very effectively for preventive deployment where there are significant early warnings generated or confirmed by the International Intelligence and Inspections Agency that one of the above is going to happen – for example, that genocide is about to occur in a particular state or that there are plans afoot for the unlawful build-up of weapons of mass destruction. To date, there has only been one clear case of successful preventive deployment by UN troops and that was in the former Yugoslav Republic of Macedonia, whose national authorities requested it.[83] Third, the army could enforce sanctions imposed by the Security Council. In the words of Kofi Annan, such sanctions constitute 'a necessary middle ground between war and words'[84] and are effective only if implemented. Action in this regard would be taken after proper monitoring by the Intelligence Inspections Agency produced hard evidence to the effect that sanctions were being flouted. Fourth, it should be used to enforce judgements of the World Court critical to maintaining or restoring international peace and security when nations fail to comply with them, thereby causing threats to the peace. Fifth, it could be used to help deal with terrorism and transnational organized crime, which are largely financed by illicit activities including drug trafficking (estimated at about $300–500 billion annually from narcotics trafficking[85]), arms trafficking and trafficking in humans. Sixth, it could be used to deal with insurgents and militias whose actions are leading to the weakening and destabilization of a given state and could lead to its ultimate collapse. Seventh, the army could be used to move food to areas that are threatened by famine. Eighth, it could help deal with the emergence of new global pandemics. Ninth, it could help handle crises arising from natural disasters such as the 2005 tsunami that wreaked havoc in places such as Banda Aceh in Indonesia, Sumatra, Thailand and India or the devastating earthquakes that occurred in the city of Bam, Iran, in December 2003 and in Kashmir in October 2005.

For a standing army to be effective in its role as enforcer of the will of the international community as executed through the Security Council, or in other legitimate ways, it must be structured to ensure complete loyalty to the United Nations. This means that it must be independent of national considerations and pressures. It should be under the command and control of the Secretary-General of the United Nations, who will act to deploy its forces only by authority of the Security Council. Its finances must also be regulated and determined by the General Assembly. Its troops and other personnel should be drawn from all regions and countries of the world.[86] Ideally, all nations should contribute troops and equipment to the army so that all will feel that they have a stake in its success. Ensuring the army's independence from national considerations and its loyalty to the United Nations is essential to avoid the current problem noted in the Brahimi Report that concern about nationalities of commanders of forces in any given situation results in delays in getting teams together for deployment.[87]

In addition, it is critical that the army be held to high standards of accountability for the unlawful actions of its personnel. The current system, which leaves it to member states to prosecute any members of their national contingents who commit crimes in the states where they are deployed,[88] must be changed. To this end, there should be a transparent system for both the hiring and firing of its personnel. Moreover, crimes committed by soldiers during the course of their deployment should be made punishable by an international court, under a new set of international rules that should be created to regulate their behaviour. This would ensure an equal-handed and uniform approach in dealing with UN soldiers regardless of their country of origin and would enhance the level of trust that the citizens of all countries would have in the army and in the international system of collective security.

Several new ideas have emerged about how to shape a system to provide rapid and effective military backing to the Security Council and the United Nations. These ideas range from the timid to the ambitious. At the cautious end of the spectrum is the idea proposed by the former Secretary-General in his report 'In Larger Freedom' that the international community simply strengthen the existing framework of United Nations arrangements.[89] However, in view of several weaknesses inherent in the UN Standby Arrangements System (UNSAS) discussed in part 2 of this book, including its voluntary nature and the conditional nature of the commitments made under it, the system would have to be seriously revamped to make it an effective tool in the hands of the Security Council.

In the middle of the spectrum is the idea that countries or groups of countries create brigade-size forces of about 5,000 each that are capable of dealing with a crisis or an emergency. This is considered more effective than having a number of combat units that cannot work together.[90] An example of such a force is SHIRBRIG, the Multinational Standby High Readiness Brigade for UN Operations, that is designed to train troops together specifically for UN peacekeeping. Its units are all part of the UNSAS system. It is capable of deploying its advance forces into an area within 14 days and its main forces within 30 days. SHIRBRIG itself is not a complete solution, however. Among its main drawbacks is that it operates only in consent-based operations under Chapter VI of the UN Charter and not in coercive military actions launched by the Security Council under Chapter VII. More importantly, each participating country of SHIRBRIG decides on a case-by-case basis whether its forces will participate in any given SHIRBRIG operation.

A scaled-up version of SHIRBRIG is the idea propounded by former UN Secretary-General Boutros Boutros-Ghali in his 1995 book *An Agenda for Peace*. He advocates establishing a rapid reaction force of battalion-sized units. Although these units would be stationed in their own countries, they would be able to fight together because they would have the benefit of common training, equipment and procedures as well as a shared system of communication. Their existence would enable the Security Council to respond quickly to a situation of threat.[91]

An even more ambitious and forward-thinking idea is that proposed by the Working Group for a United Nations Emergency Peace Service or a 'UN 911' in 2005. The Working Group proposed creating a permanent UN force of 10,000–15,000 volunteer personnel. These volunteers would receive the best training and equipment possible. They would be stationed at designated locations around the world and would be ready to respond quickly in the event of a threat or crisis, namely within 48 hours after authorization by the Security Council. The chain of command would be clear: the force would be headed by someone designated by the UN Secretary-General with Security Council approval.[92] One of the attractive and distinguishing features of this proposal is that these forces would be deployable by the Security Council without requiring approval by its member nations. It would thus be free of the fetters imposed by nations' reluctance to deploy their own national units. This would make the forces in question an instrument of the international community acting as they ought to be, in service of the common weal as determined by the Security Council which has been given the mandate to preserve peace and security, rather than being subject to the whim of each individual nation acting in its own interest.[93] The cost of setting up this emergency service is estimated to be two billion dollars with an annual cost thereafter of $900 million. This would still be less than the costs required if conflicts were allowed to escalate. In the 1990s alone the international community spent roughly $200 billion in seven major interventions.[94]

Finally, there is the idea that regional security organizations be strengthened and used as strategic reserves that can be deployed rapidly within the framework of UN arrangements.[95] Former Secretary-General Kofi Annan called for the creation of an integrated system of peacekeeping capacities that would allow the UN to work with relevant regional organizations 'in predictable and reliable partnerships'.[96] He was concerned that the United Nations and regional organizations not compete with each other for the same resources.

In deciding how to craft a new and viable system of collective security it is essential that our leaders ensure that the Security Council has at its immediate disposal standing forces and equipment. These are critical tools for the Council to be able to discharge its responsibility to maintain peace and security. The creation of a new system will require a willingness to break away from past practice, to think out of the box and be creative. At the same time, if the proposals for change are too radical they are likely to be dismissed out of hand and not accorded the proper consideration they deserve. Therefore proposals for standing forces should be crafted in a way that is both innovative but also politically palatable to our leaders.

Revive Articles 43–7 of the UN Charter

One of the questions that must be dealt with head-on is whether it is possible or wise to resurrect those articles of the UN Charter that provide for the allocation of national forces for use by the Security Council in discharging its mandate to keep the peace. One of the attractions of doing so is that the provisions of the system have already been agreed to and are enshrined in the UN Charter. On the other hand, however, we should not feel duty-bound to stick to an agreement arrived at decades ago if it is demonstrably unworkable.

Articles 43–7 are no longer adequate to provide the Security Council with the troops and equipment it needs to maintain international peace and security. The articles take us only a part of the way towards the goal to which our leaders should now strive, namely the creation of an international standing army that is independent of the whims of the nation states from which those serving in it came and that functions under the direct command of the Secretary-General, as authorized by the Security Council or some other appropriate supranational organ of the world community's will. Consequently, implementing the provisions of the Charter constitutes only the second step in a proposed three-step process ending in the establishment of an international army.

A more viable approach to providing the Security Council with the forceful means it needs takes three gradual steps. First, a network of coherent regional security organizations that encompasses the whole planet should be created. Second, an international framework along the lines provided for in the Charter should be established, requiring those regional organizations to formalize their relationship with the Security Council and make their forces available for its use. Third, going beyond the provisions of the UN Charter, the regional forces should be consolidated and integrated into an independent standing army stationed with these regional forces but serving as permanent UN units operating solely at the behest of the Security Council and completely independent of the nations within their regions.

A Coherent Network of Regional Forces Covering the Planet

Establishing regional building blocks of collective security is recommended as a good intermediate stage between our current system in which the Security Council relies on whatever national forces it can muster, forces that are very disparate in their capability and strength on the one hand, and the creation of an international standing army on the other. The regional approach has many benefits to commend it, including the important one that it is likely to be more palatable to our leaders at this stage in our growth than the creation of an international standing army. They may find it easier to cede sovereignty over their security to a regional organization in which they have an active say than they might in an international organization which they may feel is less representative of their interests. This willingness to cede sovereignty to a supranational regional body may also be made easier by the fact that there are likely to be more commonalities between countries within the region including language, culture, way of life and mentality.

The act of assuming responsibility at the regional level and working collectively to discharge it will have the positive effect of gradually creating a culture of collective action within each region. The strong incentive of self-interest will drive states to make the system work. After all, they will suffer most directly and will be most likely to lose much if there is violence, breach of the peace and instability in their region.

Regional responsibility for security would also avoid the pitfalls of allowing individual, militarily strong countries within a region to undertake policing functions. Unfortunately, states playing such a role often arrogate to themselves the right to act as the region's general policeman, ultimately overstepping their bounds no matter how well-intentioned they may have been at first. Experience has taught that relying on such states is a recipe for more problems than it solves. A prime example was Syria's provision of peacekeeping forces to help end Lebanon's civil war: they ended up staying and exercising considerable influence on Lebanese politics and economy. Fourteen years after their original entry, having outstayed their welcome, the Syrians left only after the suspicious murder of a Lebanese political figure opposed to continued Syrian intervention brought international condemnation and a broad group of nations including Russia, Germany, France, Saudi Arabia, Egypt, the United States and the Lebanese people themselves demanded withdrawal.

Work on the first and foundational step should begin as soon as possible. We should use the sprinkling of existing regional security arrangements that have been created over time, albeit randomly and without a master plan, as the basis upon which to build an integrated, coherent network of regional security arrangements that will blanket the planet. This approach will appeal to many who are fearful and suspicious of centralized authority, especially at the international level, by creating a decentralized network on the one hand, while providing a certain amount of direction and coordination on the other. Also, this approach will ensure that no one nation's military is overstretched[97] and no one nation's financial and human resources are disproportionately and unfairly taxed. This alone should make this an attractive proposition for those countries that currently have military forces stationed in several regions around the world as keepers and enforcers of the peace. Although regions with greater military and financial resources would assist those with more limited resources to build up and strengthen their regional security arrangements so they can be increasingly independent and in the meantime would contribute troops, equipment and training in times of crisis, their burden would be lighter if they did not have to step in and do it all. In the long term, taking this step would contribute to building a rapidly-deployable, efficient and effective collective security system that is decentralized yet coordinated and that inspires trust among the peoples of the world. Indeed, scholars agree that strong security structures seem to be very good mechanisms for keeping regional peace, even without active deployments.[98] They also suggest that it makes good sense to formalize regional security arrangements and have troops and equipment positioned close to where they would need to be used.[99]

The first step in this foundational process involves strengthening the troop, equipment, procedural and institutional capacities of existing regional security arrangements such as the Standby Force of the African Union and the Rapid Reaction Force of the European Union.

The second step should be for the international community to encourage the creation of new regional security arrangements in areas currently without them and to ensure that they, too, are strong in every respect. The experts on the UN's High-Level Panel supported taking such a step, especially 'in highly vulnerable parts of the world where no effective security organizations currently exist'.[100] One region that might benefit from such a regional security arrangement is Southeast Asia, as has been suggested by noted scholar Francis Fukuyama.[101] This region currently has no collective security arrangement but benefits to a certain extent from active peacekeeping engagement by Australia. Another example is the Middle East region. The Secretary-General of the Arab League, Amr Mousa, has called for the League to take 'different and daring collective action' to ensure that the League does not stagnate.[102] Moreover, foreign policy scholars Ken Pollack and Ray Takeyh have argued for a 'new security architecture in the Persian Gulf' in which Iranians, Arabs and Americans would find cooperative ways to address their security concerns.[103] Perhaps the Gulf Cooperation Council could be used as an institutional hook for creating such a regional security arrangement. As a third example, consider the region encompassing the Central American republics. Several countries in this region, including Nicaragua, Honduras, El Salvador, Costa Rica and Guatemala, have vowed to create a joint 'rapid force' to deal with violent youth gangs, terrorist threats and drug traffickers. The United States is reportedly helping them with intelligence on these issues.[104]

Experience has shown that it is easier to create regional security arrangements where there is already regional cooperation of some kind, whether economic or political. The European Union had already achieved a high degree of economic integration before it decided to create a Rapid Reaction Force in the late 1990s. Similarly, the Organization for African Unity, established in 1963, allowed for cooperation at several non-military levels. It eventually amalgamated with the African Economic Community and evolved into the African Union in 2002. It was only then that the successor organization established the African Standby Force. In Europe and Africa there were also other regional bodies for political dialogue and consensus-building. For example, in Europe there was the Council of Europe, the Organization for Security and Cooperation in Europe (OSCE) and NATO. In Africa there was the African Peer Review Mechanism and the New Partnership for Africa's Development. The value of such fora in providing a structure of regular meetings between leaders of state within a region to talk to each other directly cannot be overstated. Such meetings reduce the chance for potential misunderstanding and conflict and forge understanding and trust over the short and long term. In the cases of both Europe and Africa, regional infrastructure and policy cooperation were already in place. These in turn engendered a modicum of trust which allowed each organization to take the next step of creating a regional collective security arrangement and standby forces.

Given the experience of Europe and Africa, it might be best to begin the process of creating new regional security organizations by linking them to existing fora or institutions for economic cooperation, which abound worldwide. Where no such infrastructure exists, our leaders might begin by creating institutions to foster economic regional growth. These in turn would foster a spirit and culture of working together for the betterment of the lives of the peoples in those areas, creating the environment of trust that makes it easier to take the next step of creating a regional security organization.

Northeast Asia lacks its own regional economic grouping, even though it plays a major role in world trade.[105] Indeed, this part of the world is so vulnerable to conflict at the moment that analysts such as Michael O'Hanlon recommend establishing a formal regional collective security arrangement among Japan, the Republic of Korea (South Korea), the Democratic People's Republic of Korea (North Korea), the People's Republic of China and Russia, despite the lack of experience with multilateral institutions in this area.[106] Such an arrangement, it is proposed, would deal with threats such as piracy, terrorism and conflicts over resources in the region's waters.[107] Francis Fukuyama similarly has recommended the creation of a five-power organization in this region that would meet regularly to discuss security issues. Interestingly, he too suggests linking this discussion on security to the various economic fora currently in existence or under consideration, such as the Association of Southeast Asian Nations (ASEAN) or the Northeast Asia Cooperation Dialogue, which was established informally in the early 1990s and comprises the countries that are now participating in the six-party talks regarding North Korea's nuclear programme.[108] It is encouraging to note in this regard that interest in creating a Northeast Asia collective security arrangement has also been expressed by leaders in the region, such as President Roh Moo-Hyun of South Korea.[109]

As new regional security organizations emerge, it may be necessary for existing regional security arrangements and other security alliances such as NATO to provide financial and logistical support, such as assistance in training and provision of equipment and transportation, until they are strong enough to stand on their own feet.[110] Thus in June 2005 NATO agreed to help the African Union expand its peacekeeping mission in Darfur and has been providing the African Standby Force with air transport for its peacekeepers and civilian police into and out of Darfur since July 2005. NATO has also been assisting with the mentoring and training of officers of the African Standby Force.[111]

As we formalize and strengthen existing regional security organizations and create new ones as part of establishing a viable new system of collective security, our leaders should give serious thought to several issues. The first is whether there ought to be membership requirements for participation in a regional security organization such as the ones NATO has. To become a member of NATO, a nation must have a democratic form of government, a non-aggressive foreign policy and a military controlled by a civilian government. While some may argue that such requirements could mean excluding countries from the disciplines and benefits of the organization, there is considerable benefit to creating incentives for countries to espouse the positive principles listed above in their eagerness to be part of a regional security arrangement. Another issue our leaders must consider is whether it is better for the armed forces at the disposal of the regional organization to comprise national troops deployed as the result of the sovereign decisions taken by member states, as is the case with the European Rapid Reaction Force, or for them to belong to a regional standing army that acts at the behest of the regional organization acting as a supranational body. The latter approach ensures that the effectiveness of a regional force is not hostage to the whims of an individual state that may be tempted to act in its own narrow self-interest, rather than in the interests of the larger regional community. It also has the benefit of creating a culture in which nation states gradually become accustomed to the idea of ceding responsibility for collective security to a supranational force. This will eventually make it easier to make the transition to the final goal of a standing international army. Ultimately, however, the answer to this question will depend on how far countries are ready to go in applying first principles and relinquishing elements of their national sovereignty for a greater cause.

An additional point that needs to be made is that as the regional security organizations with their regional enforcement powers grow and evolve, they will need to work closely with the regional offices of the International Intelligence and Inspections Agency (including its early warning offices) which should be simultaneously evolving in parallel. Indeed, the work of these two sets of institutions is complementary – without proper intelligence and verification, the regional organizations will lack the information and hard evidence they need to take action when needed. On the other hand, without enforcement power to back them up, evidence of gross violations of international law and breaches of the peace produced by the Intelligence Agency cannot be effectively dealt with. Eventually these two institutions should become indissolubly linked and closely aligned parts of an efficient, equitable and well-ordered international system that is based on regional security pillars around the world.

Formalizing the Relationship between the Regional Network and the Security Council

Once we have in place a network of strong regional security organizations that cover all regions of the world, the next step would be that both the individual and component parts of this network begin to work closely and seamlessly with the United Nations within a predetermined structure to ensure peace worldwide. The germ of this idea already exists in current political thinking and was articulated in the Outcome Document of the World Summit of leaders in September 2005. The document encouraged the development of predictable arrangements between regional forces and the UN.[112]

The transition to cooperation with the UN can be achieved by allocating primary responsibility for the security of each region of the world to a security organization for that region. Moreover, the nations within each region should agree amongst themselves that a threat to the peace caused by any one member would be regarded as a threat to all and dealt with collectively. This would mean in practice that in the event of a threat to the peace, a breach of the peace or an act of aggression within that region, the responsible regional organization would be required to deploy military force to maintain or restore the peace. We have already started to see, in the Darfur region of Sudan, examples of a regional organization taking primary responsibility for conflict in its region and deploying troops when the African Union was the only body willing in the summer of 2004 to step in to try and deal with the tragedy of genocide and restore the peace.[113] In such situations, however, military intervention must have the prior approval of the Security Council, as currently required by Chapter VIII of the UN Charter, except in those rare circumstances where the urgency of the situation requires immediate action, leaving no time to seek prior approval. In the latter cases, Council approval should be sought as soon as possible after enforcement action has begun. The UN's High-Level Panel endorsed this approach.[114]

As countries establish rules for a new collective security system based on a network of regional security arrangements, our leaders need to think long and hard and honestly about the harmful implications of the current trend for regional organizations to authorize enforcement action without prior approval of the Security Council. To minimize the instances in which this will occur, our leaders should very clearly agree upon and delineate situations in which regional forces may intervene without prior Council permission. The importance of requiring regional security arrangements to seek Security Council approval in advance of regional action is extensively discussed by scholar Ademola Abass.[115] Leaders must recognize that prior Security Council authorization is needed to ensure common standards for dealing with nations that breach the peace around the world and for holding regional forces to the same standard of humanitarian behaviour. Both are requirements of justice and equity. Security Council authorization will also help defuse concerns that a regional group is unlawfully interfering in the internal affairs of a country or that it is acting as an occupying force. There were reports that such a charge was levelled by Sudan regarding the African Union's decision in the spring of 2005 to increase the number of troops in its standby force in Darfur from 2,200 to more than 7,700.[116] Since then the government of Sudan has accepted the presence of the African Union's troops in Darfur, though it flatly rejected plans made by the Security Council in August 2006 to replace those troops, which are sorely under-funded and have been unable to stem the violence in Darfur with a 22,000-strong UN mission.[117] Sudan's President, Mr Omar Al-Bashir, was reported by the media to have said that the plan to replace African Union troops with a UN force was a 'Zionist plot' intended to weaken states in the region and a move that would allow Sudan's opponents to dismember it and to plunder its resources.[118] Subsequently, Sudan agreed to a compromise for a hybrid African Union–UN force. However as of 22 July 2007, it had rejected a section of a draft UN Security Council resolution that would give the 26,000 joint African Union–UN peacekeeping troops the right to use force in the Darfur mission, claiming that such a mandate would be a violation of Sudan's sovereignty.[119]

The international scheme for action by regional forces should provide for situations in which efforts by the regional organization are not enough to maintain or restore peace. When authorizing action by a regional organization to address a particular situation, the Security Council should specify a time frame within which it will reconsider the situation and, if necessary, adopt measures to assist the regional organization. If a regional organization and its forces fail to act or, despite their best efforts, are unable to main-tain or restore peace within the given time frame, then the Security Council should step in to bolster their efforts by calling on other regional forces nearby. By setting up a system in which the Security Council is always the first port of call and must pre-authorize any military action, we can ensure that the Council will continue to have ultimate responsibility for maintaining international peace. At the same time, the system can build on the strengths of regional organizations that have played an increasingly important role in dealing with situations that threaten collective security. Encouragingly, the complementarity of regional organizations and the Security Council was recognized by states participating in a 2003 meeting of the Security Council with regional organizations held to consider ways to strengthen collective security.[120]

Regional Forces Become Integrated Units of an International Standing Army

Over the long term, as this network of regional organizations grows in strength, numbers, resources, confidence and efficiency and starts to operate smoothly and seamlessly, the various organizations will eventually be ready to comprise the building blocks of a more tightly knit multilateral security system operating under the overall guidance and direction of the Security Council. They can then start to assume greater responsibilities beyond keeping and enforcing the peace in their own regions. They can evolve from being forces owing primary loyalty to their regional organizations to becoming integrated units of an international standing army that serves solely and directly at the behest of the Security Council and is completely independent of the nation states within the region. This will require more systematic communication between the Security Council and the regional organizations, including regular meetings between the Council and the leaders of the regional organizations. It will also require joint training exercises, an integrated communications system for the various military regimes, compatible equipment and a shared language. Since there are both operational and fiscal benefits that flow from stationing forces in the regions where they are most likely to be needed (for example, by shortening the amount of time it takes to deploy troops and armour), it would make sense to structure an international standing army such that troops are positioned regionally, with each set of troops primarily dedicated to dealing with enforcement actions in that region.

Strengthen the Non-Proliferation and Arms Control Regimes and Accelerate Arms Reduction

We live in a world in which arms and weapons of all kinds abound. Not content with the massive quantities of conventional weapons we have amassed, despite the tremendous damage they can wreak, we have added nuclear, chemical and biological weapons (collectively known as weapons of mass destruction) to our growing arsenals. We seem bent on ensuring maximum pain and destruction on a vast and devastating scale. And yet it seems that no matter how varied, brutal or sophisticated our techniques, we are still not satisfied, as we continue to seek ever more sophisticated weapons of mass destruction. This feverish pursuit of such weapons has brought us to our present reality in which one of the biggest dangers facing the world is the proliferation of such weapons. The UN's High-Level Panel on Threats, Challenges and Change concluded that stopping nuclear proliferation in particular must remain an urgent priority for the world.[121] How are we to do this using a system that is buckling under pressure?[122] Nations are ignoring their commitments under non-proliferation treaties or withdrawing completely from the treaties. New dangers, such as international terrorist networks and easy dissemination of military technology, have changed the international security landscape.[123] Urgent action is needed to overhaul and strengthen the system we have or we must replace it with a new system.

Action is needed on two fronts simultaneously. We must stop developing, manufacturing and transferring technology or weapons, particularly weapons of mass destruction, any further. In other words, we must stop arms proliferation. Second, we must reduce the arms and weapons that currently exist to manageable and strictly necessary levels. It is clear that we need both disarmament and non-proliferation and we must proceed on both fronts simultaneously. As the Secretary-General of the UN put it, we should not hold one hostage to the other.[124] To achieve these goals we need to be bold and innovative. Leaders of thought in this field acknowledge that we need 'novel ideas – both substantively and operationally'.[125] They call for a 'new arms control framework'[126] and the need to 'think outside the box' if we are to survive.[127]

A successful arms control system must address three issues. First, universally agreed, clear and legally binding rules must delineate what any nation or non-state actor can and cannot do. Second, an effective system for monitoring compliance must quickly detect violations of these universal rules. Third, we must have an enforcement mechanism to ensure compliance with the rules in the event of breach. Having such a system in place will allow the international community to take effective action at the first sign of trouble. Each of these three elements is considered separately.

Establishing Clear Rules

The core group of leaders who gather together to deliberate on ways to achieve peace should appoint a commission whose sole task will be to deliberate upon and propose rules to prevent further arms proliferation and to reduce existing arms and weapons. The commission should familiarize itself with the weaknesses of the present system of treaties, as well as the special configuration of dangers facing the international community in this century. The commission's proposals should then be consulted upon by the world's leaders, who should agree upon final decisions for action. These should be embodied in the International Covenant to be ratified by all the nations of the world.

The starting point has to be the open recognition by our leaders of the fundamental reality that in the area of arms control, especially when the international community discovers a clandestine programme to develop weapons of mass destruction or to illegally transfer related technologies, two factors are key to resolving the crisis. First, the world community must act on the basis of core principles rather than expediency and each country's narrowly perceived, short-term interests. Second, more important than the actual solution adopted – whether sanctions, the use of force or some other solution – is the ability of the international community to speak with one voice and act in total unity. That show of unity will ultimately be more powerful and effective than any particular solution. Having affirmed and wholeheartedly embraced these foundational principles, the commission should consider the following proposals.

First, all rules and treaties relating to preventing the further proliferation or the reduction of arms must apply mandatorily to all nations. We can no longer afford to have an arms control system in which participation by states is voluntary.[128] Having such a system invites states to consider only their short-term self-interest at the expense of the long-term security of the international community as a whole. For example, it is ludicrous that a treaty intended to prevent the proliferation of nuclear weapons (the Treaty on the Non-Proliferation of Nuclear Weapons, also known as the NPT) would make the participation of nations known to have nuclear weapons, such as Pakistan, India and Israel, optional. The same is true with respect to the safeguards established by the International Atomic Energy Agency to monitor compliance with the Non-Proliferation Treaty. Monitoring safeguards should be mandatory.[129] It makes no sense that 30 members of the NPT should not be subject to any monitoring safeguards. Moreover, such safeguards should not be subject to a 'national security' exclusion, as is currently the case. In short, it is time that nations accept that arms control is an area in which they must be willing to cede some of their national sovereignty if they are to achieve the ultimate prize of security for all.

Second, the International Covenant should include a rule abolishing any right to withdraw from treaties embodying rules governing non-proliferation and arms reduction. This rule is a corollary of the first one that makes the application of such rules mandatory rather than optional. Achieving universal consensus around such a rule will get us out of the insane position in which we currently find ourselves, in which, for example, the Non-Proliferation Treaty itself allows a signatory to withdraw with only 30 days' notice to the other parties and to the Security Council, for reasons that are blatantly self-serving, including jeopardy to its supreme interest, and without suffering any consequences. Such withdrawal rules allow a nation to participate in a treaty such as the Non-Proliferation Treaty for as long as it suits its purposes, obtain maximum benefits from it, such as gaining access to civilian nuclear technology while secretly developing the ability to make nuclear weapons, and then to withdraw from the treaty when it decides that it has achieved enough know-how to convert its knowledge to military use. One country, North Korea, has already withdrawn from the Non-Proliferation Treaty and another, Iran, has threatened to do the same.[130] Some scholars, such as Michael A. Levi and Michael E. O'Hanlon, have recommended attaching consequences to withdrawal, for example, by requiring that the withdrawing country return the nuclear technology and assets acquired while participating in the Non-Proliferation Treaty under the threat of military action to destroy those assets or depose its government.[131] Others have suggested that the withdrawing nation be held responsible for violations of the treaty committed prior to withdrawal.[132] *The Economist* has recommended that we extend the period of notice required for withdrawal and require that all equipment acquired under the pretence of civilian use be dismantled.[133] Although these suggestions are all thoughtful, the most sensible course of action is to do away altogether with the right of withdrawal in the area of arms control treaties. Attempting to withdraw could be seen for what it truly is, a potentially grave threat to international peace, triggering the Security Council's authority to take action under its proposed newly modified mandate, including the use of force.

Third, with regard to reducing conventional weapons, the starting point for the commission should be the principle adumbrated in the Bahá'í writings that each nation be allowed to possess arms and weapons only in the amount necessary for it to defend itself and to keep the peace and maintain order within its boundaries. The world's leaders and nations have agreed once before to impose such self-restraint. The Covenant of the League of Nations drafted in 1919 and entered into force in 1920 recognized that 'the maintenance of peace requires the reduction of national armaments to the lowest point consistent with national safety . . .'[134] Beyond the level specified for each nation, no nation should be allowed to develop or otherwise acquire additional weapons. Any build-up of additional arms leads to suspicion and mistrust on the part of other nations, increasing international tensions and inevitably leading other states to acquire more weapons in turn. Indeed, many leaders of thought in this area have pointed out that one of the prime reasons so many nations want to arm themselves with nuclear weapons is to give themselves the comfort and security that they are safe and self-reliant in the face of other countries' large conventional forces and power. Thus begins the unending and destructive cycle of the arms race. To give effect to the principle enunciated by Bahá'u'lláh, the commission should carefully study the geography, history, demographics and needs of each country and propose the number of conventional arms it believes that nation requires to defend itself and maintain peace and order within its boundaries. In carrying out its study, the commission must take into account information from the country itself as well as from relevant experts. The Covenant of the League of Nations similarly required the League's council to '[take] account of the geographical situation and circumstances of each State, [to] formulate plans for such reduction for the consideration and action of several Governments'. Unfortunately, the world was not ready then to implement this forward-thinking idea. Once the commission has formulated recommendations about the level of arms each country needs for self-defence and internal order, the core group of leaders must consider them and arrive at a final decision, which must then be ratified by all the members of the international community as a matter of binding international law.

Once the number of weapons each nation may have is firmly fixed by law, the next step is to determine what weapons each state already has. The current system of soliciting annual declarations from states regarding their existing conventional weapons holdings, including their sale and purchase of such weapons, for inclusion in the UN Register of Conventional Arms is inadequate to achieve this task, as these declarations tend to be incomplete, untimely and inaccurate.[135] The commission must have broad authority to undertake a proper study, visiting any sites in any country it wishes and questioning scientists and military personnel. Once the number of arms possessed by each state has been accurately determined in this way, the commission must propose plans to the Security Council to destroy any stockpiles that are in excess of the allowed quantity within a specified time period. This destruction would be overseen and verified by the International Intelligence and Inspections Agency proposed above.

Fourth, once countries have committed themselves to non-proliferation and reduction of conventional arms, there is no reason to maintain weapons of mass destruction, and the commission should propose that all weapons of mass destruction be eliminated. To this end, there should first be a universally applicable and mandatory moratorium on the development and production of all weapons of mass destruction and a similar moratorium on the production of fissile material such as weapons-grade highly enriched uranium and separated plutonium. All nations should be subject to this rule, without exception. Conventional weapons and forces are capable of wreaking enough damage without the need for the wanton destruction of life inflicted by weapons of mass destruction. Moreover, having such weapons is itself risky as it exposes the international community to the possibility that they may be used accidentally.

It is not enough for our leaders to give lip service to the proposition that weapons of mass destruction must be eliminated, as they did in the Millennium Declaration.[136] They must act. They must completely stop developing and producing weapons of mass destruction. A first step would be to make both the Nuclear Comprehensive Test Ban Treaty and the Fissile Material Production Cutoff Treaty universally applicable. Their efforts in this regard would be more successful if they also established an international military force or a network of regional forces, as discussed in the previous section. Adopting an effective, new system of collective security in which all nations pledge to defend each other and the necessary military forces under international or regional control exist to punish wrongdoers would make nations more likely to forgo their weapons of mass destruction.

Having created an international force and fully committed to the principle of collective security, our leaders must then establish a firm time schedule for the destruction of existing weapons of mass destruction, which should proceed in parallel around the world. It might be necessary to establish an international fund to scrap such weapons, as an aid to those countries, such as Russia and North Korea, lacking financial means. This process should be overseen and verified by the International Intelligence and Inspections Agency.

While these stockpiles of nuclear, chemical and biological weapons and related materials are waiting to be eliminated, they should be kept in secure storage sites around the world to guard them against theft and possible transfer to rogue nations or dangerous non-state actors. For instance, according the UN's High-Level Panel report, there are currently 1,300 kilograms of highly enriched uranium in research reactors in 27 countries. However the total volume of highly enriched uranium is much greater when one includes the amounts that are stockpiled in storage sites around the world.[137] Many of the storage sites are inadequately secured and vulnerable to theft. Indeed, according to the report, it has been publicly confirmed that nuclear materials have been diverted from proper storage facilities some 20 times. In addition, there have been more than two hundred documented incidents of illicit trafficking in nuclear materials over the past decade and more than 650 recorded attempts to smuggle such material.[138] Some important steps have been taken recently. More needs to be done. The 1979 Convention on the Physical Protection of Nuclear Material has been changed to require states to boost security at nuclear sites and to cooperate more to track down stolen or smuggled atomic material. In 2005 many nations adopted the International Convention on the Suppression of Acts of Nuclear Terrorism and the Security Council adopted Resolution 1540, both of which require governments to punish those who illegally possess atomic devices or radioactive materials. Nonetheless, in December 2005 Dr ElBaradei called attention to the need to do more to protect existing nuclear material to prevent extremist groups from pursuing nuclear terrorism.

Fifth, the commission should encourage leaders of all nations to build consensus around the principle that no nation has the inherent right either to develop arms or sell them, lucrative though it may be. Each nation should be responsible for monitoring and controlling the manufacture and sale of arms by companies and individuals operating within its jurisdiction. The annual trade in small arms alone has been estimated at roughly $40 billion[139] and is considered one of the primary causes of instability in developing countries around the world. Leaders should immediately place all arms production under the initial supervision and eventual control of a supranational agency. This could initially be done on a regional basis until nations achieve some level of comfort with ceding sovereign control in this area. Such an agency could then ensure that arms are produced only in quantities necessary to supply the legitimate needs of states for self-defence and maintaining internal order, as agreed upon by the international community. It would also ensure that they were being shipped to their proper destinations and not being funnelled or diverted into the hands of extremist groups or violent non-state actors.

Sixth, the commission must grapple with and propose how to resolve the growing tension between the need for peaceful nuclear technology to meet the world's growing energy demands and the need to control the proliferation of nuclear materials and weapons,[140] especially in light of the recent report issued by the International Atomic Energy Agency warning of a crunch in the supply of oil and gas needed to fuel world economic growth in the years to come.[141] On the one hand, an increasing number of states turn to nuclear energy to satisfy their growing energy needs. Indeed, a meeting of energy ministers and officials from 74 countries held in Paris in March 2005 concluded that nuclear energy was going to become even more sought after to meet soaring energy needs while averting environmental disaster.[142] As countries like India and China continue to grow, their energy needs will likely not be met through the use of fossil fuels alone.[143] Even if possible, relying on fossil fuels may not be desirable, since emissions from burning such fuels have tremendous negative impact on our environment whereas nuclear energy is cleaner in the sense that it may yield fewer climate-altering green-house gases.[144]

The assessment of the Paris group is already proving a reality. Nations are actively pursuing options for building reactors for nuclear energy. They are also experimenting with new ways of producing nuclear energy. To this end an international consortium comprising six partners – the United States, Russia, China, Japan, South Korea and the European Union – was announced in June 2005. The consortium will build an International Thermonuclear Experimental Reactor in France. The $10 billion project is, apparently, seen by many scientists as crucial to solving the world's future energy needs.[145] Other indications of the drive by nations to obtain their energy from nuclear sources abound. Russia has drafted an ambitious power plan to build two nuclear reactors every year, with the goal that nuclear power provides for a quarter of its energy needs (up from a current 16 to 17 per cent) by the year 2030.[146] Britain is reported to be considering building new nuclear power stations to reduce greenhouse gas emissions, which have risen by 2.1 per cent since 2002, as well as to counter concerns that it will consume more energy than it can produce or afford to import.[147] In March of 2006 the United States promised to supply India with both nuclear fuel and civilian technology, avowedly to satisfy India's growing demands for electrical power.[148] Iran's stated purpose for its nuclear facilities is to satisfy its needs for electricity, a right it claims under the NPT.[149]

On the other hand, allowing even civilian nuclear reactors to proliferate raises the risk that nuclear materials and technology will be diverted to military use or fall into the hands of unscrupulous groups or individuals who would have no compunction about using it in violent ways. Many in the international community have such concerns about Iran's nuclear development programme. Iran's claim to a right to develop its own civilian nuclear technology exemplifies one of the weaknesses of the current non-proliferation regime. Iran and several other countries interpret Article IV of the Non-Proliferation Treaty to permit them access to civilian nuclear technology. However, all that the NPT actually promises its members is the right to enjoy the benefits of civilian nuclear power while at the same time strictly banning weapons-related activity.[150]

One solution to the dilemma of satisfying energy needs without proliferating potentially dangerous nuclear technologies lies in placing all nuclear reactors, be they for civilian or military use, and all nuclear fuel production, especially those parts of the fuel cycle that involve making highly enriched uranium and reprocessing plutonium, under the authority of a supranational or international agency. This agency should also be responsible for ensuring that production of all nuclear material for military use is halted and that nuclear fuel for civilian use is equitably distributed as needed. This far-reaching proposal appears to be supported by the director of the world's nuclear watchdog the IAEA, who has himself proposed putting the manufacture and sale of nuclear fuel under multinational control, with the IAEA acting as a 'reserve fuel bank' for accredited nations.[151] The second prong of the proposal is also supported by the UN High-Level Panel, whose report recommends that the IAEA act as a guarantor for the supply of fissile material to civilian nuclear users.[152] Although Mr ElBaradei's proposal has not yet been espoused by the international community, there are indications that the world is tentatively exploring new approaches that may eventually lead down this path. For example, Russia has proposed to enrich uranium for Iran on Russian soil and ship it to Iran, then ship the used fuel back for reprocessing in Russia, with Iran having a management and financial interest but no technical interest in the production.[153]

Monitoring Compliance with Arms Control Rules

Once our leaders have agreed upon universal rules that are to be legally binding on all nations, they must create a system to monitor compliance with the rules. Rules alone are of little use, as the international community discovered in the 1990s upon learning, to its great surprise, that two signatories to the NPT, Iraq and North Korea, possessed advanced clandestine nuclear weapons programmes, despite the IAEA safeguards system which they had signed up to obey. For the collective security system to be truly effective and viable there needs to be a reliable and shared intelligence system that allows the international community to detect early signs of breach coupled with a robust monitoring and verification system to ensure compliance. As the Secretary-General of the United Nations has pointed out, what we need is to have more consistent monitoring, more effective implementation, and firmer enforcement, for states to have confidence in multilateral mechanisms.[154] To this end, the International Intelligence and Inspection Agency should be given the mandate to monitor compliance by all nations with both the non-proliferation and arms reduction rules.

The IAEA, which has hitherto been the world's nuclear watchdog, could be made a part of this agency, as could the Organization for the Prohibition of Chemical Weapons (OPCW) and any agency that might be created to oversee and monitor the control of biological weapons. The monitoring arm of the agency should have well-defined powers so that it can act decisively, without hesitation, confident in its mandate. Its sole concern should be to discover the facts on the ground. We should also have an early warning system that alerts the international community to possible breaches of the arms controls rules, as discussed earlier in part 3 of this book. Like other components of the International Intelligence and Inspection Agency, the early warning should be set up as a network of national early warning offices feeding information to regional intelligence and inspection offices, which in turn report activities to the International Intelligence and Inspections Agency. Early warning and intelligence must be coupled with efficient, effective and equitable monitoring of the situation to ascertain whether dangerous technologies or weapons are being illicitly developed or transferred.

To discharge its responsibilities properly, the International Intelligence and Inspections Agency and its various arms, including the IAEA or its equivalent, must not concern itself with political considerations or succumb to political pressures. Doing so would undermine its credibility and open the facts it reports to question and doubt. Especially in those situations in which enforcement action is needed, it is essential that the agency be able to produce hard, verifiable and reliable evidence. Depoliticizing institutions such as the IAEA, whose role is to ascertain facts, would make the system more credible in the eyes of the international community and therefore more effective.

The International Intelligence and Inspections Agency should have very broad powers to conduct mandatory, intrusive inspections and searches in any country without being required to give advance notice. It should be able to conduct random, no-notice or short-notice inspections at will. This power must include the ability to interview and talk to scientists involved in developing national weapons programmes, especially weapons of mass destruction. Experience has taught us that the authority granted by the original safeguards agreements under the NPT and even that granted by the Additional Protocol to the NPT have proved insufficient to ferret out clandestine programmes to develop illicit nuclear weapons. Indeed, experts in the area claim that UNSCOM's intrusive powers of search have hitherto been the most successful model. Here, too, nations initially reluctant to cede national control will need to accept that ceding some control is necessary to assure international security. To help overcome concerns about national sovereignty, the International Inspections and Intelligence Agency must truly be a supranational agency, whose employees are hired solely for their technical expertise without any political considerations. Care must also be taken to ensure that, like the International Court, the officials and staff of the Agency are genuinely free and seen to be free from political pressure of any kind.

Although the umbrella International Intelligence and Inspections Agency may choose to rely on regional offices to conduct its work in each region, nations concerned about ceding too much sovereignty might more readily accept another model. This model involves systematically encouraging and helping nations to set up their own regional inspection and monitoring agencies. The idea is to create a network of such agencies around the world that could eventually be coordinated and then brought under the umbrella of the International Intelligence and Inspections Agency. Each regional agency would be composed of officials and staff drawn from that region. Each regional agency would be responsible for monitoring compliance with non-proliferation and arms reduction rules in the countries within that region. An example of an existing regional inspections agency that seems to function well is EURATOM, the European Atomic Energy Community, which reports its findings to the IAEA. Other existing regional agencies include OPANAL, the Agency for the Prohibition of Nuclear Weapons in Latin America and the Caribbean, and ABACC, the Brazilian-Argentine Agency for Accounting and Control of Nuclear Materials. As discussed at length earlier in part 3 of this book, scholars in the arms control field, such as Chen Zak, have argued that regional verification bodies are likely to be more successful than an international one. Ultimately, the various regional agencies would report their findings to the umbrella agency, which would in turn coordinate the information and refer non-compliance and breaches to the Security Council for enforcement action.

Once the International Intelligence and Inspections Agency or a network of regional inspection agencies has been established and empowered to conduct intrusive arms control inspections, these bodies must not be afraid to use their powers for fear that an inspection may not yield proof of a violation. So what if a no-notice search yields no evidence of a violation? Such an outcome should not necessarily reflect poorly on the international or regional agency, unless it is not doing its job, but rather it would demonstrate that our collective security system was functioning effectively.

Another requirement for effective, equitable and efficient monitoring is that all countries cooperate fully and deal transparently with the regional agencies and with the International Intelligence and Inspections Agency. Indeed, a general rule should be adopted that any dissembling, lying or cat and mouse games of the kind we have seen with respect to several countries like Iraq, Iran and North Korea would attract meaningful penalties.

Enforcing the Rules on Non-Proliferation and Arms Reduction

To be effective, any system to regulate the development, production and distribution of arms and to bring about their reduction must be backed by a robust enforcement power. Experience has shown that without effective enforcement the rules are likely to be flouted with impunity. One of the fundamental weaknesses in the present arms control system is that there is no mechanism to ensure that the treaties are consistently enforced. Even if there were a will to implement the treaties, there is no adequate tool – there is no international force – to implement the rules. This, in itself, causes insecurity that drives nations to amass arms, hoping for self-reliance and security. In an increasingly interdependent and interwoven world, nations still act as though they can each go it alone, even though experience shows, time and again, that they cannot. The absence of an international force means that the most a nation found to be in breach of these rules needs to fear is a referral to the Security Council. But referrals and threats thereof long ago ceased to deter anyone, since experience has demonstrated that even once the referral is made the Security Council is unlikely to act because one or more countries will exercise the veto power. Moreover, even if action were to be taken by the Security Council it is usually limited to imposing economic sanctions, which nations have become adept at circumventing and the international community has not been diligent about enforcing.

It is time that our leaders agreed on the rules of enforcement. These pre-agreed rules should specify the steps to be taken by the international community through the agency of the Security Council in the event that the International Intelligence and Inspections Agency produces clear, convincing and verifiable evidence that a country has breached its obligations under the arms control rules, for example by illicitly developing nuclear weapons. Advance agreement on the enforcement steps will help us to avoid situations in which one country or a small group of countries must persuade the rest of the world anew of the consequences that should apply to a country threatening the peace. The absence of clarity about enforcement steps leads to comments such as those by Mr Lavrov, the Foreign Minister of Russia, discussing problems that would ensue were the IAEA to refer Iran to the Security Council for violating nuclear non-proliferation rules. He explained, 'There is no collectively discussed and agreed strategy of what we all will be doing in the Security Council if the issue is there,' adding that European countries had said that no force would be used but the United States had said that no options were excluded.[155]

Under the rules of enforcement the Security Council should be able to intervene very early, as soon as it receives early warning reports from the Intelligence Agency about the development or transfer of dangerous technologies or weapons of mass destruction. Early action will stop the situation from deteriorating to the point where the options available for dealing with the problem have become very limited. The rules must specify in clear, unambiguous and simple language precisely what circumstances will trigger action by the Security Council on behalf of the international community and precisely what those actions will be. Such circumstances could include those recommended by scholars Michael Levi and Michael O'Hanlon: producing highly enriched uranium, acquiring advanced weapons of mass destruction, building new plutonium reprocessing facilities and failing to secure weapons of mass destruction and related technology. As to the range of actions the Security Council may take, it is clear that it must include the use of force. Indeed, limiting proliferation and reducing arms are so critical to the peace and security of our world that breach of non-proliferation and arms reduction rules should be treated as a threat to the peace, a breach of the peace or an act of aggression, giving the Security Council the right to call upon the international forces or regional forces to intercede. This is a perfect example of a circumstance in which force must be made a servant of justice. Nations that flout the non-proliferation rules and threaten the stability and peace of the planet must be brought to task quickly, effectively and forcefully. Forceful responses will send a strong message to other would-be proliferators and flouters of the arms control rules.[156]

Basing enforcement decisions on clear rules rather than vague policies would make it easier to deal with similar factual situations similarly and easier to avoid the lurking dangers of expediency. Proliferators must be dealt an equal hand regardless of how powerful or popular they are or how useful they can be in the short term to some nations. Moreover, threats must not be minimized simply because they do not directly affect the interests of powerful nations. Similar threats should be taken equally seriously, regardless of where they occur. An equitable rule-based system will be seen to be fair and even-handed and not determined by expediency and double standards. This, in turn, will bolster the credibility of the collective security system and strengthen its efficacy. Moreover, once the rules have been established, the international community must follow through on threatened consequences or else it will never be taken seriously. We must avoid repeating past mistakes. In 1992, for instance, the president of the Security Council issued a statement to the effect that the Security Council 'would regard any proliferation of WMD as a threat to international peace and security' and that its members 'would take appropriate action on any violation reported by the IAEA'.[157] Unfortunately, this statement lost all credibility when China vetoed the IAEA's first request for a special inspection. Unsurprisingly this was also the last time the IAEA requested permission to conduct a special inspection.

In addition to enforcement of the rules by the Security Council, individual states can and should be required to help implement the arms control treaties by passing legislation that criminalizes activities involving the development or possession of biological, chemical or nuclear weapons. Preliminary steps have already been taken in this regard, including the adoption in 2004 of Security Council Resolution 1540. The Security Council, invoking its powers under Chapter VII of the Charter, decided that all states were responsible for adopting and enforcing domestic laws which forbid non-state actors 'to manufacture, acquire, possess, develop, transport, transfer or use nuclear, chemical or biological weapons and their means of delivery, in particular for terrorist purposes'.[158] This resolution was followed in 2005 by the passage of the International Convention on the Suppression of Acts of Nuclear Terrorism which requires all states parties to adopt measures, including domestic legislation, that would punish the criminal acts specified in the treaty in accordance with their gravity.

Formalizing and integrating certain counter-proliferation mechanisms, such as interdiction and export control, could also be added to the international enforcement framework. For example, the Proliferation Security Initiative organized by the United States and ten other countries (Australia, France, Germany, Italy, Japan, the Netherlands, Poland, Portugal, Spain and the United

Kingdom) in the autumn of 2003 has been very successful at stemming the tide of proliferation by interdicting the shipment of materials used to develop weapons of mass destruction, especially in the coastal waters of participating nations. This initiative could be expanded beyond the core group of 15 countries and the additional 65 that have agreed to participate on an *ad hoc* basis. Tightening export controls could also help, although to achieve maximum effect, this tightening should be done in a systematic and coordinated fashion around the globe, rather than piecemeal by individual nations. Finally, the work of the Nuclear Suppliers Group, which currently meets in secret, should be integrated into the international arms control framework and made transparent to ensure that it is functioning consistently with the internationally agreed-upon rules.

Revisit and Fix Permanent Borders

It is evident that any viable system of collective security must include a mechanism for the international community to effectively identify and resolve border and territorial disputes, since these often act as triggers for violent conflict. To date, however, we have wilfully blinded ourselves to festering territorial and boundary disputes, often resulting from inherited arbitrary colonial boundaries and colonial economies.[159] We can no longer be content to leave it to the nations involved in a boundary dispute to submit it voluntarily to the International Court of Justice or, alternatively, to wreak havoc on their peoples by military means. Nor can we continue to stand back and allow decisions of the World Court to be ignored with impunity. To create a secure world we must craft creative solutions to long-standing patterns of problems such as boundary disputes rather than reacting to individual crises as they arise and then cobbling together ineffective short-term solutions as we go.

To this end, we clearly need to adopt a more pro-active approach resulting in a system that aims to achieve the following. First, a more viable system would identify potential trouble spots early on and solicit input speedily from all the parties involved.

Second, we need to agree on principles and rules to be applied in all cases involving border or territorial disputes. Third, an international body should be appointed, preferably a new entity other than the Security Council or the World Court, with a clear mandate and the requisite authority to apply these principles and rules. Fourth, an enforcement mechanism should ensure that parties to a boundary or territorial dispute comply with the final decision of the international body tasked with resolving these disputes.

The first step in creating this system is to establish an international boundary commission whose sole task will be to examine closely all conflicting territorial and irredentist claims (claims seeking restoration of territories that formerly belonged to a country). Nations and peoples should be encouraged to submit all such claims to the commission for it to examine all relevant evidence and issue binding decisions to resolve the disputes. In addition, the network of regional early warning agencies proposed above should regularly apprise the commission of festering problems within their region. The commission should have the power to request and, if necessary, compel parties to submit their disputes for resolution.

The second step is to craft clearly articulated principles and rules regarding boundary demarcation to be applied by the commission in a fair, consistent and systematic manner to all boundary disputes no matter where they arise. This will take us beyond the Court of Justice's current, broad and vague mandate to apply certain sources of law when deciding all cases involving the application of international law including boundary and territorial disputes cases. These sources of law are set out in Article 38 of the Statute of the International Court of Justice and include international conventions, international customary law to the extent that it reflects a general practice accepted as law, the general principles of law recognized by civilized nations, and judicial decisions and teachings of the most highly qualified publicists of the various nations. In addition, where the parties agree, the Court may decide a case using principles of equity. The breadth and generality of these sources of law require the Court to sift through a morass of rules and principles every time it decides a case, including a boundary dispute, to decide which ones are most appropriately applicable to that case.

Consequently, the Court will apply different combinations of rules and principles even when it is dealing with boundary cases. By contrast, giving the commission a specific set of rules and principles that are relevant to boundary disputes alone facilitates the work of the commission and also ensures that the same rules and principles are applied across the board to all boundary disputes. Countries are consequently more likely to submit such disputes to the commission, believing that they will be treated fairly and held to the same standards as any other nation.

In the third step towards greater security of agreed boundaries, the commission must carefully and dispassionately consider all the claims before it. It should draw upon the wealth of information we are fortunate to have at our disposal in this age of information. This information should include historical facts about how the present boundaries came to be created, such as inheritance by newly independent states of pre-independence administrative boundaries set up by a former colonial power or effective control by one of the parties. But these traditional factors, supplemented by general treaty law, do not fully resolve boundary questions. The International Court of Justice has hitherto preferred to decide land boundary cases by relying on just these three factors, yet, as some scholars argue, the results have not yielded the stability and predictability that the Court has sought.[160] The boundary commission must go beyond these legalistic approaches and also take into consideration other vital factors like the geography of the region, including mountain ranges, rivers, oceans and other bodies of water; geological considerations such as the existence of raw materials and valuable resources such as oil, gold, diamonds and timber in the land or waterways; the economic underpinnings of that region including land cultivation, industry or mining; the internal and international transportation routes used to carry goods, including pipelines, road, railways and ports; the ethnic composition of the peoples and their cultures, including their languages, religions and other cultural characteristics. After considering these factors, the commission should publish a reasoned recommendation demarcating the applicable boundaries and explaining the basis for its recommendation.

Once the commission has recommended boundary demarcations for all the pending territorial disputes, the world's leaders should consider and approve the commission's recommendations and incorporate them in the body of a new Boundary Treaty that is agreed upon by all nations. As time passes, new disputes may arise because of a change in circumstances – for instance because a river has changed its course. To ensure that such disputes are resolved in a timely fashion, the commission after its initial work resulting in the Boundary Treaty, should invite submission of new disputes for its consideration on an annual basis. In addition it should rely on alerts provided to it by the network of early warning agencies about newly emerging boundary disputes. The commission should submit its recommendations to the world's leaders who should consider them and, every five years, publish their final decision as annexes to the Boundary Treaty.

The fifth and final step is to ensure that boundary decisions are enforceable. To this end, the treaty resulting from this process to establish boundaries around the world must empower the Security Council to intervene and, if necessary, to use the military forces at its disposal (be they regional forces or the international standing army) to enforce the decision. Violation of the Boundary Treaty should also be included in the Security Council's mandate as a circumstance that constitutes a breach of the peace empowering the Council to use force if necessary to restore the peace.

Some scholars have suggested that territorial and boundary tensions may be mitigated if we encourage people to view themselves as members of a regional grouping, similar to citizens of countries making up the European Union, while also strengthening the military resources available to the United Nations. These scholars argue that minorities would flourish within such regional groupings, diminishing their desire to break away into small states. The European Union has adopted several policies and programmes for minority communities precisely to help reduce separatist tensions and pressures within or across certain of its member states. Just as the European Union has supported minority communities that might otherwise have felt suppressed within their nation states, so too other regional groupings might yield similar results.[161]

In additional to cultural, ethnic and other community tensions, a major cause of boundary and territorial disputes is competition for natural resources. One way to reduce the desire for control over and access to raw materials and other crucial resources, such as oil, uranium and water, would be to place them in the hands of a supranational body, akin to the European Coal and Steel Community, that will ensure their equitable distribution amongst the nations of the world. This recommendation will be discussed in more detail shortly. An example of a dispute that might have been avoided by taking such measures is the one that arose between Libya and Chad over the Aozou Strip, a purported source of uranium in northern Chad. The dispute was submitted to the Court by both countries in 1990 and the Court eventually found in favour of Chad.[162]

Overhaul the World Court

A strong International Tribunal or World Court must play a pivotal role in any effective system of collective security. The international community must be able to rely on such a Court to maintain the peace by resolving disputes and preventing them from degenerating into destabilizing conflicts. To be effective the Court must command the respect and trust of nations and other international actors. If the Court functions as it ought and resolves international disputes quickly, effectively and equitably, it will inspire the trust of those with potential international grievances and lead them to seek the help of the World Court to settle these disputes rather than resort to force.

The hope for the Court when it was first created was 'that international judicial settlement would be the substitute for war'. However, as Judge Schwebel pointed out in his address to the General Assembly of the United Nations in 1998, this 'has been shown to have been unrealistic'.[163] International judicial settlement has not produced peace. On the contrary, it is peace that has been conducive to the settlement of international disputes by international adjudication. The pattern that has emerged is that when international tension runs high, states generally avoid judicial settlement but when international tensions are low, states have been more inclined to settle their disputes by turning to the Court.

Judge Schwebel's assessment may accurately depict the historical role of the World Court within the flawed international system of past decades but we are not doomed to repeat this history; on the contrary, we can learn from history what needs to be changed. The real question is whether the World Court can be revamped enough for nations to turn to it when tensions are high and world peace is most threatened. This book suggests that the ideal envisioned by the framers of the UN Charter when creating the International Court of Justice is still attainable if the fundamental flaws outlined in a previous chapter are rectified.

Rectifying these flaws must begin with an open acknowledgement by our leaders that the Court as presently structured no longer serves the interests of humanity and must be revamped and strengthened if it is to play its pivotal role in creating and maintaining international peace and security. Our leaders must also be willing to make the fundamental changes necessary by applying the core operational principles identified early in this book around which they have reached consensus. These include the principle of oneness, the principle of justice, equity and fair treatment, the principle that force must be used in service of justice and the principle of the necessary curtailment of unfettered national sovereignty. These principles suggest five steps that should be taken.

First, the World Court must regain the respect and trust of those subject to its jurisdiction who must regard it as representative of the world community of nations, acting fairly and in their collective interest. Indeed, without such trust, any attempt to strengthen the Court may meet with ever-increasing resistance, as reflected by concerns of academic and legal practitioner Philippe Sands that the emergence of an increasingly powerful international judiciary raises important questions, such as who the judges are, how they are appointed and what limits their powers.[164] A basic requirement for such trust must be that the judges of the World Court be, and be viewed, not only as competent jurists and beyond moral reproach but also as completely unbiased. A recent academic study casts doubt that the past composition of the Court achieved this aim. Professors Eric Posner and John Yoo studied the voting patterns of judges in disputes involving the country that 'appointed' them. They found that in 90 per cent of the cases, judges did vote for their 'appointing' country, with the remaining judges voting in favour of a random country only 50 per cent of the time.[165] So stark were these findings that the study's authors asked themselves why states continue to use the Court at all. And, indeed, they observed that the use of the Optional Protocol accepting compulsory jurisdiction of the Court has been declining for about 20 years.[166]

In addition to being and being seen to be unbiased, judges of the Court must also be free of political pressure from their nations of origin and the states and various peoples involved in the Court's decisions. This subject has also been scrutinized by academics. Some of them have concluded that international courts, including the European Court of Justice, the dispute resolution panellists under the General Agreement on Tariffs and Trade and the World Trade Organization, often tailor their decisions to the anticipated reaction of the states parties to the dispute because the judges perceive that the very legitimacy of their court depends on the acceptance of the decision by the parties.[167] This perverse incentive does not inspire trust in the independence of a judiciary that is supposed to make impartial decisions based on the rule of law and the good of the larger community.

It is clear, therefore, that our leaders must design a new system for electing judges to the International Court that is transparent and yields judges that are both truly representative of the international community, its varied legal systems and regions, and are unbiased and independent of national and political pressures. Moreover, their decisions must be seen by all to be motivated solely by the good of the international community as a whole rather than one or more of its constituent parts.

The Bahá'í writings suggest guidelines for such a new system. Under these guidelines each nation's parliament should elect two or three national representatives in direct proportion to the size of its population. These representatives should be well versed in international law and international relations, aware of the current needs of the world and highly regarded and distinguished in their country. Their election by parliament should be confirmed by all the component parts of the legislature as well as the executive branch and the head of state, whether president or monarch. The entire body of representatives elected around the world would then elect the members of the World Court from among themselves. If these guidelines are followed, then the members of the Court will come to truly represent both the peoples of the world and their governments, putting into practice the principle of oneness.[168]

Members of the World Court should be elected for one term of about ten years, to free them of any temptation to render judgements that might garner support for their reelection to a second term in judicial office. Thereafter, they should be prohibited from seeking governmental appointments or jobs to avoid any temptation on their part to curry favour with a particular government in the hope of a plum position. Moreover, once elected they should operate completely independently, relying solely upon their own consultations and their own consciences without regard to the popularity of their decisions. Doing so will operationalize the core principles of justice, equity and fair treatment. These principles should be embodied in the statute of the World Court and provision should be made for removal by the World Parliament (discussed shortly) of a judge who is manifestly biased. Finally, all decisions taken by the Court should be taken either unanimously or, failing that, by a two-thirds majority vote to avoid deadlock.

The second step to strengthen the World Court and build its credibility is for world leaders to agree that it will have compulsory jurisdiction over all international disputes that threaten the peace of the world and that all states and certain non-state actors, including international organizations, will be subject to its jurisdiction. The Commission on Global Governance recognized a need to work towards compulsory jurisdiction[169] but the Court's jurisdiction can no longer be left to voluntary decision by individual nations or other international actors. The time has passed for us to ask states to consider recognizing the compulsory jurisdiction of the Court as was recommended both by the Secretary-General of the UN in his report 'In Larger Freedom' and by the world's leaders at the Summit held in New York in September 2005.[170] This is an area in which states must be willing to surrender a portion of their sovereignty in the interests of international peace and the greater good. If we are to have a viable World Court mandated with preserving the peace and able to act effectively, efficiently and equitably to stop disputes from escalating into violent conflict then we must grant it the powers and tools it needs to accomplish its task. If the Court is to be credible in the eyes of the world and command the respect it needs to function properly, all nations and international actors must fall within its jurisdiction and be subject to the equal application of international law. None can be given the chance to opt out of the Court's jurisdiction. Application of the principles of oneness, justice, equity and fairness of treatment demands no less. Interestingly, the relatively recent creation of an International Criminal Court has been an instructive exercise in the importance of creating an international court with jurisdiction over all states. No state can expect to have its fellow members of the international community be held responsible for breaches of international law while shielding itself from the consequences of its own illegal actions. All states must submit to equal treatment or else ill will and suspicion will ensue.

The third step to revamp and strengthen the World Court is to broaden its competence in two ways: first, by extending the range of cases it may hear as the need arises and, second, by granting actors other than nation states the standing to appear before it. Non-state actors with standing should include, for example, organs of the United Nations and, in appropriate cases, perhaps corporations and individuals. Expanded jurisdiction has been needed for a while. Indeed, its absence has given rise to the proliferation of new international courts to deal with important new categories of cases involving a broadening range of international actors. An increasing number of these courts are permanent, not time-limited or restricted to a single historical event.

The new permanent international courts have tended to be thematic. So, for example, the International Criminal Court was created as a permanent international court to prosecute and bring to justice individuals who commit the serious international crimes of genocide, crimes against humanity, war crimes and aggression. The World Trade Organization and its quasi-judicial dispute resolution panels deal with matters involving international trade, while the International Tribunal for the Law of the Sea deals with issues arising from the application of the Law of the Sea treaties. It should be noted, however, that while these *ad hoc* and permanent tribunals have filled an important need, their influence on the development of international law has been limited to the various treaty regimes under which they were created. The International Court of Justice, by contrast, has a special role to play in the development of international law: not only is it the only international court that can make pronouncements on general questions of international law but, as a practical matter, such pronouncements carry great weight with other international institutions and courts and tend to be discussed and analysed by both states and the academic community.

The existence of a plethora of international courts leads us to the fourth step for our leaders: to define clearly the hierarchy of international courts and tribunals. Some hierarchy is necessary to ensure that in a decentralized system of international courts, the coherence of international law is not threatened. For example, it is important to ensure that all similar cases be dealt with similarly and therefore equitably, by ensuring that international rules and precedents are interpreted and applied uniformly. Uniformity contributes to legitimacy of the international legal system. Moreover, there must be no overlapping jurisdiction among courts, otherwise parties to a dispute will attempt to shop around for the court they think will give them the most favourable judgement, undermining the sense of equal treatment and justice. One idea is to make the International Court of Justice an umbrella court coordinating the work of lower thematic courts, for example by assigning cases to them – those that already exist as well as those that may come into existence. Our leaders should consider creating a final right of appeal from the specialized courts, such as the dispute panels of the World Trade Organization, the International Tribunal for the Law of the Sea, the International Criminal Court and the like, to the International Court. The International Court would become the highest Court of Appeals in the international system and be granted the authority to review the decisions of lower courts. In addition, our leaders may also want to consider establishing some new thematic courts to deal with issues such as international trafficking in persons, illegal drugs and international terrorism.

The fifth step is to ensure that the World Court's decisions are enforceable. At present we lack an international culture that gives automatic and full authority to the Court's pronouncements and judgements.[171] Moreover, as pointed out by the Commission on Global Governance, it is clear that Article 94 of the United Nations Charter, which gives the Security Council the power to 'make recommendations or decide upon measures to be taken to give effect to the judgement' of the World Court, has been completely ignored.[172] Something more than the lip service of the Millennium Declaration is needed to ensure compliance with decisions of the Court and to strengthen respect for the rule of law.[173] Concrete steps are needed. World leaders should agree that failure to implement a judgement of the Court against a country will, as a matter of law, be regarded as a breach of the peace and stability of the international order. Indeed, this should be included in the Security Council's mandate as one of those circumstances to be regarded as a breach of the peace. Moreover, the stated consequence of such a breach should be that the international community will arise as a unified whole to enforce the judgement of the Court, if needed, through the agency of the international standing force or the regional forces that are at the beck and call of the Security Council.

Each decision of the World Court should give the parties a firm deadline to implement it. Once that deadline has passed without compliance, the Court would then be required to inform the Security Council immediately. The Security Council, in turn, should follow up with a final warning with a new deadline or use force to ensure compliance and maintain international order. Creating a mechanism making decisions of the World Court enforceable is critical if the World Court is to be taken seriously and is to command the respect of the nations. It is also a clear application of the principle that force must be made the servant of justice. All nations must be treated equally and all decisions must be applied equally, so that no nation is perceived as being allowed to flout the rules with impunity.

The sixth step to strengthen the World Court is to define better its relationship with other international organs, such as the General Assembly and the Security Council. Ideally, the international system will evolve to separate powers of international governance among an evolving international legislature, an international executive and an international judiciary, with each international organ having its own clearly-defined sphere of influence. Checks and balances will be needed to ensure that each international institution acts properly within the bounds of its authority. However, one of the key issues to decide in establishing proper checks and balances is whether the World Court should have the right to review the legality of decisions of the Security Council. If not, what check would there be on a Security Council that acted beyond the scope of its authority? At the same time, it is equally important to foster a respectful and seamless relationship between the various spheres of government so they can all work towards the common goal of creating a unified and peaceful planet.

Codify International Security Law

There are many compelling reasons to streamline and codify the host of international rules and laws that presently govern relationships between states, particularly those that are multilateral. These reasons, some of which were mentioned earlier, include making it easier for all states to ascertain their international obligations vis-à-vis each other, thereby enhancing the likelihood that states will discharge them. Streamlining the rules is particularly critical in areas that are governed by many complex international agreements such as the environment, which is currently governed by more than 400 regional and universal multilateral treaties covering diverse topics including desertification, climate change and biodiversity.[174] Streamlining the rules also makes it easier for states to fulfil their obligations by eliminating unnecessary multiple reporting requirements that are both confusing and burdensome to them. Moreover, clearly identifying who is obligated to do what makes it easier for the international community to monitor states' compliance with international rules. Codification also provides a certain transparency that fosters the climate of trust so critical to the viability of any system of collective security. In addition, clearly identifying and streamlining obligations also enables the international community to move from a fragmented institutional structure to a more integrated and efficient one in which the institutional components are well coordinated so that their functions are not duplicative. This, in turn, will eliminate institutional infighting over bureaucratic turf which is always wasteful and counterproductive. How should the international community go about the gargantuan task of streamlining and codifying the rules? Given the sheer magnitude of the task, involving as it does a multitude of international rules embodied both in multilateral treaties as well as in customary international law, we should begin by identifying areas that are of critical and immediate importance to international peace and security. These should include non-proliferation and arms reduction, human rights, the environment, terrorism, transnational organized crime, corruption and regulation of the world's resources.

Having identified the areas to be accorded priority, the next question is who should be given the tremendous responsibility for streamlining and codifying the rules? The appropriate body to undertake this task is the International Law Commission (ILC), which the UN General Assembly created in 1948 precisely to codify international law. Currently composed of 34 members selected for their expertise and not representing any governments, the ILC has developed extensive expertise in codifying international rules in areas of law other than international security. It should be asked by agreement of the world's leaders to focus its energies now on streamlining and codifying international law in the aforementioned areas that bear directly on collective security.[175]

The ILC should propose a draft code on each of the subjects assigned to it. The world's leaders should then convene to consider and vote on each draft. In the past the ILC's work has been incorporated into treaties open for voluntary signature by states choosing to adhere to the codification or not. Given the need for uniformity and universality in these critical areas of collective security, however, states should not be permitted to opt out of the codified rules. Instead, when first entrusting codification to the ILC, all states should agree in advance to be bound by the codifications if a majority votes to approve the ILC's draft. If approved by a majority of the world's leaders at this convention, all states would, indeed, be bound by the new codification.

All nations must stand firmly behind these foundational obligations. We can no longer afford to leave it to individual states to decide whether they wish to accede to certain international agreements that are fundamental to assuring international peace and security, such as treaties dealing with the non-proliferation of weapons of mass destruction or the Convention against Genocide. Experience has taught us over and over again that a voluntary system does not work. Indeed, as the former Secretary-General of the United Nations noted in his report 'In Larger Freedom', some important conventions have been prevented from even entering into force because many states refuse to sign on.[176] It is now time for our leaders to take the next decisive step in our collective process of maturation by making it both a moral and a legal imperative for all states to accede to such foundational treaties.

Towards World Government and Equitable Distribution of Critical Resources

We live in a dichotomous world. On the one hand nations are becoming increasingly interdependent and their destinies inextricably bound together. On the other the divisive forces of nationalism remain firmly entrenched and reluctant to give ground. Although it is both necessary and inevitable that excessive nationalism give way to greater supranational unity, the world is not yet ready to take the leap that would result in the creation of a world federation. Indeed, any proposal to create a world federation or super-state would undoubtedly be met with fierce resistance and be doomed to failure. However, an incremental approach towards ever-deepening political and economic integration of the community of nations, driven by a blend of practical necessity, collective self-interest and idealism, may be successful, as it has been in Europe. Although the European experience may not be one the entire world can or ought to replicate in all its aspects, it offers a number of useful lessons.

This final section of the book draws on aspects of the European experience to recommend a few steps our leaders should take in the short term that will take us far towards the creation of a viable system of collective security. In deciding which aspects of the European experience to draw upon, as well as the particular steps to be taken, much thought and consideration has been given to prioritizing the most urgent problems besetting the international community and to the likelihood that the solutions proposed will be acceptable to the generality of our leaders at this stage in human history.

Creation of Supranational Authority to Control, Regulate and Equitably Distribute Critical Resources

In a world where the well-being of people and the development of economies so keenly depend on having certain critical resources such as oil, gas, nuclear energy and water, it no longer makes sense for those nations who happen to sit on a particular resource that everyone needs to decide how the resource is managed and distributed. It certainly seems unfair that the rest of the world should be at the mercy of those nations as they dictate terms often based on short-term self-interest and fluctuating expediency. It also makes no sense to allow a major cause of boundary disputes and conflicts in general to continue when removing it would make the world a more peaceful place. It is high time for the leaders of the world to unite in establishing a supranational authority responsible for controlling, regulating and distributing these critical resources. Although they are likely to face stiff resistance from nations and private concerns that currently control such resources, our leaders need to recognize that application of several core principles proposed in the early section of part 3 of this book – including the oneness of peoples and nations, justice, equity and fair treatment of all peoples, the curtailment of excessive national sovereignty, and international cooperation and unity of action – dictates that critical resources be subject to control, regulation and distribution by a supranational authority. Centralizing the world's critical resources in the hands of one authority will also require our leaders to create a proper system of oversight, transparency and accountability to forestall possible corruption within the system.

The supranational authority should be designed as an umbrella authority with four separate arms. The first arm would have control over major natural energy resources such as oil and gas. Happily, our leaders have the extremely successful European Coal and Steel Community to look to as a model. There, sovereignty over the coal and steel sectors of the six original member states was shared under the auspices of a jointly controlled High Authority. One of the aims was to integrate French and German markets to ensure the supply of coal and steel on equal terms to each country. Nor was this as easy as it may seem, since Germany enjoyed far greater and cheaper coal reserves and steel production facilities than did France at the time, yet the leaders of that day recognized the benefits to both societies of removing the age-old source of envy and material means for armed conflict between these two nations. Similarly, one of the goals of the energy arm of the proposed supranational authority would be to ensure the supply of critical energy in the form of oil and gas on equal and fair terms to all nations. The agency would monitor levels of both supply and demand and ensure that there is sufficient oil and gas production to satisfy the world's needs. By doing so it would avoid problems, such as wild fluctuations in price arising from the confluence of tight supply and surges in demand, as exemplified by the unexpectedly high rise in demand for oil in both India and China in recent years. Interestingly, recognition of the need to foster greater oil market transparency has led to the recent creation of the International Energy Forum, in which both countries hungry for energy and the world's big oil producing countries participate. As Saudi Arabian Oil Minister Ali al-Naimi put it in explaining the need for this project, 'The absence of accurate and clear information is one of the biggest problems facing the markets and the petroleum industry – especially in vital subjects such as supply, demand, production and stockpiles.'[177] One of the ways the agency would guarantee ample supply is by making sure there is adequate investment in the oil industry and its infrastructure, including oil rigs, refinery capacity, tankers and exploration for new oil reserves.

Creating such a supranational energy agency would resolve some other critical problems facing the international community and yield some other important benefits. Because two-thirds of the world's oil reserves are concentrated in five countries of the Persian Gulf, the price of oil is particularly vulnerable to sudden changes, such as political instability, embargoes and terrorist attacks in this area of market concentration. Such changes engender fear in energy markets, causing the price of oil to soar. The creation of a supranational energy agency would stabilize oil prices, putting an end to wild and economically disruptive fluctuations. It would also resolve the problem of 'resource nationalism'. Nations would no longer feel driven to secure as large a share as they can of their own equity in oil out of fear that their energy needs may otherwise not be satisfied in the long term.[178]

The existence of a supranational energy agency would also put an end to the practice of energy-rich nations using oil and gas as crude bargaining chips in international relations. They would no longer be able to buy the political support of other nations in their pursuit of proscribed activities by offering lucrative deals to secure access to oil or natural gas while denying others similar access. By the same token, nations in need of energy would no longer be tempted to barter away their principles or to turn a blind eye to unprincipled behaviour by energy-rich nations out of fear that they will lose access to crucial energy supplies. Having such an agency with proper oversight, accountability and tight controls would also avoid the problems of corruption and inefficiency that have generally arisen when individual governments unaccountable to a higher authority have played a prominent part in developing oil resources.

The second arm of the supranational authority would be responsible for managing all the key resources that can be used to create nuclear energy and weapons, such as uranium and plutonium, together with the facilities for processing them and all nuclear reactors. It would also be responsible for distributing nuclear fuel in an equitable manner and would act as a reserve fuel bank to guarantee the supply of fissile material to civilian nuclear users. Another one of its important functions would be to impose and enforce international standards regarding the tracking and disposal of nuclear waste and spent fuel. Stronger tracking is needed to avoid situations like that reported in 2005 when nuclear energy authorities lost track of spent fuel from three nuclear plants in the US – Vermont, Connecticut and California – said to be missing.[179] Tracking such waste is critical to ensuring that it does not fall into the hands of dangerous state or non-state actors.

Water is another resource that is essential to the well-being of peoples worldwide. It is predicted that by the year 2015, 1.8 billion people will lack access to water. Control over this crucial resource should be given to the third arm, which would monitor the supplies and the need for clean water worldwide and be responsible for ensuring that all the peoples of the world have fair access to clean water supplies.

A fourth arm should also be set up to regulate and monitor the mining and extraction of certain other priceless resources. Our leaders would first need to agree upon a list of such resources. In doing so they should draw on the information provided and conclusions made in the reports of several expert panels appointed by the Security Council in recent years that demonstrate the nexus between certain conflicts such as the ones in Liberia, the Democratic Republic of Congo, Angola and Sierra Leone, and the exploitation of natural resources.[180] Based on these reports and other studies conducted by NGOs[181] working in this area, the list ought to include diamonds, gold, coltan, cobalt and timber because the desire to control such resources has been shown to trigger conflicts. Their illicit mining and trade by warring factions has funded and sustained civil wars within many countries and has proved to be one of the biggest drivers of conflict and violence in the developing world. African countries have been particularly prone to suffer this kind of conflict, one example being Angola, where unrestrained diamond mining funded the UNITA rebels for many years while oil extraction funded the government side. Indeed, research by Paul Collier, an Oxford economist, establishes the nexus between resource wealth and conflict very clearly. It suggests that in any given five year period the chance that an African country will have a civil war rises from less than one per cent in countries lacking resource wealth to almost 25 per cent in those having such wealth.[182] However, resource conflicts are by no means limited to Africa. Other places such as Baluchistan, Burma and Papua are also currently prey to such conflict.

One of the crucial responsibilities of the high authority's fourth arm would be to craft and enforce rules governing natural resource extraction. The rules would be designed to ensure that resources do not fund rebel groups or insurgents, for example, by requiring transparency and accountability of financial transactions related to the mining or extraction activities. Initial attempts to ensure this kind of transparency and accountability have already been made but need to be further refined and tightened. For instance, the Kimberley Process brought together governments of producing and consuming nations, the diamond industry and certain NGOs to stem the flow of 'conflict diamonds'. The parties entered an agreement requiring producing countries to track all rough diamonds from mine to export and to certify that diamonds leaving their countries are not tainted by conflict. Consuming countries agree to purchase only those diamonds that have been certified as conflict-free and diamond companies allow individual purchasers of cut diamonds to buy only conflict-free diamonds as evidenced by a certificate they provide for each individual diamond. Another attempt at transparency can be found in the Extractive Industries Transparency Initiative for oil, gas and minerals (EITI). The EITI requires both companies and governments to publish regular and detailed reports of all payments received by the governments from the companies for the resources in question and to open their books to stringent audits. Yet another initiative to ensure transparency is the EU's Forest Law Enforcement, Governance and Trade initiative (FLEGT) by which the EU seeks to identify legal timber in the country of origin and license it for export to the EU.[183] In addition to crafting and enforcing rules such as these for natural resource extraction and trade, misuse of resources or breach of related rules established by the high authority should be made crimes under international law, punishable by a designated international court.

The supranational mining and extraction agency should also consider the environmental damage caused by improper mining and extraction and attempt to arrive at solutions to mitigate such damage. For example, in the area of metal and gold mining, the prevalent use of cyanide solution to separate gold from rock is making some mines almost like nuclear waste dumps that must be tended in perpetuity.[184] The scale of the damage is apparent when one considers that miners move up to half a million tons of earth a day at some of the largest mines and sprinkle the resulting mounds with the poisonous cyanide solution.[185] The mining agency may want to prohibit this method and study economically viable alternatives that are less damaging to the environment.

In creating this fourth arm the international community should draw upon its experience in creating the global treaty regime to organize and control activities relating to the mineral resources in the international seabed, including regulating the exploration, mining and extraction of deep sea resources. The lessons learned from the creation and operation of the relevant international body, the International Seabed Authority, and its related forum for adjudicating disputes, the International Tribunal for the Law of the Sea, should be drawn upon. Our leaders should examine and learn from both the successes and failures, weaknesses and strengths of the international seabed regime. Eventually, it would make most sense to bring the control over the mining of deep sea, land and territorial water resources under one supranational umbrella organization.

Create a World Parliament

In the aftermath of the Cold War two driving forces have emerged: globalization and democratization. And yet strangely, despite the clamour of people everywhere that they should be entitled to participate in decisions that affect their lives, we still lack an international legislature that is democratically elected. It is time for a core group of our leaders to take the initiative to propose a World Parliament to represent both citizens and their governments, and to labour diligently for the support of all their fellow leaders. The World Parliament should be created either by amending the UN Charter or by a separate universal treaty. Given the international community's recent experience with the successful creation of both the European Union and the International Criminal Court, both by treaty, the latter might be a more feasible and realistic option.

Drawing on the experience of European integration, the legitimacy of this Parliament in the eyes of the peoples of the world should be assured from the beginning by making it truly representative of both the people and their governments. From the outset, members of the World Parliament should be directly elected by the people of each country and confirmed by their respective governments. Leaders should not take the intermediate step of composing it initially of representatives of national parliaments, in the expectation of gradually evolving into a directly elected parliament, the path trodden by the European Union. However, the relationship of the World Parliament to the UN General Assembly would need to be clarified. Because the General Assembly represents governments and is not directly elected by the world's citizens, an alternative approach would be to begin by creating a bicameral international legislature in which the General Assembly would represent the governments of nations and the World Parliament would represent their citizens. This possibility was mooted by international law professors Richard Falk and Andrew Strauss in an article they wrote for *Foreign Affairs* in 2001.[186] Over time, the two bodies could be melded into one that is directly elected by the citizens of all nations and confirmed by their governments.

Nonetheless, the international community should agree in advance upon some minimum membership requirements for countries that wish to participate, akin to those required for membership in the European Union. These should include the requirement that nations whose citizens elect members to the

World Parliament hold regular elections by secret ballot, with universal participation. At the very least, they must openly acknowledge that they are striving to attain these standards and demonstrate that they are making identifiable progress in that direction. In addition, they must not violate fundamental human rights standards.[187]

It is important to tackle openly and honestly an idea that has been much talked about recently: increasing the role of civil society in the deliberations at the United Nations. The term 'civil society' has come to be regarded as synonymous with non-governmental organizations (NGOs). However, the reality is that NGOs are ultimately unelected, self-appointed organizations that do not necessarily represent the majority or even any minority of the people. NGOs each have their own agendas and sources of funding and their nature, impact and interests have become almost impossible to measure, according to scholars studying them.[188] They tend to function more like lobbying organizations and, by effectively networking and mobilizing their members, they can wield disproportionate influence on decision-making and on the shaping of global policies. Why should self-appointed organizations have access to international decision-makers and have their voices heard when the general citizenry do not? The principles of oneness, justice, equity and fairness require that all voices be given the opportunity to be heard. Ultimately, regardless of the undoubted value of NGO input and without detracting from the important role they can play in enhancing awareness, educating the public and advocating on behalf of groups, NGOs cannot be a substitute for a truly representative World Parliament directly elected by the peoples of the world. The World Parliament should have certain rights, however limited at first, to pass legislation that would be binding on the international community. It should not serve merely in an advisory capacity. Drawing on the European experience, the spheres of jurisdiction within which the Parliament can legislate could initially be defined narrowly and eventually expanded, as the Parliament learns to exercise this legislative power and as the nations and people of the world build their confidence in this body. With time, the member states whose citizens are represented in Parliament and whose governments are also represented either as members of the bicameral Assembly or because they have confirmed the elected representatives of their citizens, will be increasingly willing to grant more powers to Parliament, relinquishing exclusive sovereignty in certain areas and sharing it in others, as they come to recognize the overriding benefits of a supranational approach to legislating internationally, as opposed to a merely intergovernmental one. It is likely that the evolution of the World Parliament will mirror the continuing tension between intergovernmentalism and supranationalism that has characterized the evolution of the European Union. In time, however, the chances are that the forces of supranationalism will gain the upper hand, as they appear to have done in Europe.

Towards World Federation

The creation of a World Parliament that will evolve into a world legislature is simply one piece of the international institutional infrastructure needed to ensure our collective security. Other components of this infrastructure are embodied in the recommendations made in the last part of this book. Indeed, if implemented in their totality, these recommendations will form the skeletal frame of an emergent system of world government. By urging our leaders to take the recommended steps, rather than challenging them to leap directly towards some form of world government, we, the world community, will help them to develop the needed world system gradually and based on an understanding of the need for its creation. Consequently, taking these recommended steps should not trigger the visceral fear of world government that many experience when the topic is raised.

But some form of world government is inevitable if we are to address the myriad security problems plaguing us. The steps recommended in earlier chapters will help to ensure that the world government that will emerge will have three separate centres of power that are needed to ensure a proper separation and balance of powers and functions, as well as an adequate system of checks and balances. One of these centres of power will be the world legislature discussed above. In time, this legislature will oversee the work of the supranational authority responsible for controlling, regulating and distributing the critical resources of the planet. It will also oversee the work of the boundary commission proposed in this book as well as the commission that will recommend changes and improvements to the non-proliferation and arms reduction regimes.

The second centre of power will be a World Executive. Granting the Security Council a strong mandate to act decisively and to use force in specified circumstances, as well as providing it with proper procedures and guidelines, will strengthen the Council to enable it to grow into a proper World Executive. Eliminating the right of veto and ensuring that the Council adequately represents the nations of the world will help to improve its legitimacy and its effectiveness. In addition, providing the Security Council with the tools it needs to carry out its executive functions – including the recommended International Intelligence and Inspections Agency and the regional or international forces it needs to enforce its decisions – will go a long way towards strengthening this centre of international power.

The third centre of power will be the World Court. Overhauling the International Court of Justice, particularly by changing how its judges are elected, granting it compulsory jurisdiction and ensuring that its decisions are enforced by force if necessary, will strengthen it and increase its stature, thereby ensuring a strong third centre of power. Once the three centres of power in the international order have each evolved and been strengthened, our leaders will need to ensure that they work closely and harmoniously with each other and mutually reinforce one another.

The foundation of the system of collective security proposed in this book, as well as the glue to bind it together in a congruent whole, are the core principles of oneness, justice and equity, the elimination of expediency, the curtailment of unfettered national sovereignty, the use of force in the service of justice and the unity of thought and action. Indeed, it is applying these core principles to the most serious problems affecting the security of the planet that leads to the recommendations proposed in this book for the creation of an efficient, effective and viable system of collective security that will bring us the peace for which humanity has waited so long.

Conclusion

Conclusion

The aim of this book has been to engage ordinary citizens, women and men, around the world in the conversation that has been going on in fits and starts for over a century regarding the shape and direction in which an evolving system of collective security and international order should grow. It has sought to pull together various isolated strands of thinking by individuals and groups and to consider them within the broad framework of a vision of collective security offered by the Bahá'í writings. In doing so, the book has sought to show how the apparently disparate work of men and women around the world keenly concerned with finding solutions to the problems of humanity fit together like pieces of a jigsaw puzzle to create a broad-based road map to peace. Working in synergy, these ideas can help create a new and viable system of collective security. Finally, inspired by the Bahá'í vision and drawing on ideas in the Bahá'í writings and of thinkers in areas that affect collective security, the book makes a series of concrete recommendations for action.

By engaging people everywhere – by using their ideas and asking them to participate in the debate – we can build a new system of collective security that will garner the trust and support of the people of the world and thereby impel our leaders to take the actions necessary to meet the needs and desires of their citizens. As Dwight Eisenhower said in 1959, '. . . people in the long run are going to do more to promote peace than are governments. Indeed, I think that people want peace so much that one of these days governments had better get out of their way and let them have it.'[1]

Bibliography

Books

Abbas, Ademola. *Regional Organisations and the Development of Collective Security: Beyond Chapter VIII of the UN Charter.* Oxford: Hart, 2004.

'Abdu'l-Bahá. *The Secret of Divine Civilization.* Wilmette, IL: Bahá'í Publishing Trust, 1990.
— *Selections from the Writings of 'Abdu'l-Bahá.* Haifa: Bahá'í World Centre, 1978.

Bahá'í International Community. *Turning Point for All Nations: A Statement of the Bahá'í International Community on the Occasion of the 50th Anniversary of the United Nations.* New York: Bahá'í International Community United Nations Office, 1995.

Bahai Scriptures: Selections from the Utterances of Baha'u'llah and 'Abdu'l-Baha. Ed. Horace Holley. New York: J.J. Little and Ives, 1928.

Bahá'u'lláh. *Epistle to the Son of the Wolf.* Wilmette, IL: Bahá'í Publishing Trust, 1988.
— *Gleanings from the Writings of Bahá'u'lláh.* Wilmette, IL: Bahá'í Publishing Trust, 1983.
— *The Proclamation of Bahá'u'lláh.* Haifa: Bahá'í World Centre, 1967.
— *Tablets of Bahá'u'lláh.* Wilmette, IL: Bahá'í Publishing Trust, 1988.

Basic Facts about the United Nations. New York: United Nations Office of Public Information, 2004.

Blix, Hans. *Disarming Iraq.* New York: Pantheon, 2004.

Boutros-Ghali, Boutros. *An Agenda for Peace.* New York: United Nations, 2nd ed. 1995.

Commission on Global Governance. *Our Global Neighbourhood.* New York: Oxford University Press, 1995.

Coudenhove-Kalergi, Richard N. *Pan-Europa.* Vienna: Pan Europa Verlag, 1923.

Dallaire, Lt. Gen. Romeo. *Shake Hands With the Devil: The Failure of Humanity in Rwanda*. New York: Carroll & Graf, 2004.

Dedman, Martin J. *The Origins and Development of the European Union 1945–95*. London: Routledge, 1996.

Dinan, Desmond. *Europe Recast: A History of European Union*. Basingstoke: Palgrave MacMillan, 2004.

Evans, Gareth. *Cooperating for Peace: The Global Agenda for the 1990s and Beyond*. St Leonards, NSW: Allen and Unwin, 1993.

Eyffinger, Arthur. *The International Court of Justice,* Kluwer Law International, 1996.

Fontaine, Pascal. *A New Idea for Europe: The Schuman Declaration 1950–2000*. Luxembourg: European Commission, 2000.

Gray, Christine. *International Law and the Use of Force*. Oxford: Oxford University Press, 2004.

Hoopes, Townsend and Douglas Brinkley. *FDR and the Creation of the U.N.* London: Yale University Press, 1997.

Lawson, Stephanie. *The New Agenda for Global Security: Cooperating for Peace and Beyond*. London: Allen & Unwin, 1995.

Levi, Michael and Michael O'Hanlon. *The Future of Arms Control*. Washington DC: Brookings Institution Press, 2005.

Lights of Guidance: A Bahá'í Reference File. Compiled by Helen Hornby. New Delhi: Bahá'í Publishing Trust, 2nd ed. 1988.

Merrills, J. G. *International Dispute Settlement*. Cambridge: Cambridge University Press, 4th rev. ed. 2005.

O'Hanlon, Michael and Mike Mochizuki. *Crisis on the Korean Peninsula: How to Deal with a Nuclear North Korea*. New York: McGraw-Hill, 2003.

Rosenne, Shabtai. *The Law and Practice of the International Court 1920–2004*. Leiden: Brill, 4th rev. ed. 2004.

Sands, Philippe. *Lawless World: America and the Making and Breaking of Global Rules*. Harmondsworth: Allen Lane, 2005.

Shaw, Malcolm N. *International Law*. Cambridge: Grotius, 4th ed. 1997.

Shoghi Effendi. *The Advent of Divine Justice*. Wilmette, IL: Bahá'í Publishing Trust, 1990.
— *God Passes By*. Wilmette, IL: Bahá'í Publishing Trust, rev. ed. 1995.

— *The World Order of Bahá'u'lláh*. Wilmette, IL: Bahá'í Publishing Trust, 1991.

Streit, Clarence K. *Union Now: A Proposal for a Federal Union of the Democracies of the North Atlantic*. London: Harper & Brothers, 1939.

The Universal House of Justice. *The Promise of World Peace*. London: Bahá'í Publishing Trust, 1985.

Zak, Chen. *Iran's Nuclear Policy and the IAEA: An Evaluation of Program 93+2*. Military Research Papers no. 3. Washington DC: The Washington Institute for Near East Policy, 2004.

Media Articles, Journals, Reports and Speeches

'Accepting Nobel, ElBaradei Urges a Rethinking of Nuclear Strategy'. *New York Times*, 11 December 2005.

'African Union Lifts Togo Sanctions'. Associated Press, 27 May 2005. *New York Times* online. www.nytimes.com.

'African Union Lifts Togo Sanctions'. *Economist*, 28 April 2005.

'African Union to Triple Sudan Peacekeepers'. Associated Press, in *New York Times*, 28 April 2005.

Ames, Paul. 'Annan Seeks Overhaul of Security Measures'. Associated Press, 13 February 2005.

'Annan Opens World Summit with plea not to let down billions around the globe'. UN News Centre, 14 September 2005. www.un.org/apps/news.

'APEC Wants Bigger Push on N. Korea Nuclear Talks'. Reuters, *New York Times*, 19 November 2005.

Asia Times, 8 March 2005.

'AU Agrees to Enlarge Darfur Force'. *Aljazeera*. 29 April 2005. www.globalpolicy.org.

'AU Extends Darfur Troops Mandate'. BBC, 21 September 2006. http://news.bbc.co.uk/2/hi/africa/5362762.stm.

Bahree, Bhushan. 'IEA Warns of Impending Crunch in Gas Supply'. *Wall Street Journal*, 9 July 2007. www.wsj.com.

'Bracing for Penalties, Iran Threatens to Withdraw from Nuclear Treaty'. *New York Times*, 12 February 2006.

Brauer, R. H. 'International Conflict Resolution: The ICJ Chambers and the Gulf of Maine Dispute'. *Virginia Journal of International Law*, vol. 23, 1982–3.

Brinkley, Joel. 'U.S. Official Says North Korea Could be Bluffing on Nuclear Arms'. *New York Times*, 16 February 2005.

Carter, Ashton B. Speech at the annual meeting of the World Economic Forum in 2 February 1999. www.weforum.org/site/knowledgenavigator.nsf.

Charney, Jonathan I. 'The Impact on the International System of the Growth of International Courts and Tribunals'. *Journal of International Law and Politics*, vol. 31, 1999.

Churchill, Winston. Speech given in Zurich, 19 September 1946. www.ena.lu/mce.cfm.

Cowell, Alan and Eamon Quinn. 'Two Former Enemies are Sworn in to Lead Northern Ireland's Government', 9 May 2007. www.nytimes.com.

'Crisis in Darfur'. Report of the International Crisis Group, May 2007. www.icg.org.

'Curbing Proliferation: How to Stop the Spread of the Bomb'. *The Economist*, 28 April 2005.

Diehl, Paul F. 'Once Again: Nations Agree Genocide Must Be Stopped. Can They Find the Mechanism to Do It?' *Washington Post*. 15 May 2005.

Dinmore, Guy. 'US Draws Up List of Unstable Countries'. *Financial Times*, 28 March 2005. www.globalpolicy.org.

Eisenhower, Dwight. Speaking to UK Prime Minister Harold Macmillan in a television broadcast, London, 31 August 1959. www.eisenhower.archives.gov/ss1.htm.

'ElBaradei: Protect Nuclear Material'. Associated Press, 6 December 2005.

Erlanger, Steven. 'Backing Fatah and Abbas, Egypt Organizes Summit Meeting for Palestinian Leader'. 22 June 2007. www.nytimes.com.

— and Graham Bowley. 'Palestinian President Dissolves Government'. *New York Times*, 14 June 2007. www.nytimes.com.

Evans, Gareth. 'Aceh is Building Peace from Its Ruins'. *International Herald Tribune*, 23 December 2005. www.crisisgroup.org.

— 'Darfur: What Next?' Keynote address to the International Crisis Group/Save Darfur Coalition/European Policy Centre Conference: 'Towards a Comprehensive Settlement for Darfur', Brussels, 22 January 2007. www.icg.org.
— 'Genocide or Crime: Actions Speak Louder than Words in Darfur'. *The European Voice*, 18 February 2005. www.crisisgroup.org.
— 'Meeting the Challenge of War. Report of Rapporteur for Security and Geopolitics'. World Economic Forum, Davos, January 2003. www.icg.org.
— 'The Responsibility to Protect: Evolution and Implementation'. Keynote address to the London School of Economics/Kings College London Conference on Ethical Dimensions of European Foreign Policy, London, 1 July 2005. www.icg.org.
— 'The Responsibility to Protect: When It's Right to Fight'. *Progressive Politics*, July 2003.
www.progressive-governance.net/publications/publications.aspx?id=804
— 'UN Reform: Why It Matters for Africa'. Address to Africa Policy Forum, Addis Ababa, 26 August 2005. www.crisisgroup.org.

'Experts Discuss Nuclear Power as Energy'. Associated Press, 21 March 2005.

Falk, Richard and Andrew Strauss. 'Toward Global Parliament'. *Foreign Affairs*, vol. 80, no.1, January/February 2001.
— and David Krieger. 'United Nations Should be Less Reliant on US'. *Daily Bruin*, 13 November 2002.
www.Globalpolicy.org/unitedstates/unpolicy/gen2002/1118dep.htm.

'Famine Relief – Starving for the Cameras: People Dying from Hunger Like Those in Niger Should Not Have to Wait for the TV Crews to Arrive'. *The Economist*, 18 August 2005.

Fattah, Hassan M. 'Conference of Arab Leaders Yields Little of Significance', *New York Times*, 24 March 2005.
— 'Syria Ends Military Domination of Lebanon'. Associated Press, 26 April 2005. *New York Times* online. www.nytimes.com.
— 'U.N. Envoy and Syrian President Meet'. *New York Times*, 12 June 2005.

'FBI Opens Anti-gang Office in Central America'. Reuters, *New York Times*, 4 May 2004.

'From Brussels Without Love'. *The Economist*, 24 February 2005.

Fukuyama, Francis. 'Re-Envisioning Asia'. *Foreign Affairs*. January/February 2005.

'Global or National: The Perils Facing Big Oil'. *The Economist*, 28 April 2005.

'Global Oil Producers Discuss Supply'. Reuters, 19 November 2005, *New York Times* online. www.nytimes.com.

Goormaghtigh, John. 'European Coal and Steel Community'. *International Conciliation*, vol. 30, 1997.

Graham, Bradley. 'Pentagon Strategy Aims to Block Internal Threats to Foreign Forces'. *Washington Post*, 19 March 2005.

Grono, Nick. 'Addressing the Links between Conflicts and Natural Resources'. Speech at the Conference on Security, Development and Forest Conflict, Brussels, 9 February 2006.
— 'Natural Resources and Conflict'. Speech at the EIS Symposium on Sustainable Development and Security, European Parliament, Brussels, 31 May 2006.

'Hamas Arms Roundup Still Leaves Plenty of Guns in Gaza'. Associated Press, 21 June 2007. www.iht.com/articles/ap/2007/06/21/Africa/ ME-GEN-Palestinians-Arms-Roundup.php.

'Hamas Controls Gaza, Says It Will Stay in Power'. CNN, 14 June 2007. www.cnn.com/2007/WORLD/meast/06/14/gaza/index.html.

'Hamas Hails "Liberation" of Gaza'. BBC, 14 June 2007. http:///news.bbc.co.uk/2/hi/middle_east/6751079.stm.

Hamilton, Adrian. 'The Idea of the Nation State is Fatally Flawed'. *The Independent*, 19 August 2004. www.globalpolicy.org.

Harrison, Selig S. 'Did North Korea Cheat?' *Foreign Affairs*, January/ February 2005.

Hill, Felicity. 'The Military Staff Committee: A Possible Future Role in UN Peace Operations?' Global Policy Forum. www.globalpolicy.org/security/peacekpg/reform/2001/msc.htm.

International Law Reports. Cambridge. Individual reports cited below. See Documents: International Court of Justice documents (abbreviated as ILR).

'Interview with Dr Mohammed ElBaradei, Director General of the International Atomic Energy Agency' (interview on 2 December 2003). *The Fletcher Forum*, Winter 2004.

'IRA "has destroyed all its arms"'. BBC, 26 September 2005. http://news.bbc.co.uk/1/hi/northern_ireland/4283444.stm.

'Iran and Nuclear Diplomacy – A Yes or a No?' *The Economist*, 28 June 2007.

'Iran Plans to Build a Second Nuclear Plant'. Associated Press, 5 December 2005.

'Iran Says It's Not Afraid of Security Council'. 8 November 2005. *New York Times* online. www.nytimes.com.

'Iranian Warns Against Added Nuclear Sanctions'. Associated Press, 6 June 2007. www.nytimes.com.

'Iran's Nuclear Politics: Mahmoud and the Atomic Mullahs'. *The Economist*, 30 June 2005.

Jahn, George. 'Iran Makes Major Nuclear Concessions'. *Washington Post*, 13 July 2007.

Johansen, Robert C. 'Put Teeth in "Never Again" Vow with Fast, Full-Scale UN Response'. *Christian Science Monitor*, 7 September 2004.

Kagan, Robert. 'The Crisis of Legitimacy: America and the World'. The 21st Annual John Bonython Lecture, the Grand Hyatt, Melbourne, Tuesday 9 November 2004.

Kissinger, Henry. Luncheon talk at the Metropolitan Club, Washington DC, 21 April 2005.

Knowlton, Brian. 'Bush's "Priceless" War'. *Asia Times*, 25 February 2005.

Koh, Professor Harold. 'Is International Law Useful to the US?' Speech at American Society of International Law panel, Washington DC, 30 March–2 April 2005.

Langille, Peter. 'Preventing Genocide: Time For a UN 911'. *Globe and Mail*, 19 October 2004. www.globalpolicy.org/security/peacekpg/reform/2004/1019timefor.htm.

Lavery, Brian. 'I.R.A. Destroys What It Says Were the Last of Its Weapons'. *New York Times*, 27 September 2005.

Lederer, Edith M. 'Annan Appeals to World Leaders at Summit'. Associated Press, 15 September 2005. http://aolsvc.news.aol.com/news.

Maitra, Ramtanu. 'India Takes its Arms Beefs to the UN'. *Asia Times*, 24 February 2005.

McDoom, Opheera. 'Sudan Rejects Use of Force by UN-AU Darfur Mission'. Reuters Africa, 22 July 2007. http://africa.reuters.com/wire/news/usnB269619.html.

McGann, James and Mary Johnstone. 'The Power Shift and the NGO Credibility Crisis'. *Journal of World Affairs*, Winter/Spring 2005.

Moodie, Michael. 'Confronting the Biological and Chemical Weapons Challenge: The Need for an "Intellectual Infrastructure"'. *The Fletcher Forum*, vol. 28, no. 1, Winter 2004.

'NATO's Assistance to the African Union for Darfur'. NATO OTAN, 15 June 2007. www.nato.int/issues/darfur/index.html.

New York Times database 'Arms Control'. 31 October 2005.

'NI Deal Struck in Historic Talks'. BBC, 26 March 2007. http://news.bbc.co.uk/1/hi/northern_ireland_/6494599.stm.

'Nigeria: Rehabilitation, harassment concerns mar Bakassi pullout'. 27 September 2006. http://www.irinnews.org.

'Nigerian troops leaving Bakassi'. 11 August 2006. http://news.bbc.co.uk/2/hi/Africa.

'North Korea's Nuclear Test: The Fallout' (produced by the International Crisis Group). *Asia Briefing*. 13 November 2006. www.icg.org.

'Nuclear Confusion'. *The Economist*, 22 October 2005.

Paul, James and Celine Nahory. 'Theses Towards a Democratic Reform of the UN Security Council'. *Global Policy Forum*. 13 July 2005. www.globalpolicy.org/security/reform/2005/0713theses.htm.

Perlez, Jane and Kirk Johnson. 'Behind Gold's Glitter: Torn Lands and Pointed Questions'. *New York Times*, 24 October 2005.

Polgreen, Lydia. 'West Africa Wins Again, with Twist'. *New York Times*, 27 February 2005.

Pollack, Kenneth and Ray Takeyh. 'Taking on Tehran'. *Foreign Affairs*, March/April 2005.

Posner, Eric A. 'All Justice, Too, Is Local'. *New York Times*, 30 December 2004.

— Speech at the American Society of International Law panel, Washington DC, Spring 2005.

'Quartet Urges Palestinians to Dismantle Militias'. Reuters, *New York Times*, 20 September 2005.

Quinn, Eamon and Alan Cowell. 'Ulster Factions Agree to a Plan for Joint Rule'. 27 March 2007. www.nytimes.com.

'S. Korea to Play Neutral Role in Asia'. Associated Press, *New York Times*, 10 April 2005.

Sanger, David E. 'Atomic Agency Concludes Iran is Stepping Up Nuclear Work'. *New York Times*, 14 May 2007.

— 'Month of Talks Fails to Bolster Nuclear Treaty'. *New York Times*, 28 May 2005.

Schneider, Mark. 'The Responsibility to Protect: The Capacity to Prevention and the Capacity to Intervene'. Statement to the Woodrow Wilson International Center for Scholars, Washington DC, 5 May 2004.

Schwebel, Judge Stephen M. Address to the General Assembly of the United Nations, 27 October 1998. www.icj-cij.org/icjwww/ipre.../SPEECHES/SpeechPresidentGA98.htm.

Sciolino, Elaine and William J. Broad, 'At the Heart of the United Front On Iran, Vagueness on Crucial Terms'. *New York Times*, 18 June 2006.

'Security Council Tightens Sanctions against Iran over Uranium Enrichment'. 24 March 2007. www.un.org/apps/news.

Solana, Dr Javier. 'Securing Peace in Europe'. Speech at the Symposium on the Political Relevance of the 1648 Peace of Westphalia, Munster, 12 November 1998. www.nato.int/docu/speech/1998/s981112a.htm.

Steinberg, Richard H. 'Judicial Lawmaking at the WTO: Discursive, Constitutional, and Political Constraints'. *American Journal of International Law*, vol. 98, April 2004.

Strauss, Scott. 'Darfur and the Genocide Debate'. *Foreign Affairs*. January/February 2005.

Sumner, Brian Taylor. 'Territorial Disputes at the International Court of Justice'. *Duke Journal*, vol. 53, 2004.

'Talks between Iran and Europe End without Agreement'. Associated Press, *New York Times*, 3 March 2006.

Tan, Col Jimmy. 'Regional Security Partners: The Potential for Collective Security'. Paper. National War College, 1999.

Tyson, Ann Scott. 'Two Years Later, Iraq War Drains Military – Heavy Demands Offset Combat Experience'. *Washington Post*, 19 March 2005.

'UN Assembly Approves Weakened Summit Blueprint'. Reuters, 13 September 2005. *New York Times* online. www.nytimes.com.

'The UN Gets Tougher: After Years of Inaction, UN Peacekeepers Crack Heads'. *The Economist*, 10 March 2005.

'The UN and Iran: Playing with fallout'. *The Economist*. 24 May 2007.

'UN Passes Iran Nuclear Sanctions'. 23 December 2006. http://news.bbc.co.uk.

'UN Security Council Report on Its Recent Visit to Sudan'. *Sudan Tribune*, 17 June 2005. www.globalpolicy.org.

The Universal House of Justice. Letter to a National Spiritual Assembly, 9 February 1967.

'U.S. and India Reach Agreement on Nuclear Cooperation'. *New York Times*, 2 March 2006.

Vedantam, Shankar. 'Nuclear Plants Not Keeping Track of Waste', *Washington Post*, 12 April 2005.

Wadhams, Nick. 'Sudan Won't Allow Darfur Peacekeepers to Use All Means Necessary'. Voice of America, 23 July 2007. http://voanews.com/english/2007-07-23-voa35.cfm.

'Who's in Charge?'. *The Economist*, 28 April 2005.

Wright, Robin. 'Nation Must Withdraw From Lebanon or Face Isolation'. *Washington Post*, 11 March 2005.

International and National Documents

Covenant of the League of Nations. www.Yale.edu/lawweb/Avalon/leagcov.htm#art8.

Letter from Secretary-General to the President of the General Assembly, and identical letter to the President of the Security Council, both 21 August 2000 (A/55/305–S/2000/809).

'Responsibility to Protect'. Report of the International Commission on Intervention and State Sovereignty. http://www.iciss.ca/menu-en.asp.

Schuman Declaration of 9 May 1950. http://europa.eu/abc/symbols/9-may/decl_en.htm.

Terms of Reference of High-Level Panel on Threats, Challenges and Change.

International Court of Justice documents:

Australian Declaration Under Paragraph 2 of Article 26 of the Statute of the International Court of Justice 1945, lodged at New York on 22 March. http://beta.austlii.edu.au/au/other/dfat/nia/2002/20.html.

Case Concerning the Territorial Dispute (Libyan Arab Jamahiriya/ Chad). http://www.icj-cij.org/docket/index.php?p1=3&p2=3&code =dt&case=83&k=cd.

Corfu Channel Case, ICJ Reports, 1948. www.icj-cij.org/docket/ index.php?p1=3&p2=3&code=cc&case=1&k=cd); ILR, vol. 15, pp. 349, 354.

ICJ Reports, 1949, p. 4; ILR, vol. 16, p. 155.

ICJ Reports, 1974, p. 3; ILR, vol. 55, p. 238.

ICJ Reports, 1974, p. 253; ILR, vol. 57, p. 350.

ICJ Reports, 1978, p. 3; ILR, vol. 60, p. 562.

ICJ Reports, 1980, p. 3; ILR, vol. 61, p. 530.

Land and Maritime Boundary (Cameroon v. Nigeria: Equatorial Guinea intervening), 2002 ICJ 303 (10 October). http://www.icj-cij. org/presscom/index.php?pr=294&pt=1&p1=6&p2=1.

Land and Maritime Boundary between Cameroon and Nigeria (Cameroon v. Nigeria: Equatorial Guinea intervening). http://www. icj-cij.org/docket/index.php?p1=3&p2=3&code=cn&case=94&k=74.

Maritime Delimitation and Territorial Questions (Qatar v. Bahrain), 2001 ICJ 40 (16 March). http://www.icj-cij.org/presscom/index.php? pr=234&pt=1&p1=6&p2=1.

Maritime Delimitation and Territorial Questions between Qatar and Bahrain (Qatar v. Bahrain). http://www.icj-cij.org/docket/index.php ?p1=3&p2=3&code=qb&case=87&k=61.

The Nuclear Tests cases (Australia vs. France; New Zealand vs. France), ICJ Reports, 1974. p. 253. http://www.icjcij.org/docket/ index.php?p1=3&p2=3&k=78&case=58&code=af&p3=4.

Sovereignty over Certain Frontier Land (Belgium/Netherlands). http://www.icj-cij.org/docket/index.php?p1=3&p2=3&code=bnl&ca se=38&k=32.

Sovereignty over Certain Frontier Land (Belgium/Netherlands), 1959 ICJ 209 (20 June). http://www.icj-cij.org/presscom/index.php ?p1=6&p2=1&p3=-1&pt=1&y=1959.

Statute of the International Court of Justice. http://www.icj-cij.org/ documents/index.php?p1=4&p2=2&p3=0.

Temple of Preah Vihear (Cambodia v. Thailand). http://www.icj-cij. org/docket/index.php?p1=3&p2=3&code=ct&case=45&k=46.

Temple of Preah Vihear (Cambodia v. Thailand), 1962 ICJ 6 (15 June). http://www.icj-cij.org/presscom/index.php?p1=6&p2=1&p3= -1&pt=1&y=1962.

Territorial Dispute (Libya/Chad), 1994 ICJ6 (3 February).

Territorial Dispute (Libyan Arab Jamahiriya/Chad): Judgement of the Court (03/02/1994–1994/4). http://www.icj-cij.org/presscom/ index.php?p1=6&p2=1&p3=-1&pt=1&y=1994.

United Nations documents:

Charter of the United Nations: http://www.un.org/aboutun/charter/.

CONVENTIONS AND TREATIES

Convention on the Prohibition of the Development, Production and Stockpiling of Bacteriological (Biological) and Toxin Weapons and on their Destruction (Biological Weapons Convention (BWC) or Biological and Toxin Weapons Convention (BTWC)). http://www.unog.ch/80256EE600585943/(httpPages)/ 04FBBDD6315AC720C1257180004B1B2F?OpenDocument.

Treaty on the Non-Proliferation of Nuclear Weapons (Nuclear Non-Proliferation Treaty (NPT)). http://www.un.org/events/npt2005/npttreaty.html.

GENERAL ASSEMBLY AND SECURITY COUNCIL RESOLUTIONS

Corfu Channel case, UNSCR, 9 April 1947.

S/1501.

S/RES/1718 (2006).

United Nations Millennium Declaration (A/res/55/2).

UNSCR 82 (1950).

UNSCR 598.

UNSCR 660 (1990).

UNSCR 667 (1990).

UNSCR 678 (1990).

UNSCR 687 (1991) (S/RES/687 (1991)). http://www.fas.org/news/un/iraq/sres/sres0687.htm.

UNSCR 1540 (2004): www.un.org/docs/sc.

UNSCR 1706.

UNSCR 1737 (23 December 2006); S/RES/1737(2006).

UNSCR 1747 (24 March 2007); S/RES/1747(2007).

World Summit Outcome, 24 October 2005 (A/60/L.1); A/RES/60/1.

PRESS RELEASES

Address delivered by Secretary-General Kofi Annan to the General Assembly, 23 September 2003, SG/SM/8891, GA/10157. www.un.org/News/Press/docs/2003.

'Security Council Condemns Continuing Exploitation of Natural Resources in Democratic Republic of Congo', SC/7925, 19 November 2003.

'Security Council Meets with Regional Organizations to Consider Ways to Strengthen Collective Security'. Press Release SC/7724, 4 November 2003.
www.un.org/news/press/docs/2003/sc7724.doc.htm.

REPORTS

'In Larger Freedom: Towards Development, Security and Human Rights For All'. Report of the Secretary General (A/59/2005). http://www.un.org/largerfreedom/report-largerfreedom.pdf.

Final report of the Panel of Experts on the Illegal Exploitation of Natural Resources and Other Forms of Wealth in the Democratic Republic of the Congo, S/2003/1027.

'A More Secure World: Our Shared Responsibility'. Report of the Secretary-General's High-Level Panel on Threats, Challenges and Change, United Nations 2004 (A/59/565). www.un.org/secureworld/panelmembers.html;
http://66.102.9.104/search?q=cache:pQYiL3caa4EJ:www.un.org/secureworld/report.pdf+Threats,+Challenges+and+Change,+%60A

+More+Secure+World:+Our+Shared+Responsibility%27+(A/59/56
5)+secretary+general+comments+diverse&hl=en&ct=clnk&cd=1&
gl=uk (accessed 16 June 2007).

Report of the Panel of Experts Appointed Pursuant to Security Council resolution 1306 (2000) in relation to Sierra Leone, S/2000/1195, 20 December 2000.

Report of the Panel of Experts Pursuant to Security Council resolution 1343 (2001) concerning Liberia, S/2001/1015, 26 October 2001.

Report of the Panel of Experts on Violations of Security Council Sanctions Against UNITA Pursuant to Security Council resolution 1237 (1999) of 7 May 1999 (S/2000/203, 10 March 2000).

Report of the Panel on United Nations Peace Operations (A/55/305 - S/2000/809).

Secretary-General. Address to the General Assembly, 23 September 2003. http://www.un.org/webcast/ga/58/statements/sg2eng030923.htm.

United States:

The Atlantic Charter. Department of State Executive Agreement Series no. 236. http: usinfo.state.gov/usa/infousa/facts/democrac/53.htm.

International Boundary Study by US State Department, no. 40 (revised), 23 November 1966.

Websites

African Union Mission in Sudan: http://enwikipedia.org/wiki/African_ Union_Mission_in_Sudan.

Bahá'í Community: www.bahai.org.

Bakassi: http://en.wikipedia.org/wiki/Bakassi.

International Law Commission: www.un.org/law/ilc.

Multinational Standby High Readiness Brigade for UN Operations: http://shirbrig.dk/html/main.htm.

Organization for the Prohibition of Chemical Weapons: www.opcw.org/ factsandfigures.

Report of the Panel on UN Peace Operations: www.un.org/peace/ reports/peace_operations/.

'Responsibility to Protect': www.iciss.ca/report-en.asp.

Secretary-General's Address to the 2005 World Summit, New York, 14 September 2005. http://www.globalpolicy.org/secgen/annanindex.htm.

UN Millennium Development Goals: www.un.org/millenniumgoals/.

World Summit Outcome (A/60/L.1): www.google.co.uk/search?sourcei d=navclient&ie=UTF-8&rlz=1T4SKPB_enGB211GB211&q=World +Summit+Outcome+A%2f60%2fL%2e1.

References and Notes

Introduction
1. Evans, 'Meeting the Challenge of War', p. 1.
2. 'A more secure world', p. 14.
3. 'One nation cannot defeat the extremists alone' and '[I]t will take the cooperation of many nations to stop the proliferation of dangerous weapons.' Donald Rumsfeld in Ames, 'Annan Seeks Overhaul of Security Measures', Associated Press article, 13 February 2005.
4. Tyson, 'Two Years Later, Iraq War Drains Military', Washington *Post*, 19 March 2005, A.01.
5. Knowlton, 'Bush's "Priceless" War', *Asia Times*, 25 February 2005.
6. O'Hanlon, 'Crisis on the Korean Peninsula'.
7. Kofi Annan says there is a yearning in many quarters for a new consensus on which to base collective action. See 'In Larger Freedom', p. 3.
8. Polgreen, 'West Africa Wins Again, with Twist', *New York Times* News Analysis, 27 February 2005; and 'African Union Lifts Togo Sanctions', *New York Times* online, 27 May 2005. Mr Gnassingbé subsequently ran for office as one of two candidates. He won 60 per cent of the votes, amidst claims that the elections were rigged. 'Who's in Charge?', *Economist*, 28 April 2005; and 'African Union Lifts Togo Sanctions', ibid.
9. 'Syria Ends Military Domination of Lebanon', 26 April 2005; Fattah, 'U.N. Envoy and Syrian President Meet', *New York Times*, 12 June 2005.
10. Wright, 'Nation Must Withdraw From Lebanon or Face Isolation', Washington *Post,* 11 March 2005.

Part 1: Blueprint for a Viable System of Collective Security
1. Those interested in learning more about Bahá'u'lláh or the Bahá'í Faith should refer to Shoghi Effendi, *God Passes By* and www.bahai.org.
2. The Universal House of Justice, *Promise of World Peace*, para. 36.

3. ibid. para. 37.
4. Shoghi Effendi, *World Order*, p. 36.
5. ibid. p. 193.
6. ibid. p. 43.
7. ibid.
8. ibid. p. 202.
9. Shoghi Effendi, in the Universal House of Justice, *Promise of World Peace*, para. 44.
10. Shoghi Effendi, *World Order*, p. 198.
11. Goormaghtigh, 'European Coal and Steel Community', *International Conciliation*, pp. 398–400.
12. Shoghi Effendi, *World Order*, p. 41.
13. 'A More Secure World', p. 17.
14. Shoghi Effendi, *World Order*, p. 42.
15. 'Abdu'l-Bahá, *Secret*, pp. 70–1.
16. ibid. p. 71.
17. ibid. p. 65; and Shoghi Effendi, *World Order*, p. 40.
18. *Bahai Scriptures*, p. 280.
19. Bahá'u'lláh, in Shoghi Effendi, *World Order*, p. 203.
20. ibid. p. 42.
21. ibid. p. 36.
22. 'Abdu'l-Bahá, *Secret*, p. 64.
23. ibid.
24. ibid.
25. ibid. pp. 64–5.
26. Shoghi Effendi, *World Order*, p, 40; 'Abdu'l-Bahá, *Secret*, p. 65.
27. 'Abdu'l-Bahá, *Secret*, p. 65.
28. ibid.; Bahá'u'lláh, *Gleanings*, p. 249; Bahá'u'lláh, *Tablets*, p. 165; Bahá'u'lláh, *Proclamation*, pp. 115, 165.
29. 'Abdu'l-Bahá, *Secret*, p. 65.
30. ibid.
31. 'Abdu'l-Bahá, quoted in, Shoghi Effendi, *World Order*, p. 192.
32. Bahá'u'lláh, quoted in ibid.
33. Bahá'u'lláh, *Epistle*, p. 14; Bahá'u'lláh, *Gleanings*, p. 288.
34. 'Abdu'l-Bahá, *Secret*, p. 65.
35. Shoghi Effendi, *World Order*, p. 202.
36. ibid. p. 41.
37. ibid. p. 192.
38. ibid. p. 41.
39. From a letter written on behalf of Shoghi Effendi to an individual, 19 November 1945, in *Lights of Guidance*, no. 1074, p. 319; and 'Abdu'l-Bahá, *Selections*, pp. 306–7.
40. 'Abdu'l-Bahá, *Selections*, pp. 306–7.

41. Shoghi Effendi, *World Order*, pp. 41 and 203.
42. ibid.
43. ibid.
44. 'Abdu'l-Bahá, *Selections*, pp. 306–7.
45. Shoghi Effendi, *World Order*, p. 40.
46. ibid. p. 37.
47. ibid. p. 203.
48. ibid. p. 204.
49. ibid.
50. ibid. pp. 40–1 and 203.
51. ibid. pp. 40–1.
52. ibid. p. 163.

Part 2: What Have We Built So Far?

1. Shoghi Effendi, *Advent*, pp. 72–3.
2. Shoghi Effendi, *World Order*, p. 169.
3. United Nations Millennium Declaration (A/res/55/2), p. 1.
4. ibid.
5. ibid. p. 2.
6. ibid.
7. UN Millennium Development Goals, www.un.org/millenni-umgoals/.
8. United Nations Millennium Declaration (A/res/55/2), p. 1.
9. Report of the Panel on United Nations Peace Operations (A/55/305-S/2000/809).
10. Identical letters dated 21 August 2000 from the Secretary-General to the President of the General Assembly and the President of the Security Council (A/55/305–S/2000/809).
11. ibid.
12. Report of the Panel on United Nations Peace Operations (A/55/305 – S/2000/809), p. 10.
13. ibid. p. 14.
14. ibid. p. 15.
15. Report of the Panel on United Nations Peace Operations (A/55/305-S/2000/809), p. 17.
16. ibid.
17. ibid. p. 46.
18. 'A More Secure World' (A/59/565).
19. Terms of Reference of High-Level Panel on Threats, Challenges and Change.
20. Secretary-General Address to the General Assembly, 23 September.

21. 'A More Secure World: Our Shared Responsibility' (A/59/565).
22. Note by the Secretary General, para. 25, in ibid.
23. 'A More Secure World: Our Shared Responsibility' (A/59/565), p. 16.
24. ibid. p. 1.
25. ibid. pp. 1–2.
26. ibid. p. 17.
27. ibid. p. 18.
28. ibid. p. 4.
29. ibid. pp. 2–3.
30. ibid. p. 17.
31. ibid. p. 3.
32. ibid. p. 19.
33. ibid. p. 32.
34. ibid. p. 3.
35. ibid. p. 62.
36. ibid. p. 38.
37. ibid. p. 35.
38. ibid.
39. ibid.
40. 'In Larger Freedom' (A/59/2005).
41. ibid. p. 6.
42. ibid. p. 53.
43. ibid. p. 3.
44. ibid. p. 6.
45. ibid.
46. ibid.
47. ibid. p. 25.
48. ibid. p. 31.
49. ibid. p. 33.
50. ibid.
51. ibid. p. 35.
52. ibid. p. 34.
53. ibid. p. 25.
54. ibid. pp. 28–9.
55. ibid. p. 36.
56. ibid. p. 38.
57. ibid. p. 48.
58. ibid. p. 40.
59. ibid. p. 23.
60. ibid. p. 40.
61. World Summit Outcome (A/60/L.1).
62. 'UN Assembly Approves Weakened Summit Blueprint', Reuters, 13

September 2005; and Lederer, 'Annan Appeals to World Leaders at Summit', Associated Press, 15 September 2005.

63. Alas, owing to cynical nominations for membership, the new Human Rights Council is already being discredited in some quarters.

64. Shaw, *International Law*, p. 357.

65. ibid. p. 354.

66. ibid. p. 355.

67. There is another way in which parties to a border dispute can attempt to resolve it without going to the Court. That method involves agreement between the parties to establish an independent boundary commission which will arbitrate the dispute and render a final decision not subject to appeal. This was the course agreed to by Ethiopia and Eritrea as part of the Algiers peace settlement between them.

68. Maritime Delimitation and Territorial Questions between Qatar and Bahrain (Qatar *v.* Bahrain); and Maritime Delimitation and Territorial Questions (Qatar *v*. Bahrain), 2001 I.C.J. 40 (March 16).

69. Sovereignty over Certain Frontier Land (Belgium/Netherlands); Sovereignty over Certain Frontier Land (Belgium/Netherlands), 1959 I.C.J. 209 (June 20).

70. Temple of Preah Vihear (Cambodia *v.* Thailand); Temple of Preah Vihear (Cambodia *v*. Thailand), 1962 I.C.J. 6 (June 15).

71. International Boundary Study by US State Department, no. 40 (revised), 23 November 1966.

72. Land and Maritime Boundary between Cameroon and Nigeria (Cameroon *v.* Nigeria: Equatorial Guinea intervening); Land and Maritime Boundary (Cameroon *v*. Nigeria: Equatorial Guinea intervening), 2002 I.C.J. 303 (Oct. 10).

73. See http://en.wikipedia.org/wiki/Bakassi; and http://www.answers. com/topic/bakassi; 'NIGERIA: Rehabilitation, harassment concerns mar Bakassi pullout' at http://www.irinnews.org; and 'Nigerian troops leaving Bakassi' at http://news.bbc.co.uk/2/hi/Africa).

74. Case Concerning the Territorial Dispute (Libyan Arab Jamahiriya/ Chad); Territorial Dispute (Libya/Chad), 1994 I.C.J. 6 (Feb. 3).

75. *Asia Times*, 8 March 2005.

76. Australian Declaration Under Paragraph 2 of Article 26 of the Statute of the International Court of Justice 1945, lodged at New York on 22 March.

77. UN Security Council Resolution 687 (1991) (S/RES/687 (1991)).

78. *Basic Facts about the United Nations*, p. 102.

79. Evans, 'Responsibility to Protect', in *Progressive Politics*.

80. 'In Larger Freedom' (A/59/2005), p. 6.

81. Kagan, 'The Crisis of Legitimacy', p. 1.
82. ibid.
83. ibid.
84. 'In Larger Freedom' (A/59/2005), p. 35.
85. ibid.
86. Evans, 'Meeting the Challenge of War', p. 1.
87. ibid.
88. ibid.
89. Evans, 'Responsibility to Protect', in *Progressive Politics*.
90. 'Responsibility to Protect', Report of ICISS Commission.
91. ibid. p. 69.
92. 'A More Secure World: Our Shared Responsibility' (A/59/565), para. 203.
93. 'In Larger Freedom' (A/59/2005), p. 35.
94. ibid.
95. World Summit Outcome (A/60/L.1), p. 31.
96. Bahá'u'lláh, *Epistle*, p. 89.
97. Bahá'u'lláh, *Tablets*, p. 22.
98. From a letter of the Universal House of Justice to a National Spiritual Assembly, 9 February 1967, in *Lights*, no. 1354, p. 407.
99. 'Responsibility to Protect', Report of ICISS Commission, sect. 1, para. 35.
100. ibid. sect. 2.
101. Solana, 'Securing Peace in Europe'.
102. 'In Larger Freedom' (A/59/2005), p. 4.
103. ibid. p. 7.
104. ibid. p. 6.
105. ibid. p. 3.
106. 'Abdu'l-Bahá, quoted in Shoghi Effendi, *World Order*, p. 39.
107. 'In Larger Freedom' (A/59/2005), p. 6.
108. ibid. p. 3.
109. ibid. p. 25.
110. ibid. p. 39.
111. ibid. p. 6.
112. The Universal House of Justice, *Promise of World Peace*, para. 2.
113. 'In Larger Freedom' (A/59/2005), p. 3.
114. *Basic Facts about the United Nations*, p. 259.
115. 'In Larger Freedom' (A/59/2005), p. 51.
116. Nuclear Non-Proliferation Treaty, Article X (1).
117. ibid. Article III.
118. *Basic Facts about the United Nations*, p. 103.
119. 'Iran Says it's not afraid of Security Council', *New York Times* online, 8 November 2005.

120. Security Council Resolution 1737 of 23 December 2006, S/RES/1737(2006); and 'UN passes Iran nuclear sanctions' at http://news.bbc.co.uk.

121. Security Council Resolution 1747 of 24 March 2007, S/RES/1747(2007); and 'Security Council tightens sanctions against Iran over uranium enrichment' at http://www.un.org/apps/news.

122. 'Iranian Warns Against Added Nuclear Sanctions', Associated Press, 6 June 2007, at www.nytimes.com.

123. 'The UN and Iran: Playing with fallout', Economist, 24 May 2007.

124. Nuclear Non-Proliferation Treaty, Article VI.

125. Basic Facts about the United Nations, p. 112.

126. 'A More Secure World' (A/59/565), p. 40.

127. Website of the Organization for the Prohibition of Chemical Weapons at http://www.opcw.org/factsandfigures.

128. Biological Weapons Convention, Article II.

129. BBC News, 2 March 2006; see also 'Nuclear Confusion', The Economist, 22 October 2005, p. 31.

130. Secretary-General Address to the 2005 World Summit, New York, 14 September 2005.

131. New York Times, 31 October 2005 (see database under Arms Control).

132. UN Charter, Article 24.

133. UN Charter, Article 39.

134. UNSCR 82; S/1501.

135. UNSCR 502.

136. UNSCR 598.

137. UNSCR 660 (1990).

138. 'A More Secure World: Our Shared Responsibility' (A/59/565), p. 31.

139. ibid.

140. Hill, 'Military Staff Committee', p. 2.

141. ibid. pp. 4–5.

142. UNSCR 82 (1950); S/1501.

143. UNSCR 660 (1990).

144. UNSCR 667 (1990).

145. UNSCR 678 (1990).

146. Shaw, International Law, p. 868, note 217.

147. 'The UN gets tougher: After years of inaction, UN peacekeepers crack heads', The Economist, 10 March 2005. See also www.un.org/Depts/dpko/missions/monuc/facts.html.

148. 'A More Secure World: Our Shared Responsibility' (A/59/565), p. 32.

149. ibid.

150. Press release SG/SM/8891 GA/10157, 23 September 2003, www.un.org and http://www.un.org/webcast/ga/58/statements/sg2eng030923.htm.
151. 'Responsibility to Protect', section entitled 'Synopsis – The Responsibility to Protect: Principles for Military Intervention'.
152. UN Charter, Article 92.
153. Statute of the International Court of Justice, Article 34.
154. UN Charter, Article 93; see also Eyffinger, *International Court of Justice*.
155. Shaw, *International Law*, p. 755.
156. ibid. p. 761.
157. Rosenne, *Law and Practice*, vol. 1, chapter 10.
158. Corfu Channel case, ICJ Reports, 1948, pp. 15, 31–2; 15 ILR, pp. 349, 354; and UNSCR 9 April 1947 recommending that parties submit their case to the World Court.
159. The Nuclear Tests case, ICJ Reports, 1974, p. 477.
160. UN Charter, Article 94.
161. Shaw, *International Law*, p. 766.
162. ICJ Reports, 1949, p. 4; 16 ILR, p. 155.
163. ICJ Reports, 1974, p. 3; 55 ILR, p. 238.
164. ICJ Reports, 1980, p. 3; 61 ILR, p. 530.
165. ICJ Reports, 1974, p. 3; 55 ILR, p. 238.
166. ICJ Reports, 1974, p. 253; 57 ILR, p. 350.
167. ICJ Reports, 1978, p. 3; 60 ILR, p. 562.
168. ICJ Reports, 1980, p. 3; 61 ILR, p. 530.
169. Shaw, *International Law*, p. 748.
170. Judge Oda, quoted in ibid. p. 749. ICJ Reports, 1987, pp. 10, 13, 97; ILR, pp. 139, 142.
171. Merrills, *International Disputes Settlement*, p. 126 and Brauer, 'International Conflict Resolution', 23 Va JIL, 1982–3, p. 463, quoted in Shaw, *International Law*, p. 748.
172. Shaw, *International Law*, p. 776.
173. The Atlantic Charter.
174. ibid. eighth principle.
175. ibid.
176. Hoopes and Brinkley, *FDR and the Creation of the U.N.*, p. 27.
177. The final version concluded by expressing the intention of Roosevelt and Churchill to 'aid and encourage all other practicable measures which will lighten for peace-loving peoples the crushing burden of armaments'. The Atlantic Charter.
178. Hoopes and Brinkley, *FDR and the Creation of the U.N.*, pp. 45–6.
179. ibid. p. 19.
180. ibid. p. 110.

181. Cited in ibid. p. 20.
182. ibid. p. 56.
183. ibid. pp. 65–6.
184. ibid. p. 113, footnote 7, which refers to Postwar Planning Draft Statement, 15 March 1944, State Department Postwar Planning Committee, Box 141, National Archives, Washington DC.
185. Dinan, *Europe Recast*, p. xiii.
186. Dedman, *Origins and Development of the European Union*, p. 61.
187. Churchill, speech given in Zurich, 19 September 1946, http://www.ena.lu/mce.cfm.
188. Dinan, *Europe Recast*, p. 24.
189. Fontaine, *New Idea for Europe*, p. 12.
190. Goormaghtigh, 'European Coal and Steel Community', *International Conciliation*, vol. 30, p. 348, note 48.
191. ibid. p. 57, quoting Robert Marjolin, a contemporary observer describing the ECSC.
192. Schuman Declaration, 9 May 1950.
193. Dinan, *Europe Recast*, p. 98.
194. ibid. p. 199.

Part 3: What We Should Build Next

1. Luncheon talk of Henry Kissinger, 21 April 2005 at the Metropolitan Club, Washington DC.
2. The Universal House of Justice, *Promise of World Peace*, para. 37.
3. Evans, 'Responsibility to Protect', in *Progressive Politics*, July 2003.
4. 'In Larger Freedom' (A/59/2005), p. 6.
5. Sands, *Lawless World*, p. xvi.
6. From Bahá'u'lláh, Kalimát-i-Firdawsíyyih, in *Tablets*, p. 67.
7. Kofi Annan in 'Annan Opens World Summit with plea not to let down billions around the globe'. UN News Centre, www.un.org/apps/news, 14 September 2005.
8. Sanger, 'Month of talks fails to bolster nuclear treaty', *New York Times*, 28 May 2005.
9. Professor Harold Koh, Dean of Yale Law School, speaking at ASIL panel called 'Is International Law Useful to the US' at 30 March–2 April 2005 meeting in Washington DC.
10. 'Abdu'l-Bahá, *Secret,* pp. 70–1
11. ibid. p. 71.
12. Evans, 'Responsibility to Protect', *Progressive Politics*, July 2003. www.icg.org.
13. Levi and O'Hanlon, *Future of Arms Control*, p. 12.
14. Blix, *Disarming Iraq*, pp. 4 and 11.
15. 'In Larger Freedom' (A/59/2005), p. 34.

16. Graham, 'Pentagon Strategy Aims to Block Internal Threats to Foreign Forces', in *Washington Post*, 19 March 2005, p. A02.
17. ibid.
18. 'Iran's nuclear politics: Mahmoud and the atomic mullahs', *Economist*, 30 June 2005.
19. 'In Larger Freedom' (A/59/2005), p. 33.
20. See Gareth Evans's address in Addis Ababa to the Africa Policy Forum, 'UN Reform: Why It Matters For Africa', 26 August 2005.
21. Address delivered by Secretary-General Kofi Annan to the General Assembly, 23 September 2003.
22. Strauss, 'Darfur and the Genocide Debate', *Foreign Affairs*, January/February 2005, p. 129.
23. Ashton B. Carter, speaking at an annual meeting of the World Economic Forum in 2 February 1999.
24. Evans, 'Aceh is Building Peace From Its Ruins' in *International Herald Tribune*, 23 December 2005.
25. 'IRA "has destroyed all its arms"', BBC article reported at http://news.bbc.co.uk/1/hi/northern_ireland/4283444.stm.
26. 'NI deal struck in historic talks', reported by the BBC, 26 March 2007, at http://news.bbc.co.uk/1/hi/northern_ireland_/6494599.stm; and 'Ulster Factions Agree to a Plan For Joint Rule', reported on 27 March 2007 by Eamon Quinn and Alan Cowell at www.nytimes.com.
27. 'Two Former Enemies are Sworn in to Lead Northern Ireland's Government', reported by Alan Cowell and Eamon Quinn, 9 May 2007, www.nytimes.com.
28. In an ironic twist, having itself refused to give up its arms, upon seizing power in the Gaza strip in June 2007, Hamas called for a voluntary drop-off of arms, which proved unsuccessful. See 'Hamas arms roundup still leaves plenty of guns in Gaza', reported by the Associated Press, 21 June 2007 at http:/www.iht.com/articles/ap/2007/06/21/Africa/ME-GEN-Palestinians-Arms-Roundup.php.
29. See 'Quartet Urges Palestinians to Dismantle Militias', Reuters, in *New York Times*, 20 September 2005.
30. 'Hamas hails "liberation" of Gaza', reported by BBC, 14 June 2007, at http:///news.bbc.co.uk/2/hi/middle_east/6751079.stm.
31. 'Hamas controls Gaza, says it will stay in power', reported by CNN, 14 June 2007, at http://www.cnn.com/2007/WORLD/meast/06/14/gaza/index.html; and 'Palestinian President Dissolves Government', reported by Steven Erlanger and Graham Bowley on 14 June 2007 at www.nytimes.com.
32. 'Backing Fatah and Abbas, Egypt Organizes Summit Meeting for

Palestinian Leader', by Steven Erlanger, reported on 22 June 2007 at www.nytimes.com.

33. See, for example, the UK's articulation of the doctrine of humanitarian intervention described by Christine Gray in her book *International Law and the Use of Force*, pp. 29–30.

34. Evans, 'The Responsibility to Protect'.

35. World Summit Outcome (A/60/L.1).

36. 'A More Secure World' (A/59/565), pp. 66–7.

37. 'In Larger Freedom' (A/59/2005), p. 52. The Charter has been amended twice to enlarge the membership of the Security Council and the Economic and Social Council.

38. Paul and Nahory, 'Theses Towards a Democratic Reform of the UN Security Council'.

39. Report of the Panel on United Nations Peace Operations (A/55/305-S/2000/809), p. 10.

40. S/RES/1441 (2002), clauses 4, 11 and 12.

41. Blix, 'Disarming Iraq', p. 183.

42. Sciolino and Broad, 'At the Heart of the United Front On Iran, Vagueness on Crucial Terms', *New York Times*, 18 June 2006.

43. 'A More Secure World: Our Shared Responsibility' (A/59/565), p. 12.

44. 'Interview with Dr Mohammed ElBaradei, Director General of the International Atomic Energy Agency', *Fletcher Forum*, p. 38.

45. 'A More Secure World: Our Shared Responsibility' (A/59/565), p. 34.

46. Blix, 'Disarming Iraq', p. 207.

47. ibid. p. 182.

48. Pollack and Takeyh, 'Taking on Tehran', in *Foreign Affairs*, March/April 2005, pp. 30–1.

49. 'Iran and nuclear diplomacy – A yes or a no?', *Economist*, 28 June 2007.

50. Sanger. 'Atomic Agency Concludes Iran is Stepping Up Nuclear Work', *New York Times*, 14 May 2007, and Jahn, 'Iran Makes Major Nuclear Concessions', Washington *Post*, 13 July 2007.

51. 'Iran and nuclear diplomacy – A yes or a no?', *Economist*, 28 June 2007.

52. Blix, *Disarming Iraq*, p. 33.

53. ibid. p. 179.

54. Evans, 'Genocide or Crime: Actions Speak Louder than Words in Darfur', *The European Voice*, 18 February 2005 and Evans, 'Darfur: What Next?'

55. Strauss, 'Darfur and the Genocide Debate', *Foreign Affairs*, January/February 2005, p. 131.

56. S/RES/1706 (2006).
57. International Crisis Group, 'Crisis in Darfur'.
58. 'UN Security Council Report on Its Recent Visit to Sudan', *Sudan Tribune*, 17 June 2005.
59. 'From Brussels Without Love', *Economist*, 24 February 2005.
60. *Economist*, 26 February–4 March 2005, pp. 48–9.
61. Brinkley, 'U.S. Official Says North Korea Could be Bluffing on Nuclear Arms', *New York Times*, 16 February 2005.
62. Harrison, 'Did North Korea Cheat?', *Foreign Affairs*, January/February 2005, pp. 100–1.
63. S/RES/1718 (2006), and 'North Korea's Nuclear Test: the Fallout', *Asia Briefing*, 13 November 2006.
64. 'A More Secure World: Our Shared Responsibility' (A/59/565), p. 16.
65. Zak, *Iran's Nuclear Policy and the IAEA*, p. 53.
66. Blix, *Disarming Iraq*, p. 47.
67. Zak, *Iran's Nuclear Policy and the IAEA*, p. 44.
68. Dinmore, 'US Draws Up List of Unstable Countries', *Financial Times*, 28 March 2005.
69. 'A More Secure World' (A/59/565), p. 34.
70. 'Famine Relief – Starving for the Cameras: People dying from hunger like those in Niger should not have to wait for the TV crews to arrive', *Economist*, 18 August 2005.
71. Zak, *Iran's Nuclear Policy and the IAEA*, p. 66.
72. ibid. p. 67.
73. ibid.
74. ibid. p. 68.
75. ibid.
76. Brahimi Report, pp. 14–15.
77. Diehl, 'Once Again: Nations Agree Genocide Must be Stopped', *Washington Post*, 15 May 2005, p. B01.
78. 'A More Secure World' (A/59/565), pp. 18–19.
79. Diehl, 'Once Again: Nations Agree Genocide Must be Stopped', *Washington Post*, 15 May 2005, p. B01.
80. Falk and Krieger, 'United Nations Should be Less Reliant on US', *Daily Bruin*, 13 November 2002.
81. Dallaire, *Shake Hands with the Devil*, p. 374.
82. Statement of Mark Schneider to the Woodrow Wilson International Center for Scholars, 'The Responsibility to Protect – The Capacity to Prevention and the Capacity to Intervene', Washington DC, 5 May 2004.
83. 'A More Secure World: Our Shared Responsibility' (A/59/565), p. 8.
84. 'In Larger Freedom' (A/59/2005), p. 30.

85. 'A More Secure World: Our Shared Responsibility' (A/59/565), p. 53.
86. Bahá'í International Community, *Turning Point for All Nations*, para. III, B, 2.
87. Brahimi Report, p. 16.
88. 'In Larger Freedom' (A/59/2005), p. 31.
89. ibid.
90. Brahimi Report, p. 19.
91. Diehl, 'Once Again: Nations Agree Genocide Must Be Stopped', Washington *Post*, 15 May 2005, p. B01.
92. Johansen, 'Put Teeth in "Never Again" Vow With Fast, Full-Scale UN Response', in *Christian Science Monitor*, 7 September 2004; Langille, 'Preventing Genocide', *Globe and Mail*, 19 October 2004, p. 3.
93. Diehl, 'Once Again: Nations Agree Genocide Must Be Stopped', Washington *Post*, 15 May 2005, p. B01.
94. Data from the Carnegie Commission on Preventing Deadly Conflict and from the International Commission on Intervention and State Sovereignty, cited in Johansen, 'Put Teeth in "Never Again" Vow with Fast, Full-Scale UN Response', in *Christian Science Monitor*, 7 September 2004, p. 2.
95. 'In Larger Freedom' (A/59/2005), p. 31.
96. ibid.
97. Tan, 'Regional Security Partners'.
98. O'Hanlon and Mochizuki, *Crisis on the Korean Peninsula*, p. 153.
99. ibid. p. 164.
100. 'A More Secure World: Our Shared Responsibility' (A/59/565), p. 85.
101. Fukuyama, 'Re-Envisioning Asia', *Foreign Affairs*, January/February 2005, p. 75.
102. Quoted in Fattah, 'Conference of Arab Leaders Yields Little of Significance', *New York Times*, 24 March 2005.
103. Pollack and Takeyh, 'Taking on Tehran', *Foreign Affairs*, March/April 2005, p. 29.
104. 'FBI opens anti-gang office in Central America', Reuters, *New York Times*, 4 May 2004.
105. 'APEC Wants Bigger Push on N. Korea Nuclear Talks', Reuters, *New York Times*, 19 November 2005.
106. O'Hanlon and Mochizuki, *Crisis on the Korean Peninsula*, p. 149.
107. ibid. p. 155.
108. Fukuyama, 'Re-Envisioning Asia', *Foreign Affairs*, January/February 2005, p. 75.
109. 'S. Korea to Play Neutral Role in Asia', Associated Press, *New York Times*, 10 April 2005.

110. 'A More Secure World: Our Shared Responsibility' (A/59/565), p. 86.
111. 'NATO's Assistance to the African Union for Darfur'.
112. 2005 World Summit Outcome, A/RES/60/1, 24 October 2005, Article 93, p. 23.
113. African Union Mission in Sudan at http://enwikipedia.org/wiki/African_Union_Mission_in_Sudan.
114. 'A More Secure World: Our Shared Responsibility' (A/59/565), p. 85.
115. Abbas, *Regional Organisations and the Development of Collective Security*.
116. 'AU Agrees to Enlarge Darfur Force', *Aljazeera*, 29 April 2005.
117. Security Council Resolution 1706.
118. 'AU extends Darfur troops mandate', 21 September 2006.
119. 'Sudan rejects use of force by UN–AU Darfur mission', 22 July 2007, Reuters Africa; and Wadhams, 'Sudan Won't Allow Darfur Peacekeepers to Use All Means Necessary', 23 July 2007, Voice of America.
120. 'Security Council Meets with Regional Organizations to Consider Ways to Strengthen Collective Security', Press Release SC/7724, 4 November 2003.
121. 'A More Secure World: Our Shared Responsibility' (A/59/565), p. 39.
122. Evans, 'Meeting the Challenge of War'.
123. 'A More Secure World: Our Shared Responsibility' (A/59/565), p. 40.
124. 'In Larger Freedom' (A/59/2005), p. 28.
125. Moodie, 'Confronting the Biological and Chemical Weapons Challenge', *The Fletcher Forum*, Winter 2004, vol. 28, no. 1, p. 43.
126. Levi and O'Hanlon, *Future of Arms Control*, p. 1.
127. ElBaradei, 'In-depth Interview with the Director General of the International Atomic Energy Agency', *The Fletcher Forum*, Winter 2004, vol 28, no. 1, p. 42.
128. Levi and O'Hanlon, *Future of Arms Control*, p. 13.
129. 'Curbing Proliferation', *Economist*, 28 April 2005, p. 12.
130. 'Bracing for Penalties, Iran Threatens to Withdraw from Nuclear Treaty', *New York Times*, 12 February 2006.
131. Levi and O'Hanlon, *Future of Arms Control*, p. 136.
132. 'A More Secure World: Our Shared Responsibility' (A/59/565), p. 45.
133. 'Curbing Proliferation', *Economist*, 28 April 2005, p. 12.
134. Covenant of the League of Nations, Article 8.
135. *Basic Facts about the United Nations*, p. 116.

136. Millennium Declaration, Section II, article 9.
137. 'A More Secure World: Our Shared Responsibility' (A/59/565), p. 39, article 112.
138. 'ElBaradei: Protect Nuclear Material', Associated Press, 6 December 2005.
139. Maitra, 'India Takes its Arms Beefs to the UN', *Asia Times*, 24 February 2005.
140. 'A More Secure World: Our Shared Responsibility' (A/59/565), p. 44.
141. Bahree, 'IEA Warns of Impending Crunch in Gas Supply', *Wall Street Journal*, 9 July 2007.
142. 'Experts Discuss Nuclear Power as Energy', Associated Press, *New York Times,* 21 March 2005.
143. ibid.
144. 'The Atomic Elephant', *Economist,* 30 April 2005, p. 53.
145. 'France Will Get Fusion Reactor. To seek a Future Energy Source', 29 June 2005.
146. 'Russia Drafts Ambitious Nuclear Power Plan', Associated Press, 28 February 2006.
147. 'The Atomic Elephant', *The Economist*, 30 April 2005, p. 63.
148. 'U.S. and India Reach Agreement on Nuclear Cooperation', *New York Times*, 2 March 2006.
149. 'Iran Plans to Build a Second Nuclear Plant', Associated Press, 5 December 2005.
150. 'Curbing Proliferation: How to Stop the Spread of the Bomb', *Economist*, 28 April 2005, p. 12.
151. 'Accepting Nobel, ElBaradei Urges a Rethinking of Nuclear Strategy', *New York Times*, 11 December 2005.
152. 'A More Secure World: Our Shared Responsibility' (A/59/565), p. 44.
153. 'Bush and Putin Want Iran to Treat Uranium in Russia', *New York Times*, 19 November 2005.
154. 'In Larger Freedom' (A/59/2005), p. 25.
155. 'Talks between Iran and Europe End without Agreement', Associated Press, *New York Times*, 3 March 2006.
156. Blix, *Disarming Iraq*, pp. 82 and 179.
157. Zak, *Iran's Nuclear Policy and the IAEA*, p. 40.
158. UNSCR 1540 (2004), Article 2.
159. 'A More Secure World: Our Shared Responsibility' (A/59/565), p. 11.
160. Sumner, 'Territorial Disputes at the International Court of Justice', *Duke Journal*, 2004, vol 53, p. 1779.
161. Hamilton, 'The Idea of the Nation State is Fatally Flawed', *Independent*, 19 August 2004.

162. Territorial Dispute (Libya/Chad), 1994 ICJ 6 (February 3).

163. Address by Judge Stephen M. Schwebel, President of the International Court of Justice, to the General Assembly of the United Nations, 27 October 1998.

164. Sands, *Lawless World*, pp. xvii–xviii.

165. Posner, 'All Justice, Too, Is Local', *New York Times*, 30 December 2004.

166. Prof. Eric A. Posner, American Society of International Law (ASIL) Panel, Washington DC, Spring 2005.

167. Heiner Schulz, ibid. See also Steinberg, 'Judicial Lawmaking at the WTO', *American Journal of International Law*, vol. 98, April 2004, p. 247.

168. 'Abdu'l-Bahá, *Selections*, pp. 306–7.

169. Commission on Global Governance, *Our Global Neighbourhood*.

170. 'In Larger Freedom' (A/59/2005), p. 36; and World Summit Outcome (A/RES/60/1), 24 October 2005, p. 30.

171. Charney, 'The Impact on the International System of the Growth of International Courts and Tribunals', *Journal of International Law and Politics*, vol. 31, pp. 702–3.

172. Commission on Global Governance, *Our Global Neighbourhood*.

173. United Nations Millennium Declaration (A/res/55/2), p. 3.

174. 'In Larger Freedom' (A/59/2005), p. 51.

175. *Basic Facts about the United Nations*, p. 261 and http://www.un.org/law/ilc/.

176. 'In Larger Freedom' (A/59/2005), p. 36.

177. 'Global Oil Producers Discuss Supply', Reuters, reported by *New York Times* online, 19 November 2005.

178. 'Global or National: The Perils Facing Big Oil', *Economist*, 28 April 2005.

179. Vedantam, 'Nuclear Plants Not Keeping Track of Waste', *Washington Post*, 12 April 2005, p. A19.

180. Final report of the Panel of Experts on the Illegal Exploitation of Natural Resources and Other Forms of Wealth in the Democratic Republic of the Congo (S/2003/1027) and subsequent press release by the Security Council entitled 'Security Council Condemns Continuing Exploitation of Natural Resources in Democratic Republic of Congo' (SC/7925), 19 November 2003; Report of the Panel of Experts Appointed Pursuant to Security Council Resolution 1306 (2000) in Relation to Sierra Leone (S/2000/1195), 20 December 2000; Report of the Panel of Experts pursuant to Security Council Resolution 1343 (2001) concerning Liberia (S/2001/1015), 26 October 2001; Report of the Panel of Experts on Violations of Security Council Sanctions Against UNITA pur-

suant to Security Council Resolution 1237 (1999) of 7 May 1999 (S/2000/203), 10 March 2000.

181. These NGOs include Global Policy Forum, Global Witness, World Vision, Human Rights Watch, International Peace Academy, Save the Children Alliance and the International Crisis Group.
182. Grono, 'Natural Resources and Conflict', EIS Symposium on Sustainable Development and Security, European Parliament, Brussels, 31 May 2006.
183. Grono, 'Addressing the links between conflicts and natural resources', Conference on Security, Development and Forest Conflict, Brussels, 9 February 2006.
184. Perlez and Johnson, 'Behind Gold's Glitter', *New York Times*, 24 October 2005.
185. ibid.
186. Falk and Strauss, 'Toward Global Parliament', *Foreign Affairs*, vol. 80, no. 1, January/February 2001.
187. Bahá'í International Community, *Turning Point for All Nations*, p. 8.
188. McGann and Johnstone, 'The Power Shift and the NGO Credibility Crisis', *Journal of World Affairs*, Winter/Spring 2005.

Conclusion

1. Dwight Eisenhower speaking to UK Prime Minister Macmillan on a television broadcast, London, 31 August 1959.

Index

This index is alphabetized word for word, hence 'civil society' precedes 'civilization'.

BEYOND THE CULTURE OF CONTEST

FROM ADVERSARIALISM TO MUTUALISM IN AN AGE OF INTERDEPENDENCE

by Michael Karlberg

How can social change come about? Is it possible to have democratic government without political parties? Can we have a productive economy without unfettered and aggressive competition? How can social and ecological ills be addressed without resorting to a 'culture of protest'?

Adversarialism has become the predominant strand in contemporary western-liberal societies. Throughout the public sphere, competitive and conflictual practices have become institutionalised norms.

In his analysis of present-day society, Michael Karlberg puts forward the thesis that our present 'culture of contest' is both socially unjust and ecologically unsustainable and that the surrounding 'culture of protest' is an inadequate response to the social and ecological problems it generates. The development of non-adversarial structures and practices is imperative.

Dr Karlberg considers various historical and contemporary expressions of mutualism, including expressions within feminism, systems theory, ecology and environmentalism, communication theory and alternative dispute resolution, and presents a case study of the Bahá'í community and its experience as a working, non-adversarial model of social practice. The prescriptions and practices of the Bahá'í community provide a viable and workable alternative to the culture of contest.

Michael Karlberg is Associate Professor in the Department of Communication at Western Washington University. His research and writing focus on the relationship between communication, culture and conflict. He also teaches in the area of 'critical media literacy', helping students understand the ways that we are influenced by, and can also influence, our mass-mediated cultural environments.

288 pages   21.0 x 13.8 cm (8.25 x 5.5 in)
Softcover   ISBN 978-0-85398-489-1

MANNA FROM HEAVEN

FROM DIVINE SPEECH TO ECONOMIC SCIENCE
by Dalton Garis

Is it legitimate to discuss religious and divine topics in terms and contexts normally reserved for purely scientific discussions? What is the relationship between economics and the teachings of the religions that have appeared in the Middle East? Why is it important to understand the difference between ideology and rational inquiry?

Dr Dalton Garis is a well-known economist with a deep knowledge of Middle Eastern religions, customs and interests. He is also a Bahá'í and explores the answers to these questions in his thought-provoking book. Correlating the Bahá'í and Muslim teachings with economics, he uses the concept of 'prophetic dialogues' or 'divine speech' to indicate true religion (as opposed to ideology) and demonstrates how it harmonizes with science. His exposition of the elements of economics is reinforced by the liberal use of passages from the Holy Qur'án and the Bahá'í scriptures, providing unique insights into economics, society and religion and stimulating a much-needed discussion on the harmony of science and spiritual teachings.

288 pages   23.4 x 15.6 cm (9.25 x 6.2 in)
Soft Cover   ISBN 978-0-85398-515-0

THE LAST WAR

RACISM, SPIRITUALITY AND THE FUTURE OF CIVILIZATION
by Mark L Perry

Overcoming racism, respiritualizing society, establishing the unity of all people and creating true civilization is the last war. To fight it, we need to understand how society got to this point:

• how racism developed

• why society became despiritualized

• what happened to our sense of oneness

and we need to develop a vision of how the world can move from its turbulent adolescence to its long awaited maturity, a time when all nations and races will become united in a global civilization.

Mark Perry uses the analogy of an archaeological dig to survey the historical roots of racism and the despiritualization of society, century by century, back from the modern day to their primitive, prehistoric past. Holding out a vision provided by Bahá'u'lláh, the founder of the Bahá'í Faith, more than a century ago, he explains how humanity can lay the groundwork for a new civilization.

Mark Perry grew up in Swarthmore, Pennsylvania. He earned a BA in music and physics at Haverford College and a MA in anthropology and a PhD in the history of culture at the University of Chicago. He and his wife and three children live in Beirut, Lebanon, where he teaches social science and cultural studies at the Lebanese American University.

352 pages   23.4 x 15.6 cm (9.25 x 6 in)
Soft Cover   ISBN 978-0-85398-491-3

BLUEPRINT FOR A NEW WORLD

USING THE POWER OF THE REVELATION OF BAHÁ'U'LLÁH TO REVITALIZE THE INDIVIDUAL AND SOCIETY

by Craig Loehle

What does it mean to build the 'Kingdom of God on earth'? Why a building process and not a miraculous process, a snap of God's fingers? Is there a model for the future society? And if so, is it something we would want?

Craig Loehle suggests that a new world view is needed for society to take the next steps of social and material progress. Such a world view, he proposes, can only be provided by a new revelation of guidance from God. He thus explores the teachings of Bahá'u'lláh, founder of the Bahá'í Faith, as this new divine revelation and examines the role Bahá'ís play as inventors in the development of the new social and economic systems that will form the pattern for a peaceful, united and just future society.

192 pages   216 x 138 mm (8.5 x 5.5 ins)
Soft Cover   ISBN 978-0-85398-514-3

GLOBAL GOVERNANCE AND THE LESSER PEACE

by Fuad Katirai

People everywhere are rapidly coming to recognize the reality of the brotherhood of humankind but still the world is burdened with systems of international governance that were created to favour the victors of a war that ended over half a century ago and which consistently maintain the ascendancy of the rich nations. The desperate need for a system of international organization and administration that is fair to all the world's people and reflects the essential oneness of mankind is now clear. But how should this be brought about?

160 pages   18.1 x 12.3 cm. (7 x 4.75 in)
Soft Cover   ISBN: 978-0-85398-453-0

HUMAN RIGHTS, THE UN AND THE BAHÁ'ÍS
IN IRAN
by Nazila Ghanea

A comprehensive account of the interaction between the United Nations human rights system and one human rights situation – that of the Bahá'ís in Iran. The Bahá'í community in Iran is the largest religious minority in the country yet does not feature in its constitution. This survey traces the course of the human rights of the Bahá'ís after the 1979 Islamic Revolution and follows the Bahá'í case as it is taken up by the United Nations Commission on Human Rights.

The main actors in this study include governmental representatives at the United Nations, Sub-Commission and Treaty-body experts, non-governmental organizations, the Special Representative appointed to monitor Iran's human rights situation, the Special Rapporteur on Religious Intolerance and other Special Rapporteurs who have covered it within their thematic mandates.

Nazila Ghanea's study provides the scene, the setting and the actors in this legal, political, social, cultural and religious drama, and observed within the United Nations human rights system. It is this drama that this book examines in its theoretical, legal, institutional and political dimension.

Nazila Ghanea has been lecturing for the past decade and is currently a fellow of Kellogg College at the University of Oxford, and University Lecturer in International Human Rights Law. She is a graduate of Leeds and Keele Universities in the United Kingdom. Her research and publications have focused on freedom of religion or belief, the UN human rights machinery and particularly the Commission on Human Rights, religious minorities in the Middle East, diplomacy and human rights and the human rights of women. She has participated in over fifteen UN fora around the world as consultant, delegation member or independent expert. The research for this publication stemmed from her doctoral research at the University of Keele.

640 pages
Soft Cover

21.0 x 13.8 cm (8.25 x 5.5in)
ISBN: 978-0-85398-479-4

THE ECO PRINCIPLE

ECOLOGY AND ECONOMICS IN SYMBIOSIS
by Arthur Dahl

Rooted in the Bahá'í teachings and in the scientific study of living systems, Dahl correlates the findings of science and the values and spirit of religion to produce a highly original theory that shows how the same fundamental rules and structures govern the life and death of organic and social systems. From the humble bacteria to the most highly developed nation state, systems must be able to transform themselves to meet the ever-changing challenges of their environment.

This readable book clearly demonstrates how a Bahá'í with a well-trained mind can bring together the teachings of Bahá'u'lláh with the best of scientific thought to produce an accurate analysis of the world situation as well as a stunningly creative tool to help humankind move forward into its collective adulthood.

192 pages   21.4 x 13.6 cm. (8.5 x 5.25 in)
Soft Cover   ISBN: 978-0-85398-434-9